"Robert G. Callahan, II, blends personal testimony, prophetic insight, and legal acumen to offer a compelling read for all who yearn for justice and righteousness in the here and now. *Fire in the Whole* not only exposes the racism and willful hypocrisy within white American Christianity but also presents an honest and liberating pathway toward a better and more faithful Christian witness in the United States."

–**WILLIAM YOO**, Associate Professor of American Religious
and Cultural History, Columbia Theological Seminary,
and author of *What Kind of Christianity? A History of Slavery
and Anti-Black Racism in the Presbyterian Church*

"I remember the first time I heard the term *white Christianity*. It jarred me. And yet it convicted me. Naming it helped me see it. *Fire in the Whole* exposes the narratives that we feel comfortable telling ourselves to continue enjoying our comforts and faux securities. I lament the ways I've been complicit: maybe not in my intention but certainly in the cruel and dehumanizing impact. Callahan frees us from the counterfeit, names what needs to be named, guides the reader through necessary emotions, and points to our true hope. I am so thankful to bear witness to the harm named and to learn from this book. I hope it is read widely in the church."

–**AIMEE BYRD**, author of *The Hope in Our Scars: Finding the
Bride of Christ in the Underground of Disillusionment*
and *Recovering from Biblical Manhood and Womanhood:
How the Church Needs to Rediscover Her Purpose*

"Fire in the Whole is a wonderfully crafted work that lays out Callahan's case for white Christianity to reconcile with Christ and stop its spiritual abuse against the Black and Brown bodies that continue to worship within the world of white Christianity. If not, more breakups will continue until its entire system is burnt to the ground!"

—**ANGELA N. PARKER**, Associate Professor of New Testament
and Greek, McAfee School of Theology, Mercer University,
and author of *If God Still Breathes, Why Can't I?
Black Lives Matter and Biblical Authority*

"Callahan has created an important glimpse into the real impact that Christian nationalism has on real people—impact that white people often choose to ignore. But reading this challenging tome makes it impossible to look away, and for those of us white folx who really care, it is both a clarion call to action and also a strange sort of balm for our grieving souls to know that our rage, sense of bewilderment, and betrayal at what our beloved church is doing is not just valid—it's holy. If you've ever stood in your church, looked around, and wondered "What the h*** is happening?" then this book is for you. If you haven't yet had that experience, this book is especially for you. Let the fires of our anger be stoked with Callahan's words and, in response, let us burn it all down and imagine something new—something outside the chains of white pseudosupremacy and something more like Beloved Community. And let this book guide the way."

—**KERRY CONNELLY**, author of *Good White Racist?*
Confronting Your Role in Racial Injustice and
Wait—Is This Racist? A Guide to Becoming an Anti-Racist Church

"Traversing the scar tissue of white Christianity, Callahan offers clear-eyed permission to accept no less than God's perfect dream. Validating, hopeful, and loaded with wit, this is a book that heals."

—**SHANNAN MARTIN**, author of *Start with Hello*
(and Other Simple Ways to Live as Neighbors) and
The Ministry of Ordinary Places:
Waking Up to God's Goodness around You

Fire in the Whole

To assist with personal reflection and group discussion, a Spotify playlist curated by the author and downloadable versions of the guides at the end of the book are available at **www.wjkbooks.com/FireintheWhole**.

Fire in the Whole

*Embracing Our Righteous Anger
with White Christianity
and Reclaiming Our Wholeness*

Robert G. Callahan, II

WESTMINSTER
JOHN KNOX PRESS
LOUISVILLE · KENTUCKY

First edition
Published by Westminster John Knox Press
Louisville, Kentucky

24 25 26 27 28 29 30 31 32 33—10 9 8 7 6 5 4 3 2 1

Book design by Sharon Adams
Cover design by Luisa Dias

Library of Congress Cataloging-in-Publication Data
Names: Callahan, Robert G., II author.
Title: Fire in the whole : embracing our righteous anger with white
    Christianity and reclaiming our wholeness / Robert G. Callahan, II.
Description: First edition. | Louisville, Kentucky : Westminster John Knox
    Press, [2024] | Summary: "Validates the anger and betrayal felt by Black
    Christians who worship in proximity to white Christians, offers advice
    for healing church hurt, and encourages Black Christians to seek
    spiritual wholeness wherever it can be found-even outside the church"--
    Provided by publisher.
Identifiers: LCCN 2024024198 (print) | LCCN 2024024199 (ebook) | ISBN
    9780664268626 (paperback) | ISBN 9781646984053 (ebook)
Subjects: LCSH: Power (Social sciences)--Religious aspects. | Christians,
    White. | White people--Race identity--Religious aspects. | Christians,
    Black. | Spiritual healing.
Classification: LCC BL65.97 .C47 2024 (print) | LCC BL65.97 (ebook) | DDC
    261.089/96073--dc23/eng/20240628
LC record available at https://lccn.loc.gov/2024024198
LC ebook record available at https://lccn.loc.gov/2024024199

Most Westminster John Knox Press books are available at special quantity discounts when purchased in bulk by corporations, organizations, and special-interest groups. For more information, please e-mail SpecialSales@wjkbooks.com.

For my wife, my family, and all my friends
who saw beauty in my fire,
and for all the survivors who are angry.

Whenever I speak, I cry out proclaiming violence and destruction. So the word of the Lord has brought me insult and reproach all day long. But if I say, "I will not mention his word or speak anymore in his name," his word is in my heart like a fire, a fire shut up in my bones. I am weary of holding it in; indeed, I cannot.

—Jeremiah 20:8–9

I always want to, first of all, interrogate my intentions. What do I bring to this space, even while I prepare my sermons? In this space, I'll be honest, I vacillate between two places: fatigue and anger. And I have to be honest about how I come to sermon preparation in this season. I have to fight for joy because fatigue and anger are my portion right along through here. So, I have to interrogate that this is how I come to the space, to the space of study, to the space of application, to the space of exegesis. I come tired and I come angry. So, I have to come to God, "God help me not lose what I feel but help me not make what I feel what you say. Help me figure out how to work through my feelings and my expressions—my hurt, my pain, my anger, but for that not to be the dominant voice in this space. I need you to speak, but use this tired, angry vessel."

—Pastor John Faison Sr.

I am not sure I will ever be able to articulate the betrayal these last few years have felt like, watching the church that raised me fall into lockstep with Trump. It is actually shocking. The white supremacy, the brutal anti-immigrant policies, the immorality, the absolute depravity. Every value supposedly held dear—purity, lovingkindness, integrity, humility—turned out to be meaningless when they interfered with a proximity to power. So many of us feel like spiritual orphans, abandoned by our spiritual leaders and disassociated from the church that once taught us to act justly, love mercy, and walk humbly with our God. It was and remains one of the great sorrows of my adult life. If Biden is elected, the Christian leaders who threw themselves at Trump and defended his indefensible words and deeds will now be left empty handed. They got their 30 pieces of silver, but they lost their witness, their integrity, and the next generation of the church. . . . This is not a tacit endorsement of Biden. It is grief over the Christian defense and rabid support of Trump. I will never get over it. My kids will never get over it.

—Jen Hatmaker

O Lord, bless this Thy hand grenade, that with it Thou mayest blow Thine enemies to tiny bits, in Thy mercy.

—The Book of Armaments,
Monty Python and the Holy Grail

Contents

Introduction

Since I've Laid My Burden Down

Sometimes Christianity feels like a legend. There's archaeological evidence of this extinct culture that existed once, a long time ago. Like prehistoric fossils, the bones are reconstructed and displayed to give our best approximation of what it looked like in buildings across America every Sunday. But, even as a lifelong believer, traveling the path of deconstruction has often caused me to doubt whether I've ever actually witnessed Christianity living and breathing in the modern world with my own eyes.

Sometimes I fear, what if the church—the healthy assembly of people we were designed to be and long for when we pray "your kingdom come, your will be done"—is the exception in Christianity while dysfunction is the rule? And what if it's always been that way? After all, Christ tried to show the religious leaders of his own time what he intended for humanity, and they killed him for it.

Deconstruction was not part of some plan I hatched. Like many, I never *chose* to question my faith. For me, it was the inevitable result of spiritual trauma stemming from right-wing Christianity's complicity with racism. Living in the Bible Belt, that left me and my family feeling spiritually homeless. We have wandered through the wastelands of religion like nomads, searching for some assurance that not all humanity was lost in the wake of Skynet's attack on judgment day. Perhaps you can relate.

Over the past several years American Christianity, with its nefarious entanglement with politics, has gained a reputation for being

1

the opposite of everything it stands for. For the most part, this leaves minorities and their allies with an abundance of questions and few answers: How did my friends and family develop such a different understanding of Christianity than me? Can racism and nationalism's influence be extracted from evangelical Christianity? Do they not see racism in the church, or are they ignoring it? Is it too late for the church to be saved (pun intended)? Are advocates of this toxic theology even saved? If I leave this spiritually abusive space, where do I go? Is it just me?

If you feel the same way, I've got news for you: you're *not* crazy. As John Connor admonished in *Terminator Salvation, if you are listening to this, you are the resistance.*[1] If it feels like the loudest voices in American Christianity have lost their minds, it's because that's exactly what happened. The people we know and love—spiritual mentors who brought us to faith, family who taught us to read the Bible, Christian coworkers, friends we see at church every Sunday, pastors we've respected so long—truly have forgotten what they taught us the Bible has to say.

Not long ago, I identified as a Christian, an American, a Republican, and a Black man with a mixed-race family—in that order. In other words, I was one of the good ones. Like Paul, I had much to boast about: raised middle class; my Bible drill skills, unmatched; a conservative among conservatives. But that changed. When evangelicalism became a political designation—when my white conservative Christian friends embraced win-at-all-cost politics while I refused to extenuate my Christian principles—I fell from the favor of my peers and my church, and I turned my back on what often is nebulously referred to as "white evangelicalism" (though, it should be said, Christians of this sort can be found in any denomination).

Until 2015, I believed America was headed generally in the right direction. I reasoned that the moral evolution of humanity moving further from the time of the civil rights movement ensured America would eventually become too diverse—too intelligent—for stubborn weeds of racism not to be choked out by progress. The charged rhetoric and cultural polarization accompanying the election of our forty-fifth president was a weather vane demonstrating how wrong

I was. Worse, the storm wasn't coming; it was already here. You may empathize if you find yourself exhausted by the loss of loved ones (figuratively and literally) to the COVID-19 pandemic, conspiracy theories, political idolatry, racism, gun worship, marginalization of LGBTQIA+ people, and misogyny—all of which the faith community had a hand in.

While we could find many reasons that the church makes such a welcoming incubation chamber for these vices, it is my observation that white supremacy is the common denominator. And, without fail, where the church has held hands with white supremacy, all other ills abound. It is for this reason that I train my thoughts in these pages on the destructive gravity well created by the church's complicity with racism and what it will take for each of us to achieve escape velocity and break free from it.

It has taken years for me to reconstruct my faith, but I finally see the light ahead. In recovering from my enmeshment with white Christianity, I have sacrificed many things on the altar before God. Friendships. Status. Reputation. But everything the fire consumed I now see was actually a burden that hindered me. And as the fire grows, I find myself able to move freely, closer to God. As the old Black hymn goes, "I feel better, so much better, since I laid my burden down."* During this migration, I've found that we who have the mind of Christ[2] waste a lot of time attempting to reform ineffective, or now irrelevant, religious institutions from the *inside* when the truth is that they needed to be burned down—figuratively speaking.

In 1 Samuel 11, Saul undergoes his first recorded test as the leader of Israel. When he learned that God's people, whom Saul was charged with protecting, were being oppressed and besieged by a political force, the Bible says, "the Spirit of God came powerfully upon him, and he burned with anger" (1 Sam. 11:6). Surveying maps that depict the ancient topography, it's clear that the journey from Gibeah (where Saul was) to Jabesh Gilead (where the Ammonites surrounded the city) was a mountainous *jaunt*. It might

---

*I'm partial to Mississippi John Hurt's recording of this classic spiritual, "Since I've Laid My Burden Down," track 5 on *Rediscovered* (Vanguard Records, 1998).

have been tempting for Saul to write off the people of Jabesh Gilead as an acceptable loss. It would have been easy to decide that the risks to the whole outweighed the rewards to the minority. Yet anger mobilized Saul. It was righteous anger, an anger that stirred Saul to act on behalf of his neighbors. There are not a lot of things that Saul did correctly during his reign as the king of Israel. Let's give him props where props are due.

Too often, we are told that anger has no place in the hearts of Christians. As a consequence, we don't know what we're allowed to feel in regard to the wolves that have infiltrated our flocks. Evangelical Christian culture has a way of training us into timidity to protect the opinions and abuses of others at the expense of our own well-being. But, as Beth Moore once opined, "Sometimes you can put it so delicately no one even gets it. Sometimes, unless you drop it like a grenade, nobody hears it."[3] In that spirit, we are pulling the pin on the grenade here. As I journey further into reconstructing my faith, I have determined that when anger motivates us to move toward liberation, to be more inclusive, to build wider tables, and to love our neighbors better, it is righteous and holy. My pointed and sometimes satirical honesty in these pages reflects our communal need to abandon the pursuit of acceptance within white Christianity's context in exchange for clarity, liberation, and love of neighbor.

To that end, we will use the imagery of fire throughout this book in several ways: as a beacon to rally to; a safe place our community gathers around to share our vulnerabilities; flames that consume our burdens at the altar; a heat source converting our lament into action; and, finally, a light guiding our path forward into healing. While the imagery of fire serves a valuable purpose in each of its applications, the most important purpose is to facilitate our embrace of the righteous anger threatening to consume us and to help us become whole. Said another way, my goal in writing *Fire in the Whole* is to help you recognize that your anger is valid and that the time has come, at least metaphorically, to burn some stuff down. Notwithstanding, the fires of our revolution will look less like Molotov cocktails and more like burnt offerings. But rest assured, these fires will be large, as there's much to burn and much illumination is needed. By sacrificing these burdens at the altar, we can free ourselves from the stifling effects of racism in white Christianity and illuminate the path to healing.

The goal is not to tear down the church, but to free you from an imitation of it.

How to Read This Book

There's something magical about a campfire. Friends gathered around flames on a cool fall evening. Sharing laughter, singing songs together, trading sorrows, mesmerized by the flames, engrossed in deep conversations that last until the embers finally fade away. In the right company, these moments of authentic community and vulnerability can be healing. This is my goal for you here.

Fire in the Whole is organized in three parts. The first part is a type of communion—gathering all those who share these pains and frustrations in the same place around the fire. In these chapters, fire is a beacon to gather us together. Part 1 is also a lament designed to validate the pain that we who are displaced by the white church's complicity with racism feel. To assist in processing the emotions associated with that validation in Part 1 and beyond, I have compiled a Spotify playlist to accompany this book, featuring songs of hopeful rebellion from diverse genres. Their themes and titles provide a soundtrack for our reflection and observation. Access this playlist at https://spoti.fi/3QyTFvp, listen to the songs referenced, meditate on the lyrics, pray through them like liturgies, and allow the emotions they invoke to rise to the surface from the deep places we tend to secure them.

In the second part, we stoke the flames. We add fuel to the fire by openly discussing the various wounds dealt by the evangelical church. In each chapter, we focus on a specific way the church has stripped many of us of dignity, though we recognize there are many other ways than those discussed here. We name the pains we carry, and we symbolically add them to the fire in hopes that doing so will help us begin the healing process of moving forward without carrying those burdens in our minds. Here, again, there is an opportunity to bring this contemplative process to life. As an exercise to visualize the freedom we're seeking, consider gathering with others struggling with the same topics around a fire pit, writing down these grievances we share, and burning them in the fire like secular CDs purged from your teenage music library. (If you know, you know.)

Finally, in the third part, we break camp. We turn away from the flames that now consume the weight we carried here. Stepping away from this bonfire, we commit ourselves to emancipation from the toxicity of white Christianity and we look to the path ahead. We only take with us the new light we've found to illuminate our steps.

Part 1

A Fire to Gather By

Chapter 1

Lift Every Voice and Sing

*W*hat if I told you that your anger is holy? The question may feel more poignant if you imagine, as I do, that it comes from a leather-clad Lawrence Fishburne, poised in a red leather chair, wearing a killer pair of reflective sunglasses like in *The Matrix*. Growing up in church, I was *never* taught that anger was something that could be appropriate, right, and healthy. Anger, I learned, could only evince a lack of self-control, immaturity, and unhealth. Now, as an adult, in practicing law I have the opportunity to evaluate justice on a literal daily basis. My work, my faith, and my identity as an African American all lead to the inexorable conclusion that when God's heart burns with anger at injustice, ours should too. God created us with this emotion for a purpose.

Here's another epiphany: the apathy with which the church seems to just casually accept racism in its ranks is a manifestation of spiritual abuse. Twenty—or even ten—years ago, we could never imagine the rhetoric and vitriol that have become a hallmark of evangelicalism. But today, reliable statistics demonstrate that white evangelical voters were the decisive factor in President Trump's 2016 election. According to polling data compiled by Pew Research, 81 percent of people who identify as white, born-again or evangelical Christians voted for Trump in the 2016 election.[1] While those numbers dipped slightly in the 2020 election, polling also suggests that approximately seven in ten white Americans who attended religious services at least monthly supported Trump's second run.[2] According to a national poll published by Monmouth University in 2022, 61 percent of Republicans believe that the 2020 presidential election was stolen from Trump.[3] The same poll reveals that only 63 percent of Americans as a whole believe that Biden won the election without the influence of fraud.

But we hardly need those statistics, do we? We saw who the loudest and most aggressive supporters of Donald Trump were. We worshiped next to them on Sundays, endured their hysteria on social media, worked with them during the week, conversed with them at our children's soccer fields, grimaced while listening to them rant over Thanksgiving dinner, and watched them cheer as their heroes set their feet up on Nancy Pelosi's desk in the offices of the US Capitol. All observable data shows that the divisions in the body of Christ, and by extension our nation, fall squarely along racial lines. Worse, we know that these lines aren't just demarcations on issues of race. Misogyny and bigotry against LGBTQIA+ people follow closely behind; white supremacy and patriarchy walk hand in hand. We have much to lament.

Those of us most affected by these issues see their effect on the church clearly. And more often than not, we've been ridiculed, had our faith questioned, lost community, been alienated from family, been maligned by church leaders, been cast out from our congregations, and been forced to consider whether Christianity, as a whole, is a sham. But what about believers who claim not to see the problem? Truly, can anyone be so naive? The cognitive dissonance is bewildering:

- They support a completely depraved charlatan for highest political office because "God can use anyone," but they object to women in ministry?
- They say, "We're not electing a pastor," but they invite him to speak from the pulpit on a Sunday morning?[4]
- They want African angels doing miracles, but they don't want African Americans taking a knee?[5]
- They disagree with homosexuality "because it's sinful," but

they ignore the disturbing frequency of conservative Christian leaders exposed for sexual immorality?

- They'll pray and fast forty days for a spiritual breakthrough, but they can't wear a mask for forty minutes to prevent a breakthrough infection?

These glaring hypocrisies have done us great harm, but even more hurtful is the church's unwillingness to take responsibility for the damage it's done. To use the words of rapper J. Crum, "How you speak in tongues but can't apologize?"[6] After all we have witnessed and endured these last several years, we have every right to be livid. Radicalism's stranglehold on white Christianity has given us much to be angry about.

What Is White Christianity?

Before we go any further, we need to define terms. Generally speaking, when we're discussing issues of race or theology, the more specific we can be, the better. Yet it's difficult to name the species that created this rift in the church with taxonomic precision due to the interplay of politics, racism, misogyny, bigotry, and theology in American Christianity.

One of my biggest pet peeves is how white Christian nationalists and MAGA Republicans (e.g., Richard Spencer, Stephen Wolfe, and Charlie Kirk, among others) seem uniquely capable of defining groups of human beings and cultural ideologies with overly broad, sweeping terminology. While it's clearly manipulative, those who utilize the tactic do so masterfully. For example, the term "woke" used to be exclusively utilized within the Black community in reference to those who are particularly insightful regarding social issues. The term gained popularity in mainstream Christianity shortly after the 2018 release of Eric Mason's book *Woke Church: An Urgent Call for Christians in America to Confront Racism and Injustice*. As believers of all races sought insight into the racial turmoil that settled upon the United States shortly after its release, books like *Woke Church* flew off the shelves. But physics teaches us that for every action there is an equal and opposite reaction. Lest they lose their voting bloc, Republicans and conservative Christians quickly began to spin "wokeness" as a threat to democracy. In short order, the term "woke" was appropriated as a derisive pejorative by white conservatives to drive a wedge between conservative Christians and the liberal minorities they were beginning to empathize with. Soon "woke" was contemptuously utilized as a euphemism for anything related to Black culture that white America deemed threatening—regardless of whether it was related to faith. Today, the term has been deployed so broadly that it encompasses anything that the political right can label as part of the "liberal agenda," despite their continued inability to define the term. As an illustration, conservative author Bethany Mandel went viral when she was at a loss to define "woke" during an interview promoting her book, despite having weaponized the word several times during her interview and having devoted a chapter of her book to it.[7]

By contrast, those of us who strive for intellectual honesty are not allowed to paint with such a broad brush. In fact, as Christians in social and political discourse, we are burdened with a level of precision that doesn't inhibit those with political agendas. Namely, we have the obligation of aggressively critiquing what those who are corrupting our faith tradition are doing while simultaneously acknowledging that they are also created in the *imago Dei* (the image of God). Our convictions require that we fight fair, while theirs do not.

Therefore, while most Americans (particularly in the southern Bible Belt) would probably understand who we're talking about if we were to label the troublemakers exclusively as "evangelicals," the fact remains that we should acknowledge that term could be a political or theological designation. Meanwhile, outside of America, being labeled as an evangelical connotes little, if anything, more than the convictions of those ascribing to certain religious, doctrinal beliefs. There's no political baggage associated with the designation.

It's not my intent to cast too wide a net. "White evangelicals" might be a sufficiently specific description. However, I do not want to be so limiting in my definition that I let those who contribute to the problem while not embracing an evangelical theological identity off the hook. There are many white Christians in Catholic or "mainline" Protestant denominations who may not identify *religiously* as evangelicals, but nonetheless embrace the toxic blend of religious and political conservatism I am describing here. Yet, paradoxically, some of those may still identify themselves as evangelicals in exit polls. How do we precisely describe such a nebulous group? The fact of the matter is that "toxic white American capitalistic patriarchal heteronormative Christian nationalism" just *does not* roll off the tongue. Nor would it serve us well to utilize an overly broad, derogatory term simply for the purpose of creating a label, as some conservatives have done with the term "woke." So, for now, the phrase "white Christianity" must serve as shorthand to describe *those whose orthodoxy and orthopraxy are dictated by an unshakable, yet misguided, tangle of faith and right-bridled political and social conviction that are antithetical to everything Christ represents.*

Lest we define "white Christianity" too narrowly, it is crucial to understand that white Christianity is also not about Christians who are white. Rather, it is a worldview that encourages cultural homogeneity through assimilation, or even promotion of nationalism, while giving equal emphasis to a unified stance *against* cultural phenomena (such as "wokeness") that it views as threatening to that homogeneity. In this way, it is completely possible for ethnically diverse congregations (even those led by African American pastors) to perpetrate the ills of white evangelicalism as they encourage minority conformity with majority culture. There's a difference between a *multiethnic* church, which has a visually diverse collection of races and ethnicities present in the congregation but lacks diversity in theological or political thought, and a *multicultural* church where the variety of cultures present all contribute to a diverse approach to reading and interpreting Scripture through various cultural lenses. In multiethnic assemblies a premium may

be placed on storefront diversity—utilizing people of color in pro-
motional materials, websites, and front-facing positions—to attract
other minorities and create a mirage of inclusivity. But it lacks true
diversity of social, political, and theological views. Allowing ourselves to be used as tokens in such manner comes at great emotional and spiritual cost. Tokens get spent.

This power dynamic necessarily causes conflict when minorities point out ways in which the gospel conflicts with our modern,
consumerist, American cultural iteration of Christianity. Examined
in this context, *white Christianity is also that subset of Christianity that intentionally ignores, or does not consciously consider, the
effects of racism or prejudice—in either the church or society—
on the marginalized, nor cares to, having been given the resources
and information to do so.*

> **White Christianity is also that subset of Christianity that intentionally ignores, or does not consciously consider, the effects of racism or prejudice on the marginalized.**

As specific as I've attempted to
be, I confess I still struggle with the
phrase "white Christianity." For one,
as a Black person, it feels to me as
though any reference to "whiteness"
has more weight leaving my lips than
it does when Caucasians utilize it. I
envy white authors who are permitted to address the impact that white
supremacy and its twin brother, patri-
archy, have on our relationships and theology without receiving the
same level of protest that minorities receive for saying the same
things. Indeed, it feels as though our white allies are allowed to
discuss whiteness clinically, as a state of mind—an assumption of
normalcy in every facet of life that threatens historic, academic,
and religious honesty, and that, once identified, may be recognized
as problematic—whereas whiteness is understood as nothing more
than a skin color dividing cultures when minorities attempt to have
these conversations.

Moreover the burden of proof for white allies seeking to prove
that whiteness is detrimental to the body of Christ seems much
lower than for African Americans attempting to do the same. Where

a preponderance of the evidence seems sufficient for white people to prove their case, minorities making the same point must convince the same jury beyond a reasonable doubt.* Perhaps these are unavoidable biases brought by all who engage in challenging cultural conversations. Still, it's important to name these double standards in order to reduce their influence on our work.

So, now that we know how to identify those who caused us this pain, how do we identify ourselves, we who have suffered such terrible blows from religion wielded like a blunt instrument? My hope is that over the course of this book, we begin to identify ourselves as survivors rather than as victims. The distinction is in our progress toward healing. There is a difference between speaking from a place of scars and speaking from a place of wounds. Wounds are traumas that have not fully healed. On the other hand, scars reveal places where we were once wounded but healing has taken place. The healing may not be complete or even adequate. But it is no longer an active injury that impacts us in the same way.

Many things about my journey from white evangelicalism still hurt. Some traumas I will continue to work through for the rest of my life. Regarding some facets of spiritual abuse, I understand that I will be in lifelong recovery in the same way that those who go through formal efforts at recovering from addiction are taught to recognize that recovery is a lifelong process. But, for the most part, I can call myself a survivor of racialized spiritual abuse. As such I can speak about most of these issues from a place of scars. Either way, it is important that we see ourselves as survivors, even if it still hurts.

You can identify yourself as a survivor of white evangelicalism if you've left a church community feeling as though you were not free to be entirely who you are due to their complicity with racism. You

*In law, winning different kinds of cases requires different levels of proof. In a civil case, where the parties are typically fighting over money (because of a business dispute or a car accident, for example), one must prove one's case by a preponderance of the evidence to prevail. This simply means convincing the jury that the evidence tips the scales in favor of one side by an amount of 51 percent or greater. However, in a criminal case, the government must prove that the accused committed the crime beyond a reasonable doubt, the highest standard of proof that exists in law.

left; you're a survivor. If you felt as though a perspective of Scripture emphasizing liberation and social equity was tolerated, but not promoted, in the church you departed from, count yourself among our number. If your church leaders taught the Bible through a politicized lens that elevated nationalistic sentiment, quickly endorsed so-called conservative political candidates but overlooked their gross character flaws in favor of the church gaining political "influence" (read: power), you are a survivor. If, in your faith community, "unity" was more important than accountability, we can lament together. If you have been written off as "divisive" or "liberal" for reminding believers what the Bible teaches us about justice or love of our minority neighbors, look no further; you have found your people. If you feel abandoned by the very people who taught you the principles that buoy your faith, and feel you are screaming into the wind that the idea of refusing to discuss racism in the church is unfathomable, you are a survivor. These examples are endemic to the racialized psychological warfare practiced by white Christianity. Said another way, these are examples of spiritual abuse.

The Fire We Gather Around

It's only because I've dealt with the intense heat of anger that the duplicity of white Christianity generates in me that I am beginning to feel that I can walk in wholeness now. This is what I want for you. This is the work ahead of us: embracing that righteous sense of anger that burns within toward white evangelicalism, placing it in its proper context, fostering our departure, and illuminating our path to healing. And in a lot of ways the point is the journey. Perhaps the real antiracism work was the friends we lost along the way.

In the book of Revelation, we are encouraged that the faithful will persevere through the blood of the Lamb and the power of their testimony (Rev. 12:11). As we work together through this pain, we have in common that our present grief is part of the testimony we look forward to. Perhaps you recall Paul's encouragement to the Romans that our trials produce character. The translations we typically read sound like a morbid pep rally, something akin to "suffering is great! It leads to perseverance, which builds character!" The somber insights of the *First Nations Version* feel much closer to what I imagine the apostle intended for his original audience:

> But we must also find joy in our sufferings on his behalf. For we know that when the trail gets rough, we must walk with firm steps to reach the end. As we walk firmly in his footprints, we gain the strength of spirit that we need to stay true to the path. This gives us the hope we need to reach the end of the trail with honor. All of this is because of Creator's great love that has been poured into our hearts by the Holy Spirit, who is his gift to us from above. (Rom. 5:3–5)

We will overcome, but for now, it is enough to mourn, taking our lives one step—one day—at a time. Your frustrations are valid. The tension you feel in your body is real. Your depression is justified. Our anger is righteous.

As I process my grief with other people, one of the questions that just won't go away is "Where did everything go wrong?" What were the first indications that something was awry? Unfortunately, evangelicalism has given us lots of options to choose from: the disillusionment of missionaries who have given up everything to do overseas ministry work when they realize that white evangelicalism could never have adequately prepared them; culture shock after returning from abroad; exposure to diversity of thought from Christians of other cultures; a pastor's hard right turn into politics; the stigmatization of divorce and bias against single mothers; erasure of women; misogynistic demands for "biblical submission"; differing standards for men and women; pastors having affairs; unhealthy parenting practices; homophobia; political support of former president Trump; failure to respond appropriately to the COVID-19 pandemic; promotion of conspiracy theories; politicized responses to immigration; failure to respond to the poor; indifference toward mass shootings; the hypocrisy and fall of well-known Christian public figures or institutions; tolerance of psychophysical, emotional, and sexual abuse; syncretism of capitalism and evangelicalism; culture war fatigue; hysteria over critical race theory (CRT) or diversity, equity, and inclusion (DEI); accusations of Marxism; failure to acknowledge the impact of world events on minorities in the congregation; complicity with racism; adoption of culturally offensive rhetoric; promotion of white supremacist ideology cloaked in the authority of biblical teaching; refusal to correct course; inability to apologize. . . . Truly, there is much for the white evangelical church to atone for.

And atone it must. It will be up to us to hold the church accountable. As a Black man married to a white woman and raising interracial children, my need for the church to speak appropriately into societal matters like police brutality, racism, and xenophobia isn't theoretical. The hypocrisies that the church tolerates, the sheep are raised to view as normal. For example, when white public figures are caught using slurs candidly on a hot mic, or white police officers are tried for murdering minorities, one of the first defenses proffered in their favor is how well they are regarded as good Christian people. Yet their supposed faith in Christ apparently provides them no insight into how Christ calls us to love our neighbors. The faith defense is a commonly utilized ploy because it works.

How does this happen? Historians can give us specific insights into the church's evolving complicity. But every historical mile marker we point to is really just an indicator that evangelicalism has failed to teach love of neighbor as a governing dynamic of the gospel. We already know what went wrong. It is past time to shift our energies from "How did we get here?" and instead focus on a different question.

Where Do We Go from Here?

Jesus taught that the command to love our neighbors is akin to the first and greatest command of loving God (Matt. 22:34–40). It's kind of what God is all about. These are essential tenets of our faith. While we know that it is not our duty to pronounce eternal judgment on the souls of humankind, if those claiming Christ miss this, I think it's fair to question whether they are actually even Christians. If they're not following Jesus, by definition, they are not Christians.*

It is the shepherd's duty to lead the flock appropriately. If the church isn't teaching God's people how to read Scripture with an ethic of justice and live holistic Christian lives, then it's no wonder we see this cognitive dissonance. For this reason, Paul admonishes, "How, then, can they call on the one they have not believed in? And how can they believe in the one of whom they have not heard? And how can they hear without someone preaching to them?" (Rom. 10:14). If a pastor persistently challenges their church to see minorities as neighbors and image-bearers, the white police officer who sits in that pew on Sunday and pulls over a person of color on Monday would, hopefully, feel less inclined to shoot first and ask questions later. The church's failure to show up for the marginalized and give full-throated guidance on God's view here is wildly practical—a matter of life and death.

So why is it so difficult to convince so many Christian leaders to publicly denounce racism in politics and in the church? In short, because they don't want to. This will be discussed in greater detail in the chapters that follow. But suffice it to say, we would be wise to stop giving the benefit of ignorance to those at issue by appreciating how much information has to be disregarded for the church to be complicit in racism. We will never see eye to eye with folks committed to looking down their noses at us. There is freedom to be found in accepting that we are not here by accident. It's not that they don't understand. The offenders have *chosen* to champion *superficial* notions of unity. They have chosen to participate in tokenism. They have chosen to silence the voices of minorities by labeling them as being out of harmony with their

---

*The word *Christian* literally means "little Christ"—that is to say, a reflection of Jesus himself.

mission. It is even more egregious when the pastors who conde-
scend to minorities, dismissing their views of Scripture as "woke"
or a "social gospel," are no more theologically educated than those
they deride.

It is healthy and right to name the ways that the church has acted,
or failed to act, that contribute to our social, spiritual, and emotional
demise. Mourning together is an inevitable and necessary part of
deconstruction, and deconstruction is a prerequisite to reconstruction. There are no shortcuts. Our collective lament is the spark
that ignites this fire we gather around. Our beacon. As the light
increases, revealing our faces, we understand that we are not alone.
We are, each of us, seen and known. There is beauty in the sorrow.

Gathering together provides not only strength in numbers but
an acknowledgment that we collectively held a vision of Christianity that has been upended. Yet if we all once held that vision—
if we see that the church has deviated from what it should be—it
suggests that there is, among us, a picture of the church that may
yet still be achieved, one quite different from the version of Christianity we were handed and are deconstructing. We carry within us
an enduring hope of all that the body of Christ may yet become,
despite its perversion. In this regard, our recognition of the counterfeit provides evidence that there is, somewhere, a genuine article. Even if we have never fully laid eyes on it. Thus we gather.
We lament in one voice. And soon we will add fuel to the fire to
produce even greater light—to expose what is amiss for the sake
of seeing it made right.

As former Supreme Court justice Louis Brandeis once opined,
"Publicity is justly commended as a remedy for social and industrial diseases. Sunlight is said to be the best of disinfectants; electric
light the most efficient policeman."[8] Similarly, "Selfishness, injustice, cruelty, tricks, and jobs of all sorts shun the light; to expose
them is to defeat them," wrote James Bryce. "No serious evils, no
rankling sore in the body politic, can remain long concealed, and
when disclosed, it is half destroyed."[9]

If you share these sentiments, there is a community here to support you. Come, gather around this fire.

The Song We Sing

There is something wrong when church, the place we go for shelter and nurturing, becomes the place we feel least safe. This paradox has understandably forced many minorities to question whether the faith we hold is an accurate reflection of the God we worship or whether we've just projected our own desires for a benevolent God who sees the lowly and brokenhearted onto an invisible deity. For people of color, the fact that our brothers and sisters in Christ can't see, or refuse to acknowledge, that the church has become a forward operating base in a culture war that denies our dignity calls the credibility of all Christian witness into question. The added weight of seemingly irreconcilable theological quandaries to such a burden is enough to break the confidence of our faith. We have to ask, Is God real, and is God really who we thought?

As we reassess everything we have learned in our faith, as well as those we learned it from, those of us standing on shaky ground realize there are only two possibilities: either the Bible has misrepresented who Jesus is or white Christianity has misrepresented the Bible. If it's the latter, what do we do with the reverence and long-standing trust we developed for those we adored who claimed to speak on God's behalf? Just like that, welcome to deconstruction.

"Deconstruction" has become utilized almost as a pejorative, on one hand, or so muted in definition as to become unhelpful, on the other. On one end of the spectrum is a knee-jerk overreaction to the notion of believers questioning anything they've been taught. Here, it seems that most of what has conservative Christianity screaming that the sky is falling is actually nothing more than pensive reflection on faith claims that had previously gone unchallenged. Yet even this austere version of deconstruction seems threatening to those who have never questioned any aspects of their faith. On the other hand, some of the Christian influencers who have the biggest platforms to discuss deconstruction understate its significance by describing it in terms that feel cold and clinical, such as "reconsidering," "unbundling," or "re-examining inherited beliefs." These hardly acknowledge deconstruction for the foundation-rattling experience that it can be. Matt Chandler, pastor at the Village Church in the Dallas/Fort Worth metroplex, has come under fire for a number of (justifiable) reasons. One of the most memorable, in my opinion, was his assertion that "deconstruction has become some sort of sexy thing to do." This perspective has become too popular in evangelicalism—as though survivors of abuse choose to be ostracized from loved ones and question all that we've ever known.[10]

While I don't want to belittle anyone's faith journey, I can't take either the alarmist or understated view of deconstruction seriously. My experience of deconstructing didn't lead me to the left or right side of the spectrum. It took me *down.* For myself and those I've discussed deconstruction with, the process wasn't faith-*shaking*; it was faith-*demolishing.* I'm talking about psychic warfare, capture, torture, and internment. My process of deconstruction, first and foremost, was not something that I wanted to admit I was even going through.

Here's a helpful analogy. I started playing piano at an early age. My lessons began before I could read. Therefore, I wasn't able to be taught most of music theory. Things like chords, cadence, scales, intervals—the elements that are essential to improvisation—would have to wait. Nevertheless, I became very talented at reading notes and playing what was handed to me from hours of practice and rote memory. I had an extensive repertoire to play from memory, anything from Scott Joplin's "The Entertainer" to Beethoven's "Moonlight Sonata." I received many awards for my achievements in competitions. I got so good that I considered becoming a professional pianist one day. When I was sixteen, I began lessons with a different teacher, who attempted to teach me theory. By that point, however, I had more than a decade of experience learning to play with an incomplete understanding of how music worked, and I'd become adept at compensating to hide it. Having to admit what I didn't know was embarrassing. It was as though I had never known music at all. Eventually, the frustration defeated me, and I stopped playing completely. Deconstruction felt very similar to me.

As someone raised in the church, baptized at an early age, I was terrified of admitting that I harbored—was even capable of harboring—areas of doubt or unbelief in my faith. Doubt was a shameful prospect for me because as far back as I can remember, my entire life has been in, and in service to, the church. I knew the Bible inside out, but now there were things that I couldn't account for. And without understanding the theory underlying the stories and letters that I'd learned from rote memory, I was unable to improvise when the contradictions challenged me. Far from the fun, sexy, flirtatious rebellion that deconstruction is often portrayed as, there were whole weeks where I was immobilized by the impact of feeling every phase of grief simultaneously. At other times, my lament was disorienting and violent—the feeling of perpetually crashing through each of the stages of grief like floors of a building. Think of the scene in *Avengers: Age of Ultron* when Tony dons the massive Hulk-buster armor and drives the Hulk through every level of an African skyscraper, nearly leveling a city block in the process. My deconstruction process was nuclear fission, an atom-smashing undoing of that which meant the most to me. It was an unraveling of my sanity.

I began at the top of a slippery slope (despite a sincere, lifelong communion with Christ) and finished dangling from the last inch of that slope by one frostbitten finger. I am not exaggerating to say that there was a point where I questioned the historical existence of every biblical figure prior to King David and even began looking at Jesus side-eyed. I was fortunate to have pastors to go to with my questions who helped pull me back onto the ledge. Even still, I will never be the same.

What about those who don't have a safe place to work out their faith? This is the space that I want to create here.

If I can accomplish one thing throughout the course of this book, I hope to help people understand that the discriminatory spiritual abuse that the church has put them through is unacceptable. Everything that white Christianity stands for is worth being angry about. And exposing the ways the church continues to harm survivors is

God's work. The process may expose us to criticisms, such as those from Matt Chandler. But it will also liberate us from the isolated, quiet litigation of our dignity on which our sanity teeters. And we can do it *together*. Truth be told, what other option do we have? We who share this passion for Christ but utter disdain for how he is maligned by Christianity suffer the same malady as Jeremiah: too weary from opposition to our witness to carry on, but unable to stop for the fire that burns within (Jer. 20:9). Indeed, "truth telling will cost you," says Dr. Thema Bryant. "Tell it anyway. Your silence costs you more."[11] If these words resonate with you, if you've discovered vocabulary for things that once felt impossible to explain to others, you are a survivor. We all are. And you're not alone.

Those of us gathered around this campfire represent a new community beginning to understand that our lived experiences are legitimate barometers of unhealth in the church. And our lived experiences are no longer subject to intellectual debate from the culprits of spiritual abuse—racialized spiritual abuse in particular. Though we mourn, we also choose to value our peace of mind and dignity as people created in the *imago Dei*. We simultaneously rue and embrace our creation of healthy boundaries for those committed to failing to understand us—even those closest to us. We resolve that we will no longer offer justifications for those who wounded us. We will speak loudly together. We will lend our voices to the chorus of the spiritually homeless.

As we gather around this fire, let us lift every voice and sing:

Sing a song full of the faith that the dark past has taught us.
Sing a song full of the hope that the present has brought us.
Facing the rising sun of our new day begun
Let us march on till victory is won.[12]

Chapter 2

More Than Fine

If you've seen the 2003 version of *The Italian Job,* you'll recall one of my favorite exchanges in movie dialogue. Just before everything goes sideways, two thieves, Charlie Croker (Mark Wahlberg) and John Bridger (Donald Sutherland), discuss their pending $35 million heist job:

BRIDGER: I feel so optimistic. How do you feel?
CROKER: [*shrugging*] I'm fine.
BRIDGER: Fine? You know what "fine" stands for, don't you?
CROKER: Yeah, unfortunately.
BRIDGER: Freaked out . . .
CROKER: Insecure . . .
BRIDGER: Neurotic . . .
CROKER: And Emotional.
BRIDGER: You see those columns behind you?
CROKER: [*looks behind him and sees the pillars*] What about them?
BRIDGER: That's where they used to string up thieves who felt fine.
CROKER: [*gesturing*] Well, after you.[1]

"Fine" is such a funny expression. Many a comedian has (perhaps with less caution than deserved) opined that men should be wary when a woman says she's "fine" after a conflict. As the trope goes, the emotionally wounded partner may be saying she's fine, but in reality, she's been wounded and "fine" is actually shorthand for *"What do you think? There's a huge problem here. I shouldn't have to tell you what you did wrong. You should know that for yourself and there will be huge consequences later!!!"*

Similarly, when asked how I'm feeling, I have an unfortunate habit of quickly responding, "I'm fine," without stopping to think about it.

My wife: "How was your day?"

I silently recall that a client yelled at me for an hour on the phone; a judge sent a first-time offender to prison rather than giving them probation; a prosecutor won't dismiss a case though it's clear my client is innocent; and I have two trials on the same day next week and still haven't figured out how to be in two places at one time.

Me: "It was fine."

Therapy has taught me that when I say I feel "fine" there's probably something to explore that I haven't processed yet. Honestly, I'm not usually trying to deceive anyone. I just don't take the time to assess my emotions on a regular basis at all, much less in the moment I'm asked about them. (Pro tip: this is not healthy behavior. The perils of being an Enneagram 8.* Add to that the fact that people rarely actually want you to share your unrefined emotions with them and it creates a pretty solid case for my favorite default reply: I'm fine.)

Over the course of American history, minorities have been asked to stomach an unconscionable amount of injustice and pain, yet we're expected to adapt without complaint. We're supposed to be fine. And often, we even convince ourselves that we are. But as it concerns most people of color and our relationship to white Christianity, the truth of the matter is we're not fine. Nor do we feel that our genuine, unrefined honesty is welcomed. However, societal

*The Enneagram is a system that classifies personality types by numbers based on our motivations. The type 8 personality wants to be self-reliant, harboring a desire to protect themselves, prove their strength, and resist weakness. As such, type 8s tend to avoid engaging their feelings to be impervious to pain. Ironically, type 8s also hate being labled or put in boxes via personality tests. For more information, visit https://www.enneagraminstitute.com/type-descriptions/.

apathy toward our truest feelings has conditioned us to say of our church-induced pain, "We're fine."

During the 2020 presidential town hall debate, George Stephanopoulos asked candidate Joe Biden, who was then the former vice president, what it would say about America if Biden lost. Biden responded, "It could say that I'm a lousy candidate, and I didn't do a good job. But I think—I hope that it doesn't say that we are as racially, ethnically, and religiously at odds with one another as it appears the president wants us to be."[2] While I want to share Biden's hope, and notwithstanding the success of his campaign, I believe it would be naive to see things any other way.

It may be tempting for the white church to believe that time heals all wounds and that, eventually, its relationship with people of color in the aftermath of everything since 2016 will be fine. Let me assure you: it's not fine. The majority culture would do well to bear in mind that no matter their political persuasion, no matter what they say, or even how they voted, BIPOC (Black, Indigenous, and people of color) and their allies have lingering questions about how American Christians see them, in light of the latent discriminatory sentiments that the last several years of American politics have unearthed.

In truth, we're anything but fine; we're angry. Don't we have every right to be? We're furious with the way that white Christians have misrepresented the mission and values of our Redeemer. We're livid from demands that we not only tolerate, but embrace, the diminution of our intrinsic value. Those things that grieve our hearts grieve the heart of the Father as well. Heaven is angry and so we have every right to be. But can we fix it?

As a lawyer, I'm trained to reflexively answer most important questions with "it depends." Can I sue Popeyes for running out of chicken sandwiches just before I pull up to the drive-through?[3] *It depends*. Ill-advised as it may be, can I sue my wife for giving birth to an ugly baby?[4] *It depends*. What does it depend on? *Well, a number of things, and now I have to charge you by the hour. Have a seat.*

I don't mean to be exploitative; it's just hard to be succinct about the labyrinth of the law. As a result, lawyers tend to get long-winded. But here's a public secret: We also like to hear ourselves talk. A lot. To help mitigate that, aspiring lawyers are taught in law school to lay out their arguments in legal briefs by articulating the issue, rule, application, and conclusion (IRAC). Each of these key words has specific legal significance:

> **Issue.** What's the central question, or problem, on which everything turns?
> **Rule.** How does our historical understanding of the law inform this problem?
> **Application.** How do we apply that historical understanding to the facts?
> **Conclusion.** What decision should be made based on all those factors?

I've found that this system of analysis is useful in solving problems outside the legal realm as much as inside of it, so let's use it to analyze our current dilemma. We'll assess the first two in this chapter, and the latter two in the next.

The Issue

OK, so we know we're not fine. In order to remedy the problem, what's the central inquiry we need to ask? At first glance, the issue before us would seem to be whether the body of Christ can function as one unified body. I posit that this is the wrong question. A friend often reminds me that I should begin assessing problems with the end goal in mind. As Christians, our end goal shouldn't be functioning in unity. Functioning cohesively doesn't mean we're functioning correctly. But functioning correctly does necessitate cohesion. Our goal is to function *correctly*.

There are a lot of different ways to express God's love to our neighbors. Hence Francis of Assisi wrote, "Preach the gospel at all times. When necessary, use words." Even so, Jesus taught us, in explicit terms, what a correctly functioning bride of Christ looks like to *him*. Within the context of the Jewish faith, Jesus's ministry gave humanity a new calling, led by him. Christianity is *his* idea. Therefore, we are charged to conform to *his* standard and *his* expectations as they are clearly articulated in the Gospels. Most of that has to do with how we love and, therefore, it ain't that hard to do.

This is where Enneagram 9 peacemaker personalities would interject to beg for nuance: "There are differing personalities, priorities, and perspectives represented among the body. Therefore, no two people will agree on a theologically correct application of Christianity to our culture." Granted. There is room for some nuance when it comes to the particular strengths and gifts we all have. But I believe living as image-bearers is not all, nor even mostly, nuanced. In fact, in regard to loving our neighbors, *our* personalities, priorities, and perspectives are irrelevant. We're called to love regardless. Jesus believed that there was an objectively correct way to love—and he taught us how to do it.*

For our purposes, pinpointing the issue presented requires identifying the origin of our rifts that keep us from functioning correctly. Any useful excavation will reveal the lure of power at the epicenter. To gain power, culturally and politically, the church has allowed the systems of the world to direct and change it rather than the other way around. The church has had a taste of what it's like to be disempowered in society, and we don't like it.

From a secular perspective, holding hands, fingers interlaced, with political influence and ideology is a logical means to avoiding future subjugation and gaining proximity to power. However, it's clearly not in keeping with Jesus's approach to power while he was here on earth. For those of us who discern this, and seek to model Christ in our culture, the white American church has become maddeningly unrecognizable.

Whatever else we glean from the 2016 presidential election, it's clear that the biggest distinction between MAGA Republicans and those who refused to vote for Trump came down to whether the president's personal character was important to his ability to govern. For those of us raised in the church, mindful of how conservative

*Matt. 22:37–39.

Christianity reacted to former president Bill Clinton's affair with Monica Lewinsky in the 1990s, debating the importance of an elected official's character seemed incomprehensible. Yet, confronted with that contradiction, 81 percent of white evangelicals held their noses and voted for Donald Trump in 2016, according to most polls. Even more confounding, most polls indicate that somewhere between 76 and 81 percent of white evangelicals doubled down in 2020.[5] But evangelicals weren't alone. Among nonevangelicals, Trump was the preferred choice for 57 percent of white Protestants in both the 2016 and 2020 elections. In 2016 he garnered 64 percent of the votes of white Catholics, who distanced themselves from him only slightly at 57 percent in 2020, when the other candidate was a Catholic, Joe Biden.[6]

> **The problem extends well beyond the walls of the evangelical church, where many reasoned they had to hold their noses and vote for Trump. The reality, however, is that they didn't just hold their noses—they endorsed.**

The problem extends well beyond the walls of the evangelical church, where many reasoned they had to hold their noses and vote for Trump. The reality, however, is that they didn't just hold their noses—they endorsed. Their advocacy saturated workplaces, family gatherings, social media, and church services, depriving us of any neutral ground and reminding us that there's a reason the election booth is private. The safeguards protecting the secrecy and integrity of our vote ensure that our personal political convictions are ours alone and no one knows how we voted unless we tell them. Yet white evangelicals didn't just vote for Donald Trump, they defended him and encouraged others to support him. After emerging from a huddle of religious leaders gathered at Trump Tower in 2015 to pray for candidate Trump, Paula White used the full weight of her religious gravitas to lure evangelical voters, announcing that she was serving as Trump's personal spiritual adviser.[7]

Candidate Trump earned significant clout when Jerry Falwell Jr. invited him to speak at Liberty University, where Trump infamously cited "two Corinthians" after declaring, "We're going to protect

Christianity. . . . I don't have to be politically correct."[8] Republican Christians hardly batted an eye when Trump was unable to provide a Bible verse or story that informed his thinking or character when asked to do so by conservative talk show host Bob Lonsberry during a 2016 radio interview.[9] The character or faith of the Republican nominee just didn't matter. Evangelicals weren't merely stomaching immorality, they planted a flag for it.

As a result, America bore witness to increased cultural violence as the president characterized the 1619 Project as propaganda,[10] justified violence against people protesting police brutality,[11] and called the COVID-19 virus "the China virus" and "Kung flu."[12] Not to mention the rise of online hate directed at women and minorities, depriving us even of the ability to feel safe as we access social media in the security of our own homes.[13]

So what hope do we have of realigning with white conservative Christians and functioning correctly as one body of Christ? Imagine living through the Holocaust, or the Rwandan genocide, and hearing your neighbors say, "Boy, that was something, huh? Oh well. Back to business. . . ." Just as the survivors could never see their neighbors and communities in the same way, we can never see America the way we once did. The pitched cultural battle may be over, but we have borne witness to crimes against humanity that cannot be forgotten.

As a result, we who staggered, disoriented and disheveled, from under the rubble of religious white supremacy have every right to be angry toward religious leaders who publicly locked arms with the MAGA mentality, discipled their congregants in "anti-woke" politics, turned on us when we denounced their hypocrisy, and reduced our faith to debris. Without a real opportunity to assess, and a safe place to do so, it's hard to be vulnerable enough to realize, much less admit, how broken we are. But I assure you, if you identify as a survivor of the evangelical church, you are not fine.

With all of this in mind, the actual issue up for discussion in this case is: Can we compartmentalize the precepts of our faith from the ethos we display to our neighbors and still represent Christ accurately? First lesson of advocacy: when you articulate the issue clearly enough, the answer seems so obvious that it begins to sound like a rhetorical question that answers itself.

If I've done my job correctly, your instinctive response to the issue presented was, "No, of course we cannot compartmentalize the precepts of our faith from the ethos we display to our neighbors and still represent Christ accurately." But let's explore further.

The crux (pun slightly intended) of modern Christianity, as I see it, is that we're experiencing cognitive dissonance between our true identity as "little Christs" and who we've shown the world we actually are.

In the summer of 2019, my family was looking for a new church. After attending, investing in, loving, and serving at our church, Toxic Fellowship Inc. (TFI),* for more than a decade, our identities were tangled up in our membership there. At this church, my wife and I had volunteered in the children's ministry, gone on mission trips, and regularly supported missionaries. My wife led worship for a women's ministry. My law firm committed hundreds of hours of resources working with the church's anti-human trafficking ministry—so much so that the firm was written into a million-dollar grant the ministry received from the state of Texas. Two of our children were baptized at TFI. We attended their marital counseling, parenting classes, and mission conferences; read the books authored by their pastors; and owned all the worship team's albums. We'd been firmly planted in a small group with other families we went to church with, studying the Word, sharing life's hardships and joys together. We were known, and not just by the pastors and leaders; this congregation of four thousand felt much smaller as we developed meaningful relationships in the community. This church was our home.

---

*Confession: the church wasn't actually called Toxic Fellowship Inc. But doesn't that sound on-brand for modern Christian marketing? Toxic Fellowship Inc. is the pseudonym I choose to use for a specific megachurch that we attended for more than ten years. When I hear about the pain experienced by so many at the hands of evangelical churches nationwide, I can't help but think of the specific church our family attended for so long. This congregation spawned several church plants around the globe, so it feels especially appropriate for it to serve here as an avatar for so many other evangelical churches nationwide that could figuratively operate as chapters of the same organization.

TFI changed my political views as well. While I tended to vote for Democratic candidates, I'd always been socially conservative, as many Black Americans my age and older are. (This is a largely unadvertised fact, given that most Black Americans are politically left-leaning. Not all, of course, but most.) Our parents and grandparents were raised in a time when the church was the nucleus of the community and the only source of empowerment. As a result, they made sure their children were in church on Sunday—attentively seated upright in the pews of a good Black, whooping, hellfire-and-brimstone preaching, gospel-choir-singing, tambourine-shaking, organ-playing, maroon-carpeted church for hours, wearing the cheapest, warmest, most unbreathable polyester suits that money could buy, despite the fact that the building's air conditioner was perpetually broken, the outside temperature was pushing 100 degrees Fahrenheit, and we were armed with nothing more than a standard-issue square, thin paper fan with a popsicle stick handle as our last line of defense against loss of consciousness. Can I get an amen?

While historically the Black church has been conservative on matters of personal morality, Black Americans tend to vote with liberals because the Democratic Party has been the only one expressly articulating an interest in the political issues that concern us. That's not to say that the Democratic candidates followed through on their promises, but they made us feel like our voices had their ear. I think conservatism appealed to me due to the rhetoric of being culturally embattled, the values espoused by those within TFI's community, and the accompanying hubris of moral clarity.

Beyond that, it's hard to be a progressive Christian in the South—especially in an area steeped in conservative political and theological ideology, attending the city's largest white evangelical church—without constantly being dragged before an inquisition to answer the question "But how can you be a Christian and a Democrat?" At some point it just becomes easier to be a Republican. They wear you down. But I thought I was one of them. The 2016 presidential election disabused me of that notion.

During the primaries and their immediate aftermath, the

consensus among conservatives within the religious community was that neither Hillary Clinton nor Donald Trump was a suitable candidate for president. Trump displayed an obvious and well-documented lack of character, but Clinton had those emails and the audacity of being a woman seeking the highest political office in our nation. Then there was the whole issue of abortion: while Clinton was pro-choice, Trump had a hard time giving a direct answer when asked if he was ever involved with a woman who had an abortion.[14] Notwithstanding the lack of moral equivalence, it just seemed too close a call for most moderate and conservative Christians, despite the fact that Trump's fetid vocabulary and vile behavior set him far apart. Honestly, the choice should have been clear to everyone when he crooked his hands and quivered to mock news reporter Serge Kovaleski's disability. There was an acute treachery in God's people, who know Christ as a healer, laughing or sitting silently as Trump mocked a disabled man.

Explaining the religious right's shift toward Trump, Kristin Kobes Du Mez, author of *Jesus and John Wayne: How White Evangelicals Corrupted a Faith and Fractured a Nation,* notes that his key endorsements included these religious leaders:

- Jerry Falwell Jr., then president of Liberty University
- Robert Jeffress, pastor of First Baptist Dallas, where Billy Graham had been a longtime member
- James Dobson, founder of Focus on the Family, who coaxed conservative Christians into believing Trump was a recent convert to Christianity, "a baby Christian," and asked evangelicals to "cut him some slack"

It seems, in the end, that white evangelical voters wanted a strongman who could stand against all the dangers and fears stoked by partisan politics and reclaim ground they felt was lost under the tenure of the first Black president. They sought a rugged cowboy, even if only a caricature of one; a John Wayne to lead them through the wilderness to the promised land despite the severity of his moral failings. "When it came to evangelical masculinity," writes Du Mez, "the ideological extreme bore a remarkable resemblance to the mainstream. . . . It was a vision that promised protection for women but left women without defense, one that worshiped power and turned a blind eye to justice, and one that transformed the Jesus of the Gospels into an image of their own making."[15]

And so it was. Politics, and polite society, would never be the same again. We've almost forgotten that for nearly a decade there were real, live human beings who believed that Barack Obama was a Muslim terrorist with a forged birth certificate, intent on bringing sharia law to the United States and stealing everyone's guns. Yet, time having proven such fears for naught, no apologies are forthcoming.

Remember the *Access Hollywood* video in which Trump admitted to sexually assaulting a married woman whom he "grabbed by the pussy"? Were that it had gotten no worse. Characterizing Mexican immigrants as drug dealers and rapists?[16] Portraying Vietnam War hero John McCain as a loser?[17] Sexually degrading a *Celebrity Apprentice* contestant?[18] Two impeachments, multiple indictments, $355 million in civil fraud penalties, an $83.3 million jury verdict for defamation to accompany a $5 million jury verdict against him in a writer's sexual abuse and defamation claim later, there are no deal-breakers for Trump's conservative evangelical base. Not even Trump selling gold high top sneakers during Black history month as a stereotypical marketing ploy to gain Black voters or hawking a "God Bless the USA" Bible during Holy Week ahead of Easter has alienated Trump from his voter base.[19] Equally as bad, Trump's dominating cultural influence has increased our tolerance for scandals and moral deficiency in, and outside of, Christianity.

In November 2016, I recall electricity in the air throughout the faith community as evangelicals became hopeful that Republicans could reclaim the White House. This was especially true in Texas. By this point I had lived in Central Texas a long time—since long before Chip and Joanna Gaines mined the first shiplap. I'd visited many churches and maintained relationships with many of the city's religious leaders. It was disturbing how many local white pastors openly opined (despite the fact that partisan endorsement should jeopardize their churches' 501(c)(3) status) that Christians could only vote Republican in the 2016 election with good conscience. When challenged to defend that position biblically, the response was consistent: "We're choosing a president, not a religious leader. Character is unimportant." The way this reasoning was parroted by the members of those churches is testament to the influential power of the pulpit. With a straight face, God's people reasoned with me that evil was acceptable in a leader if it created a *possibility* for good elsewhere. Not just that, they labeled me divisive for stating otherwise. This point is too important to miss: for believers such as these, the body of Christ can look healthy even if Christ-followers openly condone ungodly behavior. It's not just unity they're after; they've made allegiance a sacrament.

> We must ask ourselves as believers: Can we compartmentalize our faith from the ethos we display and still represent Christ accurately?

Reiterating the issue presented, we must ask ourselves as believers: *Can we compartmentalize our faith from the ethos we display and still represent Christ accurately?* When you craft the issue well enough, the answer seems so obvious that it begins to sound like a rhetorical question.

The Rule

Before we get ahead of ourselves by answering the issue, we have to discuss the rule we apply to get the answer (even if we already know the right answer). I imagine that if you're a farmer or physician, the Bible's agrarian metaphors and healing stories come to life for you in a way that's different for the average reader. As an attorney, every biblical allusion to justice comes to me in 4K Ultra HD resolution. In fact, one of the ways that I knew, even at age eleven, that I wanted to practice law was that my understanding of Scripture informed my understanding of justice and my perception of deviations from justice. The more I learned about God, the more sensitive my justice meter became. Even when I was neck deep in Republican politics, people often assumed I was secretly a liberal and dismissed me out of hand.

The thing most Christians no longer seem able to understand is that our faith should inform our politics; our politics isn't supposed to inform our faith. The causes I champion and my insistence on radical inclusion are not a product of my political leanings. I believe the things that I believe because my reading of the Bible leads me to understand God's expectations of us in a way many churches eschew as progressive. To quote Zach W. Lambert, pastor of Restore Austin, "I'm committed to racial justice because of the Bible, not in spite of it. I'm egalitarian because of the Bible, not in spite of it. I'm dedicated to liberation because of the Bible, not in spite of it. I'm affirming of LGBTQ+ folks because of the Bible, not in spite of it."[20] At this point in my life, I almost feel like I could open the Bible randomly and find an expression of God's heart for equity and justice displayed somewhere on whatever page appears. Justice is the helix on which God has placed his DNA. In her book, *An Untidy Faith: Journeying Back to the Joy of Following Jesus,* my friend Kate Boyd points out that the word we often translate as "righteousness" in the New Testament (Greek *dikaiosynē*) can also be translated as "justice." Boyd's insight is supported by Sylvia Keesmaat and Brian Walsh, authors of *Romans Disarmed: Resisting Empire, Demanding Justice.* In their book Keesmaat and Walsh expand our understanding of the biblical book of Romans by instructing us to envision reading the word *justice* throughout Romans every time the word *righteousness* appears on the page.[21]

As I understand it, in the Greek "righteousness" implies a state of physical justification—straightening an object to conform with a standard—the way a bike shop may straighten (also called rightening or trueing) a crooked wheel. That's an important detail for God's people to know in their journey to seeking righteousness. God's emphasis on justice in the here and now communicates that how we treat one another is of infinite import because we tell the world something about who God is in the way we treat them. Imagine how different living out our faith would look if we all understood righteousness as the fruit of our care for neighbors in society. What if the flourishing of the marginalized was such a nonnegotiable for American Christians that minorities weren't relegated to living in a perpetual state of being "fine"? This is an important view of righteousness that is woefully underutilized in our faith.

If the Bible is an authoritative source for understanding God's will for the believer, God's Word has to actually mean something when it's time to apply it to our lives and community. While there is some room for the interpretation of Scriptures, Christians must be on the same page about what the red letters say and mean when it comes time to demonstrate the love of Christ to the world around us.

Revisiting the IRAC structure for legal analysis, the Scriptures—not political trends—are the rules we apply to the issues identified. To use the law as an analogy, you have to know what the law is in order to apply the law.* Because of the Bible's voluminous references to God's heart for equity, I certainly can't do a detailed list of them any, well, justice. However, here is a collection of some of my favorite references to justice for the disenfranchised that should be obvious motivators to shape our faith:

- "Do not mistreat or oppress a foreigner, for you were foreigners in Egypt." (Exod. 22:21)
- "When a foreigner resides among you in your land, do not mistreat them. The foreigner residing among you must be treated as your native-born. Love them as yourself, for you were foreigners in Egypt. I am the LORD your God." (Lev. 19:33–34)
- "And you are to love those who are foreigners, for you yourselves were foreigners in Egypt." (Deut. 10:19)
- "Cursed is anyone who withholds justice from the foreigner, the fatherless or the widow. Then all the people shall say, 'Amen!'" (Deut. 27:19)
- "Do not oppress the widow or the fatherless, the foreigner or the poor. Do not plot evil against each other." (Zech. 7:10)

*Important distinction: "the law" in a scriptural context is different from "the law" in a legal context.

- "Wash yourselves; make yourselves clean; remove the evil of your deeds from before my eyes; cease to do evil, learn to do good; seek justice, correct oppression; bring justice to the fatherless, plead the widow's cause." (Isa. 1:16–17, ESV)
- "Is not this the kind of fasting I have chosen: to loose the chains of injustice and untie the cords of the yoke, to set the oppressed free and break every yoke? Is it not to share your food with the hungry and to provide the poor wanderer with shelter—when you see the naked, to clothe them, and not to turn away from your own flesh and blood? Then your light will break forth like the dawn, and your healing will quickly appear; then your righteousness will go before you, and the glory of the Lord will be your rear guard." (Isa. 58:6–8)
- "When the Son of Man comes in his glory, and all the angels with him, he will sit on his glorious throne. All the nations will be gathered before him, and he will separate the people one from another as a shepherd separates the sheep from the goats. He will put the sheep on his right and the goats on his left. Then the King will say to those on his right, 'Come, you who are blessed by my Father; take your inheritance, the kingdom prepared for you since the creation of the world. For I was hungry and you gave me something to eat, I was thirsty and you gave me something to drink, I was a stranger and you invited me in, I needed clothes and you clothed me, I was sick and you looked after me, I was in prison and you came to visit me.'" (Matt. 25:31–36)
- "The Spirit of the Sovereign Lord is on me, because the Lord has anointed me to proclaim good news to the poor. He has sent me to bind up the brokenhearted, to proclaim freedom for the captives and release from darkness for the prisoners, to proclaim the year of the Lord's favor and the day of vengeance of our God, to comfort all who mourn." (Isa. 61:1–2; quoted by Jesus in Luke 4:18)
- "Religion that God our Father accepts as pure and faultless is this: to look after orphans and widows in their distress

and to keep oneself from being polluted by the world." (Jas. 1:27)

- "Faith without works is dead." (Jas. 2:26 KJV; see 2:14–26).

This is the authority that we rely on as believers, the rule that guides our everyday analysis. TLDR: God is pretty interested in how we treat people. But it's the little people he seems particularly concerned with—the poor, the foreign, the orphaned. More importantly, the measure of our receptivity to—and actual administration of—justice is the measure of how we represent (literally, re-present, over and over in our daily lives) the image of Christ to the world. Thus it seems impossible for Christians to hold a genuine understanding of what our faith requires of us and represent Christ well while compartmentalizing that belief from our actions.

> TLDR: God is pretty interested in how we treat people. But it's the little people he seems particularly concerned with—the poor, the foreign, the orphaned.

A sentiment that I've often heard within congregations that centered whitewashed Christianity is that when Christians interact with the unsaved, it should leave them wanting more of what we have—inner peace and joy, the implication seems to be. While the heart behind this conviction may be well intended, in application it has often felt like a marketing ploy, like a free sample offered in the grocery store to entice shoppers to buy a product. What if a more accurate barometer of righteousness for Christians is how valued the disenfranchised feel after encountering God's people? Perhaps when we invite the world to our tables, they should leave feeling full. Occupying the seat of honor.

If the faith we claim matches the ethos we publicly display, there is no reason those we encounter should walk away guarded or estranged. Rather, our love of neighbor, and their contact with the representation of Christ, should leave the oppressed better than we found them. To quote a song I love by Switchfoot, they should feel "more than fine. More than just okay."[22]

Chapter 3

Mad as Heaven

*I*n the last chapter, we began utilizing the same tools employed by lawyers for legal analysis (IRAC: issue, rule, application, conclusion) to establish that, despite any assertion otherwise, as survivors of racialized spiritual abuse we are anything but "fine." We are angry! With good reason. We identified the *issue* plaguing white Christianity and the *rule* that governs how we should address the problem, the rule being God's consistent, clearly unequivocal concern for "the least of these," the poor in spirit. Accompanying said concern is Jesus's disdain for those who prey upon the weak.[1]

Therefore, we can rest assured that heaven is equally angered, if not more so, by those who commit abuse in the name of the Lord. In this chapter, we tackle the *application*—applying the rule to the facts of our case—and articulate our *conclusion*.

The Application

What should believers glean from the idea that God seems particularly concerned with the little people in a time where church seems particularly unconcerned? Asked another way, what does God's caring deeply about justice mean for a culturally and ideologically segregated church in such a deeply fractured country? Obviously, it implies a call to action, but let's not get ahead of ourselves. First, and foremost, it says that we have the right to be angry.

41

Adopting God's perspective only implicates a call to action because we initially recognize that something is amiss. You see, if everything looked the way it was supposed to, there would be no need for a call to action. Only those slumbering are roused to consciousness by trumpet's sound. The fact that this work has been so woefully neglected by those entrusted with the duty to act that the call to action is necessary is, in itself, an offense. It's something worth being mad about. Intuitively we understand that it requires a reaction. The anger animates the call to action; principle guides our response.

As we discuss "the gospel" in our modern, Western context, we lose sight of the historical import of the term. "Gospel" is an interpretation of the Latin *evangelium* (looks a little like the word "evangelical," doesn't it?) and Greek *euangelion.* As many sermons have informed us, it means "good news" or, perhaps more aptly, "good telling." In antiquity, these were declarations made on behalf of military victors. Propaganda. Augustus Caesar's *Pax Romana,* carved in stone in Priene (in modern Turkey), declares the end of war and the goal of common good for all humankind and establishes that all the cities under his rule will celebrate his birthday as the beginning of their calendar year. This was his gospel. A more famous example is found in modernity vis-à-vis *Avengers: Infinity War.* While navigating the slalom of deceased warriors strewn across the floor of an Asgardian spaceship, Ebony Maw, Thanos's hype man and magical henchman, declares, "Hear me and rejoice. You have had the privilege of being saved by the Great Titan. You may think this is suffering. No. It is salvation. Universal scales tip toward balance because of your sacrifice. Smile. For even in death, you have become Children of Thanos."[2] What can I say? Not every gospel has the same feel.

According to Luke, when Jesus comes on the scene, he starts his public ministry with a declaration in the synagogue, on the Sabbath, in Nazareth where he was raised. Prime time, center stage. Given the scroll of the book of Isaiah, Jesus chooses the Scripture reading for the day: "The Spirit of the Lord is on me, because he has anointed me to proclaim good news to the poor. He has sent me to proclaim freedom for the prisoners and recovery of sight for the blind, to set the oppressed free, to proclaim the year of the Lord's favor." That's quite the prophetic proclamation. But to make sure that no one missed it, still commanding everyone's full attention, Jesus adds, "Today this scripture is fulfilled in your hearing" (Luke 4:14–21). In other words: "I'm *Him*."

Jesus's life and ministry herald the arrival of a new reign that rivals that of Caesar and all worldly empires. If there was any doubt in the minds of those who saw him at work, Jesus makes his intentions transparent in this scene: a new king is here and a new kingdom with him. The people of the day understood that Jesus's movement placed him in ideological opposition to the political authority of Rome, which is why even his disciples thought that he was going to establish himself imminently as a political ruler. (See Acts 1:6.) This point cannot be overstated: the gospel—our gospel—isn't just good news in the abstract. It's not just "positive information," something to be happy about. The gospel is a proclamation of the reality that Christ has come to show us a better way—demonstrated to us in every act of compassion, mercy, and forgiveness, *including* his death on our behalf and resurrection. In real time, this felt like a political declaration of victory. And it was. Christ has conquered all earthly subjugating powers (including death!), which are now beholden to his cosmic authority. And he has done all this without firing one shot. It was not by oppressive might but in the most illogical demonstration of power possible: selfless love.

Grasping all that context, it should radically affect our comprehension of the gospel (the "rule" of our IRAC bulwark) as we apply it to the issue presented and inform how we should respond to the perversion of that gospel. Of all the times in history that Jesus could have come, and among all the cultures on earth that he could have inhabited, Jesus was incarnated as a member of a marginalized ethnic group—a Jewish man in Roman occupied territory. God could have chosen the appearance, citizenship, and pedigree of any people, including the imperial military superpower that oppressed the Jewish community, to convey his message. Instead, Jesus was born within a despised culture in the humility of a trough. To avoid despotic genocide, Jesus's parents took refuge in Egypt, the land in which his ancestors were enslaved under Pharoah's whip. His ministry developed in a society under the colonization, and scrutiny, of Roman (European) occupation. Taken together, the record shows that God took great pains to communicate to humankind how keenly he identifies with the lowly.

None of this is happenstance. While Jesus referenced salvation and the kingdom of heaven endlessly, only once in all of Scripture does a person directly ask Jesus how to receive salvation. In that single instance, God-with-us has a pointed answer.[3] The story of the rich young man (Mark 10:17–22; Matt. 19:16–22; and Luke 18:18–23) is substantially the same in all three accounts: a rich young man (a ruler in one account) approaches Jesus and asks what he must do to inherit eternal life. Jesus recounts at least five of the ten commandments to him: You shall not murder; you shall not commit adultery; you shall not steal; you shall not give false testimony; honor your father and mother, and (in Mark) you shall not defraud. Of the ten commandments given to Israel by God through Moses in Exodus 20, the first four pertain directly to humanity's vertical relationship to God. The remaining six commandments pertain to our relationship with God *through* our horizontal relationship with our fellow human beings—and these are the ones Jesus names to the young man as essential for salvation.

Matthew's Gospel makes this emphasis on horizontal, interpersonal relationships even more explicit, telling us that Jesus also said, "and love your neighbor as yourself" (19:19). Notice, this is *not* one of the ten commandments given by Moses, but it is the part of the Levitical law (Lev. 19:18) that Jesus elevates as the "greatest commandment" (Matt. 22:39 and Mark 12:31). When the rich man presses that he has fulfilled these commandments, Emmanuel reveals that the only thing lacking is for him to (a) liquidate all his assets, (b) donate that capital to the poor, and (c) follow Jesus. Summing up, in the only instance wherein the Bible records a human asking God *directly* how to receive eternal life, God tells that human to concern himself with his treatment of fellow humans, particularly the poor, and to follow him.

It's one thing to want to model charity for the sake of our fellow human beings. But God instructs us that to *inherit salvation,* a necessary precondition is our willingness to sacrifice whatever we esteem as our wealth, surrender our influence, and empathize with the suffering of the marginalized. This is how we apply the rule. And, for some reason, this seems like something the privilege of white Christianity is loath to do.

What Misapplication of the Rule Looks Like

I remember the day this all became clear to me: Sunday, November 6, 2016. This was the last Sunday before the 2016 presidential election. At Toxic Fellowship Inc., the head pastor (we'll call him Pastor Khakipants) gave a sermon titled "A Biblical Response to the Election." This message was meant to provide guidance to undecided voters as well as those who hadn't voted yet. It is important to understand that TFI prides itself on sending vast numbers of missionaries from its American locations to places all over the globe with the goal of planting more TFI churches and/or seeing large numbers of conversions abroad. Mission work is what TFI publicly strives to be most known for. Despite its humanitarian objective of ministering to diverse people groups worldwide, TFI is equally known for its politically conservative views. So, in such an unconventional election, how did the biblical lens through which our pastor saw the world inform his choice of political candidates? That's what every congregant was hoping to hear to aid them in applying the gospel to their anxieties going into the election.

That morning, Pastor Khakipants recited TFI's values as irreducible tenets of Christianity. He spent considerable time on the traditional definition of marriage and the rights of the unborn (no surprises there) but provided negligible, if any, discussion of how love of neighbor calls us not only to the mission field but also to serve the immigrant, the poor, the widow, the orphan, and the oppressed. We listened intently—an assembly of thousands perched on the edges of our seats, waiting to hear the pastor's official stance.

His conclusion was that our political system is binary and neither presidential candidate completely reflected our Christian values. Finis. The air seemed to leave the auditorium as we collectively slumped, deflated. Great, so what rubric could be used to decide? All across the auditorium, body language betrayed disappointment. A pregnant pause filled the air. It seemed like the sermon had come to an end. Maybe the pastor could feel the tension rising around us from his place on stage, because he didn't stop there. What he said next created a rift in our congregation that could never be closed.

As what felt like an afterthought, or even an apology, Pastor K. delivered his coup de grâce. In the absence of a clear choice between candidates, he stated that Christians should look at the "policies beneath the candidate." In so many words, the party platform. If we did that, he assured us we couldn't go wrong. Amen? Bring up the worship team and let's close.

I'm sorry, did I hear that right? Can we rewind a minute? Too late. By the time I realized what I'd heard, we were halfway through "Oceans." Stage lights bounced off of artificial fog and the band played on. All around, people were worshiping, singing, hands raised, and smiling as though our pastor endorsing an authoritarian narcissist from the pulpit was as normal as an altar call. While there was evidence of discomfort on some faces in the room, the vast majority seemed unperturbed. Everyone in the room understood the message to be a backdoor endorsement of the Republican platform and therefore its candidate, Donald Trump. Conservatives had the validation they were looking for; any personal discomfort with Trump's character did not matter. For those with questions about how to navigate their faith during an election season, the takeaway here was that Christians who applied the gospel according to the values of TFI would vote for Trump.

Growing up in Christianity, we almost exclusively utilized the King James Version of the Bible. My understanding of Exodus 20:7, "Thou shalt not take the name of the LORD thy God in vain," was that Christians should never use a curse word that contained the word *God*. You know the one I'm talking about. Now as an adult, in a post-Trump evangelical culture, I realize that a better reading is found in the New International Version: "You shall not *misuse* the name of the LORD your God, for the LORD will not hold anyone guiltless who misuses his name." The Good News Translation is even more clear: "Do not use my name for evil purposes, for I, the LORD your God, will punish anyone who misuses my name." At the same time, this reading gives more depth to verses that establish that the name of the Lord is holy.[4] The nuances of the word *holy* may be lost on the Western church today due to how often we use it in church culture. We tend to use *holy* as a synonym for *spiritual*. But to be holy is to be set apart as something devoted entirely to God or the work of God. In other words, neither commonly used nor used for common purposes. Because God's name is holy, we take it in vain if we deploy it for something as cheap as generating votes for politicians.

When we use God like a celebrity endorsement in a political ad, we are taking the name of God in vain. And there's a consequence for that. I don't know why it's so hard for evangelicals to grasp that God is not a Republican (or to hear that without reflexively and defensively adding, "or a Democrat!!!"). The orchestrated efforts to make Republican politics synonymous with evangelical Christianity are uniquely Republican. After all, we hardly ever hear about "the religious left," though it does exist. I do not envy the fate of those Christian leaders who abuse their station and walk blithely through the world as though their souls aren't flammable. It's one thing to anger our neighbors; it's another to anger God.

Most of the people I know who have left the local branch of TFI cite the preelection sermon, or one like it, as the reason for their departure. In fact, most of the people I've met who identify themselves as "exvangelical," agnostic, or atheists since Donald Trump's election point to a similar misuse of God's name as the cause of their withdrawal from Christianity. The preelection sermon delivered at TFI was so controversial among attendees that the church has since removed the recording of that sermon from its website.

TFI boasted a number of community outreach ministries that made the pastor's political stance bewildering. As the church placed great emphasis on international missions, TFI proudly advertised that it had missionaries and church plants in the most remote regions of the world. We had a ministry for feeding the poor and unhoused, volunteers who read to local elementary school children to improve literacy rates, and residential ministries dedicated to men and women in substance abuse recovery. All of these things suggested that the church prioritized caring for the marginalized—that the issue and rule were clearly defined. Yet TFI's preelection sermon, and others like it, present a glaring misapplication of the rule.

When it comes to politics, the perceived urgency of God's people "getting it right" during an election year cannot be paramount to the explicit, unconditional compassion Jesus expects of us. There is no moratorium on Christian ethics during an election year. Moreover, succumbing to the temptation to use the pulpit to defend voting for an immoral candidate precludes a host of options shy of endorsement:

- Preaching what love of neighbor looks like in action rather than to which political figure, or party, we can delegate that responsibility
- Reminding believers that there are options beyond the binary choice of Democrat or Republican
- Encouraging believers that if their conscience is so divided as to render choosing between two candidates impossible, nothing about our faith *requires* us to cast a vote

These concepts, especially the last, seem difficult for white Christianity to stomach. Especially in the Bible Belt. If pastors are going to attempt to engage political issues with intention and intelligence, it will require the church to regularly have discussions of healthy, discerning political engagement, because the level of nuance necessary to brave those waters can't be taught succinctly in a single sermon at the height of election season.

I want to make clear that TFI had plenty of public, and private, opportunities to clarify its position on the 2016 election. In fact, I had occasion to discuss my frustrations privately with the head pastor, and most of the associate pastors, separately. Feigned ignorance and broken promises to do better were the only fruit of those meetings. Increasingly noxious behavior among church members who desperately needed discipleship in the *imago Dei* eventually demonstrated that conditions at TFI were deteriorating, and after three years of hoping for change, it was time to leave.

The Sin of Duplicity

Many people have left their congregations, or Christianity altogether, after accepting that white Christianity has too closely aligned itself with political immorality. In hindsight, TFI was problematic to us because of what it failed to do as much as what it did wrong. In 2014, news coverage of the protests in Ferguson, Missouri, dominated headlines for weeks after police officers shot and killed Michael Brown, an eighteen-year-old Black man. This was an event of great significance to minorities nationwide, and I would estimate that ten percent of our local church identified as Black and fifteen percent as Latino. Yet, at TFI, there was silence in response to this tragedy. In 2016, Texans took to the streets of Dallas to protest the police killings of two more Black men, Philando Castile and Alton Sterling. The protest turned deadly when a Black Army veteran retaliated by opening fire, killing five police officers. A standoff between the gunman and police ensued, but it was brought to an abrupt, violent end when the police utilized a remote-controlled robot armed with a pound of C-4 plastic explosive to blow up the gunman without so much as a Miranda warning. For the BIPOC community, these events were fraught with the danger of blanket anti-Black sentiment where nuance was crucial.

How did TFI speak into these events? With a sermon encouraging forgiveness, particularly on the part of Black people who felt wronged by our white brothers and sisters. However, no suggestion was made that our white counterparts should strive to live in such a way as not to inflict pain that would need to be forgiven.

As blows to the American minority community became more commonplace, less was said from the pulpit. When something *was* said, it was limited to a small production from what I called "the diversity team": one of the two Black pastors on staff joined hands on stage with a Latino staff member, a white leader from the women's ministry, and one or two of the white associate pastors. They nodded intently in the background while Pastor Khakipants led a prayer for unity and reconciliation from the front of the stage. This was followed up by the regularly scheduled programming; nothing topical, of course.

During our time at TFI, the lynching of Black Americans by police officers became so commonplace that it failed to astonish. Hashtags mounted: Eric Garner. Tamir Rice. Laquan McDonald. Walter Scott. Eric Harris. Freddie Gray. Terence Crutcher. Jordan Edwards. Botham Jean. Atatiana Jefferson. No prayers were offered for these. Hard to tell why. Perhaps there were just too many to try to keep up with. But by the time the protests and demonstrations of civil disobedience began in 2020, following the deaths of George Floyd, Breonna Taylor, and Ahmaud Arbery, they were quickly met by white Christians and their church leaders with social media posts weaponizing Romans 13: "Obey those in authority." These are things that can never be forgotten—things that anger me deeply. These are things that should anger the church. And they anger the heart of God as well.

As believers, it should infuriate us that in the so-called bosom of democracy, a presidential candidate told thousands at his rally that they should feel free to assault a protester and he would pay the legal fees. Or that at a subsequent rally, Trump told the crowd how much he'd like to punch a protester, and the next month a Black protester at one of his rallies got sucker-punched by a white man as he was escorted from the building.

As a church that touted a focus on international missions, one of TFI's most successful church plants at this time was in Haiti. Yet its leadership did nothing to denounce the president's claim that Haiti, El Salvador, and Africa were "shithole countries."[5] The response that TFI should have given to the rhetoric that the president lobbed at its mission base was utter contempt. The response it gave was 404 error, input not found.

In 2016, when the Syrian refugee crisis became international news, TFI sounded a call for volunteers. By 2017, TFI could boast of having sent thousands of missionaries and medically trained volunteers to Greece and Europe to assist Syrian refugees (who, from a strictly legal standpoint, immigrated there illegally). Yet in 2018, when a caravan of refugees fleeing violence in Central America journeyed to the United States–Mexico border *on foot,* no mission teams from TFI were dispatched. Rather, the caravan was treated as a highly politicized albatross. "They could be terrorists!" the white evangelical refrain went. "They may be criminals!" Even though this opportunity to show the world what Christian charity looked like had landed in our figurative backyard (the South Texas border), TFI could hardly spare to send a small team to hand out bottles of water. Even that kindness came late.

By weird coincidence, once the 2018 midterm elections were over, the seemingly imminent threat of Brown people entering our southern border was no longer a talking point for evangelicals and politicians. It's almost as if all the fear and anxiety spun in the racial centrifuge had done its work as a catalyst for gaining the evangelical vote and was, thereafter, rendered inert. With all eyes turned away from the border crisis, TFI could afford to provide a nominal amount of humanitarian aid without political blowback. In fact, when the church finally sent a team of ten to Tijuana in 2019 to hand out blankets, it was praised for doing so in the local newspaper. The church was capable of far more than was reflected by the meager expedition team. Indeed, this humanitarian crisis is one of the few times that evangelicals *weren't* interested in sending people into the field to ~~colonize minorities~~ glorify God. This type of duplicity *should* make us angry.

The Sin of Compartmentalization

While TFI provides an archetype of the difficulty that white Christianity has applying the rule, it is, by no means, the only congregation struggling to do so. There is no shortage of examples to which survivors of white Christianity will likely relate.

It's one thing to presume that your pastor is playing politics; it's something different to see it unfold in real time. Remember in January 2019 when the Department of Health and Human Services inspector general found that thousands more migrant children than previously thought had been separated from their parents at the border since 2017? And that sometimes those kids, in the custody of the government, just kinda got . . . lost? And, sometimes, trafficked? Totally chill, no big whoop. Granted, there were already warnings that people were being detained in cages at the border and that those inhumane conditions were ripe to produce worst-case scenarios. But now that there was irrefutable evidence of people being kept in cages, kids separated from their families, and human trafficking, all within *Republican* government care? Well, that's just too much for even the #SaveTheKids "Party of Family Values" to ignore. Pro-life, anti-immigration Republicans were caught between a rock and a hard place. On one hand, they didn't want immigrants coming into our borders from the south, but on the other hand, these are children. Mitch McConnell was the first Republican to concede that the optics were bad and something had to get done. Soon after, Republican congressmen and senators representing Texas had jumped into the fray.

I remember watching how locally elected politicians and church leaders at TFI reacted to the groundswell of bipartisan support for fixing the border crises. Thereafter, pastors of several local churches were condemning the president's treatment of immigrants at the border on social media. Volunteers and assistant pastors of TFI were next (and next to last), publicly admitting that what the government was doing at the border was bad. But last of all, Pastor Khakipants himself issued a statement decrying the separation of families at the border. *Now that's leadership.*

Once President Trump's hand had been adequately slapped, conservative Christians high-fived each other and went back to their lives. It was around this time, however, that critical race theory started to be touted within evangelical Christianity as the single greatest threat to democracy and the gospel.[6] Systemic racism, the idea that particular injustices are not isolated events but indicative of systemic societal issues, was too outlandish for many in white Christianity to consider. But how can we compartmentalize slavery or Jim Crow from the whole of America's racial history? How can we separate a long history of mistreating African Americans from our commitment to treat all people as our neighbors?

This was particularly troubling for me because it was at TFI that I was first taught that our faith cannot be compartmentalized from our lives; there is no separation between the sacred and the secular. Compartmentalization, they warned, keeps us from realizing the entirety of our amphibious nature in the *imago Dei*—we are creatures of both spirit and flesh, living between water and dry land, as it were. The sermons preached often highlighted this duality: that our love for Jesus should be evident not just in ministry opportunities, but in our pursuit of excellence and service in our societal spheres. Settling for anything less would be a distortion of God's image in the world and "miss the mark." As Martin Luther opined, "The Christian shoemaker does his duty not by putting little crosses on the shoes, but by making good shoes, because God is interested in good craftsmanship." Made sense to me.

> The failure to apply biblical principles of equity, inclusion, justice, and diversity to racially polarizing political rhetoric and increasingly publicized violence against minorities wasn't simply a blind spot. It was a low priority.

The behavior, particularly online, of those who led and attended TFI made it clear that the failure to apply biblical principles of equity, inclusion, justice, and diversity to racially polarizing political rhetoric and increasingly publicized violence against minorities wasn't simply a blind spot. It was a low priority. It was baffling to watch. Ironically, as politics created greater divisions within the body of Christ, I began to realize that now it was I who was guilty of compartmentalizing. I was compartmentalizing my faith in Jesus, and my understanding of the gospel, from my church because neither that church nor the people I worshiped beside felt safe anymore. At this point I realized how out of place I was in the church I'd called home. And few things feel more amiss than a Christian without a church. I know I'm not alone. Beloved, it's not just you. It's not just one congregation. The church is no longer an accurate reflection of Jesus. Therefore, we have every right to be mad.

Recently, while discussing my experiences with racism, I was asked why I'm so angry. Minorities quickly recognize "angry" is in the same category of adjective as "divisive," and both are just around the corner from "uppity." But I always find the selective deployment of such terms to be interesting. No one called the white insurrectionists at the US Capitol on January 6 "angry," despite their building lynching gallows, assaulting and injuring 150 police officers, and contributing to the deaths of five people. If the issue presented is not whether the church can be unified, but whether we can function correctly, white Christians would do well to ask themselves why they constantly find themselves in the position of expecting minorities to exercise restraint in response to injustice.

It's maddening to be told you're wrong for remembering how Christianity was corrupted and how the Lord's name was used in vain. Like many seeking to find their place in Christianity again, I remember religious "who's whos" like Paula White, Ramiro Peña (from Waco, mind you), John MacArthur, Sean Feucht, Brian Houston, Kari Jobe, Cody Carnes, Brian and Jenn Johnson jockeying for proximity to former president Trump—literally in Oval Office photo ops and figuratively from their pulpits. We're angry that the prophetic voice of Christianity has gone mute. We remember that the evangelical industrial complex refused to condemn *any* aspect of the former president's behavior or the actions of those acting on his rhetoric. We recall how baneful ideas bounced off each other until our churches became echo chambers that became particle accelerators.

There are people who watched video of a human being lynched

by police officers over the course of ten minutes on a public side-walk in 2020 and walked away unmoved, untransformed in their views of racism and police brutality. They discerned no connection between the historical treatment of minorities in America and a Black man pleading with police officers, "I can't breathe." While we witnessed a murder, they saw only an accidental death, not the latest of many links in a chain.[7] Worse, some believers witnessed the same homicide and called it justified. Yet they want us to believe that they have been transformed by reading about the state-sanctioned lynching of Jesus that happened more than two thousand years ago. We're not buying it.

There's a reason that people are leaving the church. In 2018, the *New York Times* published an article called "A Quiet Exodus: Why Black Worshipers Are Leaving White Evangelical Churches."[8] In October 2020, the *Atlantic* published a similar article, "The Church's Black Exodus: Pastors' Silence on Racism and COVID-19 Is Driving Black Parishioners Away from Their Congregations."[9] Despite the difficulty of this terrain we travel, we know we're not alone. We know now that the problem is systemic. We have the right to be angry. Observing the refusal of self-proclaimed Christians to modify their behavior so that the church can function correctly, how can we be anything *but* angry?

There are a lot of calls for unity within the evangelical church. These come so often from leaders who have torn the body of Christ apart, unironically asking us to be at peace with believers who feel as though they've done nothing wrong. But, quoting Dr. Martin Luther King Jr., "True peace is not merely the absence of tension; it is the presence of justice."[10] Some of us aren't ready to let white Christianity off the hook for what it has done, and is still doing, because we know that history has a way of repeating itself. "And those who don't know their history are doomed to leap from life to life, striving to put right what once went wrong, and hoping each time that our next leap will be the leap home."* So how should

---

*Shout out to those who recognize this reference to *Quantum Leap*.

those of us who witnessed the church contorting itself for the sake of power feel about not just these institutional sins but the fact that we're expected not to be mad about it? How should we feel about this idea that we can have unity, so long as we absolve wrongdoers from any accountability? Mad as heaven.

Lucille Clifton wrote a poem that I think about every time I find myself angry about the ways white Christianity attempts to stifle righteous anger:

why some people be mad at me sometimes

they ask me to remember
but they want me to remember
their memories
and i keep on remembering
mine.[11]

Conclusion

In *conclusion,* the last step in our IRAC analysis, can we Christians compartmentalize our faith from the ethos we publicly display and still represent Christ accurately? Said another way, when our orthopraxy is out of whack, can we really claim to have right (orthodox) belief?[12] Absolutely not. God's Word and the life of Jesus make this clear. Remember what we said about articulating the issue in legal analysis: if you craft the issue well enough, the answer seems so obvious that it begins to sound like a rhetorical question. Clearly, when presented with this question, believers should understand the answer is no. Confronted with this hypocrisy, white Christianity simply stopped asking the question.

As believers, we re-present Jesus to the world that we inhabit. We are, at best, representations of a greater entity, and it is only out of that identity and mission that we carry any authority or credibility. Christianity is not our thing. It's God's. Whether we like it or not, God gets the first, intermediate, and final say on what we should believe, how we behave, and how we display God's self to the world we live in. As Paul reminds us, we are not our own; we were bought with a price (1 Cor. 6:19–20). So where does the church get off presenting Christ as the champion of charlatans?

Jesus had harsh words for spiritual leaders who intentionally misrepresented his Father's love.

- "Woe to you, teachers of the law and Pharisees, you hypocrites! You shut the door of the kingdom of heaven in people's faces. You yourselves do not enter, nor will you let those enter who are trying to." (Matt. 23:13)
- "Woe to you, teachers of the law and Pharisees, you hypocrites! You travel over land and sea to win a single convert, and when you have succeeded, you make them twice as much a child of hell as you are." (v. 15)
- "Woe to you, teachers of the law and Pharisees, you hypocrites! You give a tenth of your spices—mint, dill and cumin. But you have neglected the more important matters of the law—justice, mercy and faithfulness. You should have practiced the latter, without neglecting the former." (v. 23)
- "Woe to you, teachers of the law and Pharisees, you hypocrites! You are like whitewashed tombs, which look beautiful on the outside but on the inside are full of the bones of the dead and everything unclean. In the same way, on the outside you appear to people as righteous but on the inside you are full of hypocrisy and wickedness." (vv. 27–28)

It is insufficient for white Christianity to ask what's necessary to foster unity in the church. That inquiry bypasses the underlying issue that got us into this mess. In light of the division created by white evangelical, patriarchal, Christian nationalism, the most oft proposed solution is that the church should stop talking about politics. However, evangelical congregations in particular seem unable to resist the urge to call believers to arms when the political stakes are raised once again. The urgency seems to be greatest every four years. Even still, the problem we're having is not that the church has been involved in politics.* The overlap of faith and politics is inescapable because in a representative democracy "we the people" are (in theory) vested with the ability to petition the government for redress of grievances, and a large segment of those vested with that ability also identify as having some sort of organized religious belief system. Therefore, inevitably, you will have some people motivated in their political lives by their religious beliefs. What needs to be avoided, however, is a church whose faith is informed by its political beliefs.

The gospel has inherent political implications. How the people of a democratic society should allocate government resources based on our understanding of what is fair and right necessarily interrogates our core beliefs about who we are, what we believe to be the correct state of the world, and the origin of those beliefs. For the believer, those core beliefs emanate from our understanding of the *imago Dei* and the mission that we've been called to— the reasons for which we believe that we were created. Therefore our faith necessitates our political engagement. The problem is not that the church has gotten political, but that we haven't gotten political enough and that our political ethic does not align with our biblical ethic.[13] Who we claim to be should be evident in the rhetoric we utilize, who we stand beside, the causes we lend our voices to, how we advocate, and the policies, or politicians, we endorse. This is our true and proper worship (Rom. 12:1).

Correspondingly, no one is more grieved by the distortion of the image of Christ than Christ himself. When we realize that the way the white church misrepresents Christ is not incidental, but an intentional, concerted effort to usurp our faith, we have every right

---

*Contrary to popular belief, there is no constitutional provision calling for the separation of church and state. That idea came from numerous essays penned by James Madison as well as a letter written by Thomas Jefferson. There are, however, constitutional provisions prohibiting laws against the free exercise of religion and preventing the declaration of one particular religion as a state religion.

to be livid. It's not an accident that Christ has been maligned and his children abused. It's a coup. An insurrection. We are right to be angry. Here is where the church has the opportunity to be united— not unification for the sake of hegemony, but unification to function as the church is intended. Thus writes Peter, "Finally, all of you, have unity of spirit, sympathy, love for one another, a tender heart, and a humble mind" (1 Pet. 3:8, NRSVue).

So how should we respond? It's one thing to be angry, but how do we put that anger to good use? Here it's important for us to appreciate that the appropriate reaction does not require a big production on our part. As we go ahead, responding in righteous anger may be quite simple. It may look like dedicating ourselves to the abatement of toxicity, changing the cultural lens that informs how we read the Bible, reevaluating our theology, or cutting ties with those we know are committed to perpetrating spiritual abuse. We needn't be bitter, but on the whole, we're probably not angry enough.

Part 2

Burn It All

Chapter 4

Pass Me Not

*M*artin Luther King Jr. famously stated, "The arc of the moral universe is long, but it bends towards justice."* King's optimism postulates that no matter how long it takes, justice is an inevitability—a naturally occurring, consistently observable phenomenon of the moral universe. Perhaps it could even be seen as the natural state to which all things must eventually return. This is the hope we were raised with in America. It was preached from the pulpits of the little southern Black Baptist church where I was baptized after giving my life to Christ. Sam Cooke belted it out from vinyl grooves spun on my father's record player that promised, "It's been a long, a long time coming / But I know a change gonna come, oh yes it will."[1] But most notably, it was echoed to us in the assurances of white American Christianity: "Be patient." "Things are in the works." "The right time is coming; just not yet."

When I survey the history of wins and losses for Black folks in America, however, I can't help but notice a multitude of tallies in the loss column militating toward the conclusion that justice *doesn't* happen as a matter of course. Far too often, we lose. We are passed over. When I consider the long arc we journey on, hoping it leads toward justice, I hear the words of a hymn by Fanny J. Crosby (1820–1915), "Pass Me Not, O Gentle Savior."

*King was quoting nineteenth-century abolitionist pastor Theodore Parker.

Blind from six weeks old, Fanny was reportedly a creative early on, composing works when she was as young as six years old and writing more than 8,500 gospel songs during the course of her life.[2] Hymnologist William J. Reynolds reported that the inspiration for "Pass Me Not" came from her visit to a prison during 1868. After she led a service with the inmates, one of the prisoners cried out, "Good Lord, do not pass me by." Inspired by his plea and the biblical story of the blind beggar calling out, "Jesus, Son of David, have mercy on me!" (Luke 18:38), Crosby penned a powerful hymn that takes on even greater depth when sung in the Black church. Sometimes, I meditate on renditions sung by Pastor Dewey Smith or, if I need to cry, the spine-chilling version sang by Fantasia Barrino in her autobiographical movie, *Life is Not a Fairytale*.[3] The plaintive words:

> Pass me not, O gentle Savior,
> Hear my humble cry;
> While on others Thou art calling,
> Do not pass me by.
>
> Savior, Savior,
> Hear my humble cry;
> While on others Thou art calling,
> Do not pass me by.

In my legal work, I often ponder King's theory of justice as an eventual certainty alongside Fanny Crosby's cry—particularly on those dark days when injustice has its way. I've seen enough to cast doubt on King's optimism. In fact, at what point in America's history have Black believers been able to take solace in a realistic *expectation* of justice? Far too often, we are more like the blind beggar pleading, Lord, do not pass us by!

Whether you believe that our sinful nature is a product of humanity's fall in the garden of Eden and that all of creation fell when Adam and Eve sinned,[4] or that humanity's penchant for selfishness and wrongdoing is a simple, observable fact, we must concede that the systems and structures we build are similarly tainted with the same venom. We may contrive systems such as democracy in an effort to reach the original, platonic forms, but our work is sabotaged from the onset by our own being. Yet, simultaneously, the shortcomings prove that the ideal must exist—even if not on this plane of existence. In the words of Jon Foreman, "the shadow proves the sunshine,"[5] that is, what we see provides proof of the unseen.

Justice, the basic premise that things should be fair, is a concept that should be held by all and had to have come from somewhere. The English minor turned lawyer in me tends to overthink the significance of rhetoric. For instance, the word *law* implies governance, which implies a governor. The existence of a management system implies a programmer. Something had to set the thing in motion. Aristotle referred to this unseen thing as the Unmoved Mover—the primary (first) cause. The thing that put the law in place. There are objective moral specifications after which the world was designed but to which it fails to conform. God's specifications. Genesis punctuates the impossibility of our living by those standards absent a savior. Our hope as believers is that through Christ, we, and all of creation, will one day be *justified*— straightened, made right, corrected to align with those standards that predate us. Therefore perhaps the most basic moral law that can be observed in regard to justice is that we are predisposed to deviate from it.

I consider all this as I reflect on King's postulation of the inevitable trajectory of justice in the moral universe. I believe that we tend to embrace his beautiful prose as a law of nature rather than a defiant encouragement of hope to comfort the weary. But I fear that King overstated his case. Said plainly: nothing in the historical, observable conditions of our world demonstrates a natural trajectory toward justice.[6] Rather, there is ample evidence that meticulously drawn blueprints created the architecture which bolsters racism in our society.

We didn't arrive here by accident. Throughout the development of our democracy, one incremental, prejudicial change of the law has prompted another. Each outcome operates like a domino falling and impacting a subsequent one until a carefully planned mosaic is revealed. We call this mosaic America. As that picture has developed, so too have the trends empowering the white majority to the detriment of minorities. As the evidence will demonstrate, having power and privilege tend to inhibit an inclination toward justice. In her book *White Fragility: Why It's So Hard for White People to Talk about Racism,* Robin DiAngelo clarifies that the majority culture's persistent effort to gain and maintain power in the United States is actually white supremacy. DiAngelo defines white supremacy as the "system of structural power [that] privileges, centralizes, and elevates white people as a group." As evidence, she notes that in 2016–17, 82 percent of teachers were white; 84 percent of full-time college professors were white; the gatekeepers of book publication and TV show production were 90 and 93 percent white, respectively; and 100 percent of the top US military advisers were white. Recognizing whiteness as the default setting for our nation's institutions, DiAngelo concludes that these numbers "represent power and control by a racial group that is in the position to disseminate and protect its own self-image, worldview, and interests across the entire society." Indeed, an immutable truth regarding power is that it is difficult to give up once attained and difficult to wrest from those who have attained it. Thus DiAngelo observes, "For those of us who work to raise the racial consciousness of whites, simply getting whites to acknowledge that our race gives us advantages is a major effort. The defensiveness, denial, and resistance are deep."[7]

Nowhere is that clearer in America than in the treatment of minorities. Overwhelmingly, that treatment has been at the hands of those who identify themselves as followers of Christ. Consequently, nothing in the historical, observable conditions of white Christianity can be said to demonstrate a natural bent toward justice. This is essential for us to understand as we endeavor to move from the place of questioning our sanity in white-dominant spaces, even and especially Christian ones. Justice is the exception rather than the rule, and this has important implications for how we understand racialized spiritual abuse. And once we see injustice is a meticulously orchestrated backdrop of white Christianity, it gives us permission to be angry.

Because justice is not the natural disposition of humanity generally, or America's white Christian hegemonic power specifically, remedying injustice has never been as simple as the oppressed gently reminding the oppressor that they are out of alignment with the expectations of civil society or a loving God.

The "All Lives Matter" Lie

Many of us, as schoolchildren in the United States, had to memorize these iconic words from the Declaration of Independence:

> We hold these truths to be self-evident, that all men are created equal, that they are endowed by their Creator with certain unalienable Rights, that among these are Life, Liberty and the pursuit of Happiness.

How complicated such a simple idea has become. Note that this first step on the path toward our nation's identity was paved with rhetoric establishing that the founders' view of equality blossomed from their theism. Hence the assertions that all men are *created* equal and that they are endowed with unalienable rights *by their Creator*. Those naive or privileged enough to be unscathed by evidence to the contrary will point out that while our founders wrote "all men," they surely must have meant all people—women as well as men, the poor and enslaved as well as landowning and free. It is perhaps in this same naiveté that many today insist "all lives matter" when we protest the ongoing brutality against and denial of rights to Black Americans with the words "Black lives matter!"

But our history—even our current events—tell another tale. After twenty-plus years studying and practicing the law, I remain stunned by how often, in this allegedly Christian nation, our legal jurisprudence boils down to someone saying, "Black people shouldn't be able to live as freely as white people," an ensuing battle, and a court deciding the issue. The evidence suggests that "all" does not truly mean all in the mouths of today's counterprotesters any more than it did when it flowed from the pen of Thomas Jefferson, who spoke of freedom while simultaneously holding more than six hundred people captive.[8]

The difficulty that professing Christians have with this concept makes me want to scream, "What part of your American history class did you miss that you don't understand that when America claims, 'Actually, all lives matter,' we can't take America at its word?" Some may feign ignorance, but everyone knows where the dividing lines in our nation are. Everyone recognizes the events that have defined so many lives and require us to pick sides. We all understand what's at stake in the rhetoric we use and ideals we affirm. As such, if you still have difficulty saying "Black lives matter" at this late date, I don't know that we can have a relationship. Everything that has transpired in our world from 2015 to the present has served as a litmus test for our faith, humanity, and ability to fellowship with one another. Sadly, many have failed. Sometimes I miss the simplicity of life as a modern-day house Negro—"one of the good ones"—on a "colorblind" plantation. I now see that this is what I was in my multiracial evangelical church. But I can never return, even if I wanted to. When I realized that "all men are created equal" was never intended to include me, and still does not in the eyes of many, my expulsion from the Matrix was complete.

> When I realized that "all men are created equal" was never intended to include me, and still does not in the eyes of many, my expulsion from the Matrix was complete.

The fact remains that when the founders penned the Declaration of Independence in 1776, asserting, "We hold these truths to be self-evident, that all men are created equal," it was not enough to translate to equity for all. Enslaved Blacks were legally seen as property. Ironically, while the founders made sure to include a specific clause in the Constitution giving Congress express authority to terminate chattel slavery (though not for at least twenty years into the future), the provision referred to the enslaved not as property but as *people*:

The Migration or Importation of such *Persons* as any of the States now existing shall think proper to admit, shall not be prohibited by the Congress prior to the Year one thousand eight hundred and eight. (US Constitution, art. 1, sec. 9; emphasis added)

The intellectual acrobatics necessary to legally justify buying, selling, trading, owning, and assaulting humans—handling them as chattel—when your own founding documents acknowledge their humanity is remarkable. Lord, have mercy.

Even when slavery was abolished, and laws and court decisions proclaimed that "all persons" are free, that the country would "do no act or acts to repress such persons, or any of them, in any efforts they may make for their actual freedom" (Emancipation Proclamation, 1863), the issue of equality remained unsettled, for if that proclamation had been enough, slavery would not have continued beyond that point, nor would the Negro continue to strive for civil liberties.

In 1868, when the Fourteenth Amendment to the Constitution was ratified, the phrase "all persons" was employed again to ordain that anyone born in the United States was to be considered a citizen, with all the rights, privileges, and protections thereof. Nonetheless, a mere twelve years later, the Supreme Court revisited the language of the amendment as it considered whether the amendment provided economic protection from monopolies in New Orleans, Louisiana. Referring to the amendment, the court opined:

It ordains that no State shall deprive any person of life, liberty, or property, without due process of law, or deny to any person within its jurisdiction the equal protection of the laws. What is this but declaring that the law in the States shall be the same for the black as for the white; *that all persons,* whether colored or white, shall stand equal before the laws of the States, and, in regard to the colored race, for whose protection the amendment was primarily designed, that no discrimination shall be made against them by law because of their color?[9]

Seems pretty clear. Yet people unable to envision the humanity of others become remarkably creative when it comes to defending their dominant status. After Homer Plessy, in 1892, booked passage on a "whites-only" rail car in violation of Louisiana's Separate Car Act of 1890, the US Supreme Court issued the landmark opinion of *Plessy v. Ferguson*, holding that a state's segregation law could be upheld so long as it provided facilities that were equal to those of whites, though they be separate.[10]

Like "separate but equal," the classification "colored" and the "one-drop rule" were invented to maintain segregation even when the accused had more white heritage than not. In 1910, Louisiana's Supreme Court heard the state's appeal of the case of Octave and Josephine Treadway, who had been acquitted of the charge of interracial sex on the basis of what some would consider a technicality.[11] By a vote of 3–2, the court reasoned that Josephine Treadway, being an "Octoroon" (i.e., one-eighth Black) could not be considered "a person of the Negro or Black race" within the meaning of the statute. Comparing the laws of twenty-seven other states for insight to define the word "Negro," the court ultimately opined:

> We do not think there could be any serious denial of the fact that in Louisiana the words "Mulatto," "Quadroon," and "Octoroon" are of as definite meaning as the word "man" or "child." . . . Nor can there be, we think, any serious denial of the fact that in Louisiana, and, indeed, throughout the United States (except on the Pacific slope), the word "Colored," when applied to race, has the definite and well-known meaning of a person having *Negro blood in his veins* [emphasis added].

Thus was born the distinction of the "Colored" caste. The acquittal was a scandal throughout the southern states. The entire issue litigated was race and, in this instance, defendants who were functionally Black were let off on a technicality. Pearls were clutched. Within a month, Louisiana's legislature amended the statute to define "Negro" as one-thirty-second blood fraction. Similar statutes distinguishing Black people with as little as one-thirty-second blood heritage were adopted by states wishing to avoid the embarrassment of an acquittal such as the one in Louisiana. In this sense, Louisiana was on the leading edge of legislating racism.

It was not until 1924, fourteen years later, that Virginia codi-
fied the Racial Integrity Act through the efforts of Walter Plecker,
a white physician and Virginia's registrar of vital statistics. Plecker
was motivated by his belief in eugenics and desire to curtail the
ability of light-skinned minorities to pass as white. Plecker's work
would become known as the "one-drop rule," dictating that any
child born with one drop of Black blood in their ancestry was, by
law, Black. Jesus, son of David, have mercy.

Where creativity and technicalities did not work to prevent
Black Americans' inclusion as "all people," white America simply
dragged its feet. In 1954, the US Supreme Court took up the matter
of *Brown v. Board of Education,* revisiting the "separate but equal"
doctrine established fifty-eight years earlier in *Plessy v. Ferguson.*
Under the 1896 holding of *Plessy,* states had a way to pass legisla-
tion promoting segregation so long as there were alternative facilities for minorities of equal quality. In *Brown,* the issue presented
was whether segregation in public schools deprived minorities of
equal educational opportunities though the facilities and other tangible factors were equal. The lower court acknowledged that segregation "has a detrimental effect on colored children. The impact is
greater when it has the sanction of the law, for the policy of sepa-
rating the races is usually interpreted as denoting the inferiority of
the negro group."[12] Yet it fell upon the Supreme Court to take action
on behalf of the Black plaintiffs. Overturning *Plessy,* the court recognized that *intangible* considerations dictate that the indignities of
segregation inherently prevent equality. Therefore, the court concluded, education "is a right which must be made available to all
on equal terms."[13] Segregationists felt as though the world was ending. But, because the court left open the question of *how quickly*
integration needed to happen, and its logistics, the *Brown* opinion
was little more than a paper tiger.[14] Obscurity provided an interpre-
tive escape hatch for segregationists and made enforcement difficult. Ambiguity and discretion wedded in the South.

In Little Rock, Arkansas, the school board agreed to comply with
the high court's ruling, but the plan to implement desegregation

would take two more years. In 1957, the NAACP registered nine Black students to attend Little Rock Central High School. These students, later known as the Little Rock Nine, didn't just show up on the first day of class, receive their schedules, and begin their studies. Rather, the governor of Arkansas mobilized the Arkansas National Guard to prevent these *children* from entering the school. Nothing less than the intervention of President Eisenhower, who ordered federal troops to escort the nine into Central High School, would suffice to enforce the high court's ruling in *Brown*. It literally took an army for Black children and white children to go to school together.

Nearly a decade after the *Brown v. Board of Education* decision, Alabama's segregationist governor George Wallace literally stood in the doorway of the University of Alabama, flanked by five armed police officers, to block admission of two Black students into the school for the summer 1963 term. Again, it took an army for Black folks to get an education.

Prince Edward County, Virginia, resisted the mandate to desegregate by starving its public schools of funding. The effect was that the public schools, unable to operate without funding, closed for five years while the county gave tuition credits and tax concessions to white families for the creation and operation of white-only private schools. Ten years after *Brown,* the highest court was again forced to speak into the issue of race by declaring this scheme unconstitutional, ordering the district to reopen the public schools and desegregate.[15] We see this same scheme in action today as state legislatures argue for a private school voucher system while defunding public schools. White America's refusal to accept that "all" means all has had to be relitigated over and over again.

In 1958, when a white man and a Black woman married in the nation's capital and moved to Virginia, we learned that, in the government's mind, the Fourteenth Amendment's "all persons" did not apply to interracial couples. After establishing their residence in Virginia, Mildred and Richard Loving were arrested, charged, prosecuted, and convicted of miscegenation (the interbreeding of people of different races). It took nine years,[16] multiple appeals, and (ultimately) nine Supreme Court justices to clarify, in the words of Chief Justice Earl Warren:

> The clear and central purpose of the Fourteenth Amendment was to eliminate *all* official state sources of invidious racial discrimination in the States. There can be no question but that Virginia's miscegenation statutes rest solely upon distinctions drawn according to race.[17]

The issue of equality in America's transportation system, as debated in 1896's *Plessy v. Ferguson,* needed expansion and clarification throughout the twentieth century to prohibit segregation on vehicles traveling between states. In 1946, the court decided the case of *Morgan v. Virginia,* opining that under the commerce clause of the Constitution (art. 1, §8, cl. 3), such restrictions created an untenable lack of uniformity, posed an undue burden on interstate commerce, and could not be validated by the powers reserved to the states by the Tenth Amendment.[18] However, the legality of segregation in public transportation was still being litigated in Mississippi, where state laws, local ordinances, and informal practices continued to enforce segregation in spite of federal law. Thus, citing a number of cases the court had previously decided,[19] the high court's 1962 opinion in *Bailey v. Patterson* reminded Mississippi, "We have settled beyond question that no State may require racial segregation of interstate or intrastate transportation facilities. The question is no longer open; it is foreclosed as a litigable issue."[20] Mississippi and other entities would find plenty more to litigate.

On August 28, 1963, the Rev. Dr. Martin Luther King Jr. gave his famous "I Have a Dream" speech to approximately 250,000 people during the March on Washington for Jobs and Freedom.[21] The march and King's speech shared the pragmatic goal of demanding economic equality for Black Americans. It was in *that* context that King spoke of a dream deeply rooted within the American dream and bade freedom ring from sea to sea in every state and city. It still took nearly another year, to July 2, 1964, for President

Lyndon Johnson to sign the Civil Rights Act of 1964 into law, prohibiting discrimination in the workplace due to race, color, religion, or nationality.

A mere five months later, the US Supreme Court decided *Heart of Atlanta Motel, Inc. v. United States*. In that case, the Heart of Atlanta Motel brought suit claiming the Civil Rights Act of 1964 was an unconstitutional overreach of power by Congress because it prohibited the motel from refusing to serve certain persons whom it wanted to exclude as guests—namely, Negroes. In a move that feels familiar to arguments we've heard in the modern era (particularly the line of cases following the Masterpiece Cakeshop litigation), the plaintiff argued that enforcement of the act *against the hotel* was akin to slavery because the government was forcing the hotel to do business with minorities against its will. The court opined in response,

> We find no merit in the remainder of appellant's contentions, including that of "involuntary servitude." As we have seen, States prohibit racial discrimination in public accommodations. . . . We could not say that the requirements of the Act in this regard are in any way "akin to African slavery."[22]

The next year, on August 6, 1965, President Johnson signed the Voting Rights Act of 1965 into law, in an attempt to put an end to racialized voter suppression tactics under Jim Crow. The Voting Rights Act provided a glimmer of light for the Black community in an otherwise dark year that had already brought the assassination of Malcolm X in February and "Bloody Sunday" in March, when more than six hundred activists marching in protest of voter discrimination were beaten and teargassed by police at the Edmund Pettus Bridge in Selma, Alabama. Absent the brutality witnessed that day, passage of the Voting Rights Act may have failed. But that which providence and persistence accomplished in 1965 may soon be imperiled as battering rams can still be heard at the doors of the halls of justice.

In 2013, the Supreme Court gutted the Voting Rights Act by ruling that section 4 was unconstitutional. The court's opinion in *Shelby County v. Holder* eliminated the necessity for jurisdictions that have historically utilized unconstitutional requirements to suppress minority votes (such as literacy tests) to seek federal preapproval before making changes to their voter eligibility protocols.[23] Immediately following the *Shelby* decision, Texas implemented voter identification laws designed to suppress minority votes, and many other states followed suit.[24] While attacks on the Voting Rights Act continue, for now it stands, even if barely. In 2023, the Supreme Court had the opportunity to determine that the remainder of the Voting Rights Act was unconstitutional in *Allen v. Milligan,* a case which arose (ironically) from Alabama.[25] Upholding the constitutionality of the act by the narrow margin of 5–4, the court rejected an Alabama redistricting map designed to dilute Black votes. While a win is a win, the thin majority of the *Allen* court forecasts future litigation aimed at eviscerating the voting rights of minorities.

On April 4, 1968, Martin Luther King Jr. was murdered. With King's legacy fresh in the mind of all Americans, President Johnson signed the Civil Rights Act of 1968 (also referred to as Fair Housing Act) into law seven days later. Almost immediately, a case came before the Supreme Court in which a white defendant claimed his refusal to sell a home to a Black man was not a violation of the act because the federal statute applied only to government actors, not to private citizens, and therefore he was free to discriminate in the sale or lease of private property. The court ruled that federal law could effectively prohibit discrimination in the sale or rental of property—whether public or private. In delivering the court's opinion, Justice Potter Stewart stressed that to do any less would mean "the trumpet of freedom that we have been blowing throughout the land has given an 'uncertain sound,' and the promised freedom is a delusion."[26]

It was still not enough. In the 1978 *Bakke* case, the high court affirmed, for the first time, that public universities could consider race as a positive factor in admissions decisions. In 2003, the court held that the reasoning of *Bakke* applied to a law school's desire to use race as a positive factor in its admissions process. This victory was short-lived. Affirmative action in academia was all but destroyed by the high court ruling in 2023 that race could no longer be a factor in admissions considerations.[27]

We're far from done. There's simply not enough paper or ink to discuss the litany of legal battles that have spawned a parade of hashtags and injustices in recent history that stretch to the present. Believers who remain skeptical of the need for constant vigilance in beating back racism should be reminded that the state of Mississippi became the last state of the union to ratify the Thirteenth Amendment, prohibiting slavery, in 2013.[28] Yes, you read that correctly. The tendrils of chattel slavery have grown thick around the tree of democracy such that the work of ameliorating the vestiges of America's most notorious sinful enterprise may never be complete.

> Throughout our nation's legal history we have witnessed millions of microadjustments in the law because the idea of equality for minorities has been, and continues to be, confounding for majority culture.

Lord, do not pass us by.

The Greatest Commandment in the Law

If anyone is still on the fence about whether to embrace their righteous anger, I hope that this itemization of our legal history demonstrates the intentionality of racism by the time it arrives in our churches. If we can be convinced that our experiences with racism are incidental, the racism can be overlooked or pardoned. Where it is ignored or accepted, it can be repeated and built upon. Where it is repeated and built upon, it is structural and unsafe so long as the structure exists. These mile markers show that the intricacy and immensity of racism did not manifest in the moral universe by accident. Rather, there was intelligent design. These are not just isolated incidents, bumps in an otherwise smooth path. Our history shows an unbroken chain of legal violence (not to mention physical and economic violence) that proves beyond all reasonable doubt that this is who we are. It's a rocky path; occasionally paved sections provide reprieve.

Of course, this lengthy legal history of civil rights does not even scratch the surface of issues related to misogyny, racism in the indigenous and Asian communities, or LGBTQIA+ rights—all of which have their own constitutional lineage. This is the point that I need to drive home to all my friends in white Christianity: Throughout our nation's legal history we have witnessed millions of micro-adjustments in the law because the idea of equality for minorities has been, and continues to be, confounding for majority culture. And in real time, each development was met with opposition. Yet each of these pitched battles was necessary just to enforce a core idea of Christianity that too many Christians have failed to live up to: love your neighbor.

Considering how crucial the ideals of Christianity purportedly are to those who imagine that God has ordained the United States to be a "city on a hill," it's mystifying that Christianity didn't hold greater sway over the long arc of our nation's jurisprudence. Thus the proposition that our efforts toward equality should be focused on the perspective that "all lives matter" is exceedingly dubious. If all flesh was created equal and "all lives" mattered to God's people, America should never have needed more than 2 Corinthians 5.

Comedian Michael Che has a hilarious take on "all lives matter" and the depressing notion that valuing Black lives is so divisive in our country:

> As a country we just can't agree. We just fight about everything. We can't even agree on "Black lives matter." That's a controversial statement. Not "matters more than you," just "matters." ... That's where we're starting the negotiations. We can't agree on that shit? What the fuck is less than "matters"? "Black lives exist"? Can we say that? Is that controversial?[29]

Why is it that treating minorities as human beings is such a scandal? Oh, and let me be clear: treating minorities as human beings in America is a scandal. Honestly, it always has been. Those still harboring doubts that their color-blind colleagues have a hard time seeing minorities on equal footing might consider all the areas in which inequality still persists. When we say that Black lives matter, our declaration is relevant in many facets of society.

- Black lives matter in police reform.
- Black lives matter in the criminal justice system.
- Black lives matter in education.
- Black lives matter in medicine and health care.
- Black lives matter in economics.
- Black lives matter in theology.

The list goes on and on. In all these systems, there is need to assert the dignity of minorities because in all those areas, Black and Brown people are being overlooked or targeted. The assertion that Black people matter can be applied across so many facets of Western society because so many of our societal structures tend to demonstrate the opposite. Therefore, there is a blanket need to acknowledge the worth of Black lives in America.

By contrast, I'm perplexed by T-shirts and bumper stickers that say, "Blue Lives Matter," referring to police officers. The folks who display those bumper stickers are the same ones who told me that they don't see color. So why the catchphrase? Why not just say, "I love police officers"? Why not T-shirts that read, "I heart cops"? Because it's an intentional counternarrative. Declaring that "blue lives matter" is a direct response to the assertion "Black lives matter." It's a battle cry to drown out the voices of minorities tired of enduring structural racism and police brutality. "Black lives matter" is an adage to protest police brutality. "Blue lives matter" may speak to an officer's perspective when public outcry for police accountability increases, but the phrase does not address disparities in criminal justice (or education, medicine, economics, health care, theology, etc.). In the great calculus of us vs. them, defending blue lives only seeks to balance one equation on a page full of problems to solve. So if a knee-jerk reaction to defend police officers doesn't address all the other many failures of society decried by minorities, why say it at all? Why rebut the proposition that Black lives matter (in so many areas) with the proclamation that law enforcement matters? People who declare that blue lives matter are not saying that they support the police. On a subconscious level, they are declaring that they have had enough of Black people. In their minds, the one declaration is enough to cover a multitude of sins: law enforcement matters, but nothing about the Black community matters. One could even argue that "blue lives matter" is an appeal to law enforcement to put the minorities back in their place.

While advocating that "all lives matter" is dubiously broad, a focus on "blue lives" is dangerously narrow. Regardless, we would rather be nearsighted, farsighted, color-blind, or completely blind than look the problem in the eyes.

The destructive yield of this anti-Black rhetoric is far more damaging when housed in the casing of Christianity. Meeting those we encounter in the world with unconditional love should be a low-risk endeavor, but within white Christianity, the stakes couldn't be higher. As Michael Che acknowledged, the bar has been set incredibly low in this cultural debate. Somehow folks continue to stumble over it.

Chapter 5

A New Lens for a Color-Blind Church

*I*f we glean anything from the development of the law throughout the civil rights movement, it should be how difficult the pio-
neers of that movement had it. Yet I envy the clarity of the work
set before them. There were clearly defined obstacles in front of
them that made their message coherent and their objectives clear.
They fought for things such as equal pay, the right to vote, the
right to sit in the same places as white people, the right to go
to integrated schools, and the ability to have interracial relationships. No matter your opinions on race, the evening news made
the disparity clear as minorities were blasted with fire hoses or
attacked by canines for sitting outside businesses they wanted
to patronize. Clear injustice. Because the obstacles were clearly
observable, progress could be measured by observable trans-
formations in society. In our era, discrimination is more subtle. Racism has found other rocks to hide behind. Often this is
by design.

Prior to the civil rights movement, discrimination was like a
cluster of balls on a pool table racked in triangle formation. Each
ball represented an individualized system of injustice but, united
in that grouping, they created a phalanx of discrimination. The
impact of the civil rights movement broke that unified structure
apart like a cue ball. Bam! Some balls fell in the pockets, never
to return. The right to vote, for example, was a permanent victory,

though with an asterisk.* There remain a number of balls loosely scattered across the table; each represents an independent system in desperate need of reform, and each requires its own plan of attack. Though the cohesion of the separate spheres of injustice was broken, many remain on the table. Some are difficult to hit because they're lodged against the wall. You get the picture. The issues are still out there to be addressed, but they're no longer visibly clumped together in strength.

Plenty of people are doing great work in these spheres. I'm more interested in the table itself. Our current cultural climate. The atmosphere we breathe. Ways white Christianity accommodates those spheres and communicates that no legitimate reading of the Bible warrants teaching a responsibility to attack them. The campaign to demonize a theology of liberation is so effective that our greatest efforts are taken not in debating *how* we achieve the goal but whether we should pursue it at all. Because the methods of oppression utilized today are subtle, even invisible, minorities who address specific issues head-on are perceived as overreacting, reduced to "angry Black folks" who cannot just get along with people. In ways subtle and not so subtle, minorities are accustomed to being told to stop talking, even in the church.

"Give the pastor grace for that culturally inappropriate comment."

"Everyone's so sensitive that we (white men) can't joke about race anymore."

"What you thought was racism really wasn't racism."

"You're taking it wrong."

"Racism really doesn't exist now."

"Christians don't see color."

"White privilege doesn't exist."

"I put myself through college (with mom and dad's money);

---

*There is another discussion to be had about how the right to vote is whittled away through gerrymandering, school-to-prison pipelines, targeted policing, abuse of prosecutorial discretion, wrongful felony convictions, and laws prohibiting felons from voting. Save that for another day.

I didn't get a scholarship to be here. (Like you must have. Surely that's the only way you got here.)"

"All lives matter."

It seems that white Christianity expects us to be seen and not heard. Point of clarification: In this context, "seen" means becoming a harmonious but inactive part of the background. Like trees in the landscape, but not active participants in important conversations. Unless it's February, in which case we're tolerated but not listened to. In short, we feel overlooked. This is why proclaiming "I don't see color" is unhelpful. It sounds a lot like "Everyone's voice is the same. Because I'm not really interested in the complexity and uniqueness of what you're going through, you should just conform. Your voice should sound like mine anyway. Minority perspectives are not unique, after all. Therefore, minorities have representation in this discourse—through the more intelligent, refined perspective of people who think like me. Your particular voice doesn't need to be heard." The adage "I don't see color" is shorthand for "If I assume we're the same, I can skip over you."

Neither these efforts to blanch minority empowerment nor the arguments opposing such efforts are new. In 1967, Dick Cavett invited former Yale professor Paul Weiss on his talk show to confront James Baldwin on his views on race in America.[1] Weiss emphasized his commonality with Baldwin as a scholar, and asked, "Why must you always concentrate on color, or religion, or this? There are other ways of connecting men. . . ." Weiss' interrogation was meant to make Baldwin concede that by discussing race, Black people were doing a disservice to societal progress by emphasizing our differences. In today's vernacular, Weiss essentially asked Baldwin, "Why must you say, 'Black lives matter'? Isn't it sufficient to say, 'All lives matter'?" Baldwin's response chided Weiss spectacularly.

I don't know what most white people in this country feel. But I can only conclude what they feel from the state of their institutions. I don't know if white Christians hate Negroes or not, but I know we have a Christian church which is white and a Christian church which is black. I know, as Malcolm X once put it, the most segregated hour in American life is high noon on Sunday. That says a great deal for me about a Christian nation. It means I can't afford to trust most white Christians and I certainly cannot trust the Christian church. I don't know whether the labor unions and their bosses really hate me. That doesn't matter, but I know I'm not in their unions. I don't know if the real estate lobby has anything against black people, but I know the real estate lobby is keeping me in the ghetto. I don't know if the board of education hates black people, but I know the textbooks they give my children to read and the schools that we have to go to. Now, this is the evidence. You want me to make an act of faith, risking myself, my wife, my woman, my sister, my children, on some idealism which you assure me exists in America which I have never seen.

Lord, hear our cry. Why should it be necessary to make a fuss over distinctions of race in our discussions of human flourishing? In short, because neither the social aspirations boldly proclaimed by America, nor the biblical ideals espoused by white Christianity, has gotten the job done. Therefore, my purpose in taking such pains in chapter 4 to emphasize the shortcomings of American law and white Christianity in dignifying the humanity of Black people is to ensure that our white siblings of faith never forget that we have grossly deviated from those expectations enshrined in our Bibles as well as our nation's founding documents. It is to remind us that this work is godly and simple to do. But the church is ill equipped to embark on the journey of fixing the problem if we're not even willing to acknowledge how far we have to go. There should never have been a debate, in America or within Christianity, about whose lives matter more. Yet debate we do.

We can never fully embody our identities as followers of Christ if our conversations are centered around *whether* justice is due rather than what quantum of justice is necessary to make the marginalized whole. Neither a myopic nor hyperopic view will help us regain our conscience, our moral compass, or our identity as a nation. All that is really required of us is willingness to love our neighbors with the same sanctity as we love our own lives. The church's reluctance to do so is evinced by objections to protests to police violence, refusal to acknowledge systemic racism, outrage toward Colin Kaepernick, resistance to criminal justice reform, demonization of immigrants, rejection of LGBTQIA+ inclusivity within social justice movements, and insistence that minorities within white Christianity are better seen and not heard.

> We can never fully embody our identities as followers of Christ if our conversations are centered around *whether* justice is due rather than what quantum of justice is necessary to make the marginalized whole.

Blind Spots and Prophetic Vision

What white Christianity fails to see in all of this is the unique opportunity, and responsibility, that it has in sustaining the work of the civil rights movement. To clarify King's thesis, the moral arc of the universe does not bend toward justice by happenstance; it is our obligation to ensure it curves. I fear greatly that King's work has been all but completely whitewashed in the minds of American believers. Lest we forget, King was not just a grand orator, a motivational speaker peddling a generic message of unity. He shared his prophetic vision within the context of addressing our country's demonstrable shortcomings despite pledging ourselves as one nation, under God, indivisible, with liberty and justice for all. King and those who worshiped, marched, and protested with him approached each endeavor knowing there was a near certainty of violence being visited upon them by citizens, the police, or the lynching tree.

As articulate as he was, King was not prone to mince words. Before declaring his dream, King first admonished that he had come to Washington, DC, to cash a check: "America has given the Negro people a bad check, a check which has come back marked insufficient funds. But we refuse to believe that the bank of justice is bankrupt."[2] We have elected to disregard how unpopular MLK's aggressive stance toward injustice made him during his time and how unpopular such work remains today. Though the most glaring examples of oppression may have been dispersed about the table, there's much more work to be done within our hearts and minds.

As we carry on King's legacy by calling for accountability in our institutions and greater empathy from the church, we would do well to remember that the pursuit of justice has never been quiet work. As comments from the likes of Ted Cruz demonstrate,[3] there is agonizing irony in the fact that King remains an archetype of race relations in white Christianity, yet only in the most whitewashed, sanitized fashion. I'm afraid that King's adherence to nonviolent, passive resistance as a strategy to win the hearts and minds of civilized people would hardly succeed with majority culture in the modern era. White America no longer sees anything admirable, or noteworthy, in docile forms of protest. In fact, we saw as much when some of the peaceful protests carried out in 2020 were intentionally mischaracterized as riots.

We have become such connoisseurs of documented brutality against Black bodies, and the failure of the legal system to adequately address these brutalities, that no less could be expected. We have become blood sommeliers, demanding a certain clarity from cases of Black brutality held up to light for inspection, relentlessly inspecting the typicity and packaging of the victim to determine their worth, and judging whether recognition of the event pairs well with our overarching political agendas in order to evaluate whether calling for justice in this particular instance leaves the right taste in our mouths.

King's blistering words for opponents of his movement have been forgotten. Rather, when critics of social justice hold up MLK as an example of what protests against injustice should look like, it could very well be what they really want from Black people is to see them suffering via the same passive, nonviolent response to violence we saw in King's era. Some may call videos of limp Black bodies, mercilessly beaten and dragged into squad cars, a better, more palatable, example of protest than Black athletes kneeling during the national anthem. We also call this victimization.

One of the most freeing things that I've learned in recent years is that our lived experience is not a debate.[4] I owe much to authors, podcasters, and theologians who have helped guide me to sanity throughout the course of this season. Jemar Tisby, Tyler Burns, Beth Moore, Esau McCaulley, Malcolm Foley, Ryan Holmes, Ashley Irons, Elijah Misigaro—these people (and many others) have been a life preserver for me in turbulent waters. There is no explanation or disclaimer owed to those who are looking for clarification that people who take the Bible seriously are not Marxists. No one really fears that we are communists; they fear that we are threats. Such weak criticisms are attempts to *other* minorities and shame our allies into a corner by calling them unpatriotic. It is a racially tinged McCarthyism.

Such characterizations are distractions designed to force debate about *how* we're expressing ourselves rather than confront the substance of *what* we're saying or *why* we're saying it. Our intent was never to debate the ideology of the Black Lives Matter movement; we want to talk about what happened to Breonna Taylor. We don't want to talk about critical race theory; we want to talk about what made a police officer, who knew he was being filmed, think it was all right to kneel on George Floyd's neck for almost ten minutes while the suspect begged for air, onlookers pleaded for him to stop, and cameras were rolling. And why did three of his fellow officers think it was proper to aid in such a murder? Why is it so difficult for churchgoers of a certain complexion to see and face these issues head-on? For so many minorities, we just can't help but feel the sense that our cries have not been heard within white Christianity. We're given little more to hold onto than the hymns that taught us an unending, yet seemingly unobtainable, hope.

More often than not, my white acquaintances who want to debate about the existence of racism, or the efficacy of a particular method of fighting racism, are doing so from an uninformed perspective. Well-intentioned as they may be, their challenges to how I speak about racism are rooted in (1) an assumption of disbelief based on years of indoctrination within a homogeneous background, and (2) a sterile, suppositional notion of racism as an academic exercise. In other words, they have no skin in the game. Thus they view the problem, if it exists, in theoretical terms, as a think tank might. Therefore abstract ideas such as "If we stop talking about it, it will go away" seem tenable. Of course, these notions fail in a practical application. Meanwhile, racism is a lived reality for people of color. We have observed it and are impacted by it. Where we are eyewitnesses, our detractors are merely philosophizing.* When the argument is done, they'll pack up all the sharp intellectual tools used to reopen and probe our emotional wounds, go home, and turn on an episode of *Friends*. Meanwhile we're left discarded on the table, exhausted and bleeding out.

When we ask our fellow Americans and Christians to agree that Black lives matter, we're not asking for their allegiance to a political ideology or organization. We're asking them to verify that we have the same basic human dignity as others. We're asking them to dispel our belief that they don't care whether we live or die. In fact, we're asking them to admit that we're not crazy for *assuming* white people don't care whether we live or die in light of all we've borne witness to. We're asking them to repent for standing by silently while others clearly communicate that they *don't* care whether we live or die—thereby allowing us to form the mistaken (?) impression that they agree. We're asking them to affirmatively dispel the notion that they agree with racism—because the climate we're in makes that unclear.

---

*There's a parallel to be drawn here, as "eyewitness" is a term of art. As previously explained, the testimony of a witness is direct evidence if the witness is determined to be credible. Therefore the testimony of minorities as to their experience with racism has the potential to be powerful evidence—the only issue is whether it is accepted by society. Said bluntly, society challenges our credibility.

Most importantly, we're asking them to get off their ass and do something about the fact that society doesn't seem to care whether we live or die. We're asking them to denounce those who explicitly *say* that they don't care whether we live or die—not just the ones who say it blatantly but the ones who do it with nuance as well, through microaggressions and dog whistles. And, yes, we're asking them to divorce themselves from the people in their ecosystems (church, family, and political parties) who don't care whether we live or die—choosing us over them. Because we had to do the same. We're asking them to understand that we're not debating political issues. We're not talking about legal precedents tied to the right to life and the role of government in the affairs of the private citizens. We're debating about whether they care about whether we live or die. We're asking Christians to act like Christ.

Chapter 6

We Break the Silence

*I*t feels like most white Americans would rather have a root canal than have an honest conversation about race. While I'm *mostly* exaggerating, it's worth noting that if people would rather (metaphorically) endure dental surgery to avoid discussing race themselves, how much more would they have minorities endure in silence? So while talking about racial disparities may nearly be forbidden within predominantly white churches, *complaining* about them definitely is.

Often the first line of defense raised by conservative white Christians against accusations of racism is some variation of saying, "But isn't it better than years past?" or "Yeah, but look how far we've come." These propositions usually don't follow lament of our nation's history, acknowledgment of current specific systemic problems, or a vision for improving our future. Rather, they serve as deflection. They're not saying, "Look at the good we've done and the need to do more," but rather, "Why are you complaining? Don't you have it good enough?" These are periods at the end of a sentence, attempting to end the conversation, not ellipses inviting more discussion. Educator Benjamin Young provides this insight:

> When speaking of civil and social issues of justice and liberation I have often heard the following from white Christian conservatives: "Things are much better than they were." First, "much" is doing a whole lot of work in that sentence.

And second, I'm convinced that such a sentiment ought never be expressed by someone to whom the appropriate response would be "No thanks to people like you." It seems like the white Christian conservative in America loves to reference the progress made by the very people they criticize. They cite the progress made by the marches and protests they would never join. They cite the progress made by direct action they would never make. They cite the progress made as a result of the beatings they would never take.[1]

In 1964, at the height of the civil rights movement's battle for equality, Malcolm X was presented with the same proposition—that progress is being made in our country. To this, Malcolm famously responded,

> If you stick a knife in my back nine inches and pull it out six inches, there's no progress. If you pull it all the way out, that's not progress. Progress is healing the wound that the blow made. And they haven't even begun to pull the knife out, much less, try and heal the wound. They won't even admit the knife is there.[2]

I think this is one of the reasons that pictures of the civil rights era are difficult for me to look at. When I see photos of the day when those nine brave children were turned away from the doors of Little Rock's Central High School, for example, I see the intervention of the governor and the presence of the Arkansas National Guard—but I also see the hundreds of students, women, and men who screamed at children like Elizabeth Ann Eckford (age fifteen) and have never been held to account. Equally haunting are pictures of young white men harassing John Salter, Joan Trumpauer, and Anne Moody as they sat in peaceful protest at a Woolworth's lunch counter by pouring soda, sugar, ketchup, and mustard all over them.

The most painful aspect of these images is not what they are enduring but what "good, red-blooded, God-fearing Americans" got away with. These offenders have been acquitted by anonymity in the stream of history. Their identities have been lost or forgotten to time. Let me articulate this another way: Someone's living grandparents, or even parents, are in those photos. Certainly, they are recognized by their children and grandchildren. Yet those faces have been absolved by, and permitted to ease gently into obscurity from, the passage of time. We assume, further, that their offspring have not been carefully taught in their ways. Even after Jerry Jones, owner of the Dallas Cowboys, was discovered to be one of many white faces in documented crowds protesting integration, Jones was able to avoid the heat that was deserved by characterizing himself as purely a curious observer.[3] I can see why Florida governor Ron DeSantis and others want to pretend that portions of our nation's history—*most* of its history, actually—never happened.[4]

Perhaps apathy and discarding history are learned defense mechanisms because no one should easily fathom themselves or their ancestors being so clearly on the wrong side of history. For example, so often the response of my white colleagues to discussion of the institution of slavery is "I never owned slaves.

> Someone's living grandparents, or even parents, are in those photos. Yet those faces have been absolved by, and permitted to ease gently into obscurity from, the passage of time. We assume, further, that their offspring have not been carefully taught in their ways.

My ancestors never owned slaves. Why should I be held responsible for what happened so long ago?" I find it interesting that despite slavery being a widespread phenomenon, and even with the popularity of ancestral history research and the increasing use of technology to trace family lineage, in all my years I've met only one white person who admitted their ancestors were slaveholders. Isn't that something? It reminds me of the phenomenon that occurs when you ask someone about their previous relationship and they say, "My ex was crazy." Isn't it interesting that you're always talking to the one who was sane? Everyone believes they're the good guy in their story.

It cannot go unmentioned that everyone "back then" thought they were the good guys too. Segregation was only allowed to exist in the South, even after being declared unconstitutional, because the dominant political ideology of the people was that segregation was right, just, and even godly. With the benefit of hindsight, hardly anyone who contributed to Jim Crow has failed to plead innocence: they weren't there; they supported the civil rights movement; not a racist bone in their bodies; King was great, and so on. It's always the ex that was crazy. We tend to look at history through a lens that sanitizes the existing culture and absolves culprits and coconspirators of the time. We tend to forget that when the Supreme Court attempted to codify the equality of Blacks and whites, a switch wasn't flipped displacing the momentum of white supremacy. Racists didn't tuck their tails between their legs, head home, and resolve to do better and enrich our nation. Like all viruses, they mutated and evolved.[5]

Questions like "Aren't things better now than before?" presuppose that we live in a post-racial society. We've done good. We can stop working now. Momentum will carry us the rest of the way. While some of these inquiries are probably well-intentioned, let me be clear: such questions have to be disingenuous to anyone who's watched the news or visited one strand of the World Wide Web. Recognizing there is no deficit of information available to educate those who hold these opinions liberates us from the maddening exercise of trying to convince them. We need not litigate the lie of a postracial America with ill-intentioned people. For the small remaining number of folks who do believe in a post-racial society, I understand what an attractive lie it must be. But they are responsible for the work of their own enlightenment.

If you've ever done work with the homeless, poor, sick, or suffering, you'll recall how deeply uncomfortable it was the first time you rolled up your sleeves, stepped into the "mud," and humbled yourself to the level of those you were ministering to. That's not an easy transition. Much easier to stand at the riverbank and encourage those doing the work. It's hard to look difficult things in the eye. For this reason, I think we cringe to read Isaiah's prophetic description of Christ on earth:

He was despised and rejected by mankind,
   a man of suffering, and familiar with pain.
Like one from whom people hide their faces
   he was despised, and we held him in low esteem.

Surely he took up our pain
   and bore our suffering,
yet we considered him punished by God,
   stricken by him, and afflicted.

                                        Isa. 53:3–4

As I read this passage, it's important to understand how the people viewed Jesus in a cause-and-effect relationship to his advocacy. *Why* was he despised, held in low esteem, and considered by humankind to be punished by God? *Because* he took up our pain and bore our suffering. It is extremely uncomfortable to look upon the suffering of others with such intentionality that our pupils dilate and our own visage is changed.

That being the case, if humans have the luxury of overlooking the sufferings of others, we typically do. In the context of race, those who are uncomfortable discussing race simply don't, and more specifically, they want *minorities* to stop whining about it. Talking. Whining. Same difference.

If we would just suck it up, the argument goes, racism would go away. Equity would suddenly spring forth from our judicial and educational systems. Medical morbidity and mortality rates for pregnant Black women would be spontaneously reduced. Gerrymandering would become a relic of the past—all because minorities were silent. We just have to stop talking about it. It's not victim-blaming in their eyes; it's just that if we are *silent* victims, the problem goes away . . . for them. For those who feel this way, race is the edge of the world. The final frontier. The iced wall on the rim of our flat earth. The problem, of course, for minorities affected by these issues is that they don't have the option of ignoring their experiences of injustice. For most people of color, the question isn't "Where do we see racism?" but "Is there any area of the American experience that it doesn't touch?" Racism isn't just a component of our culture; it's all-consuming. Therefore, to quote poet Kyle "Guante" Tran Myhre, "White supremacy is not a shark; it is the water."[6]

Suffering Silently

As a father of three, I now have deep appreciation for the way my parents tried to insulate us from the cruelty of the world. I was appalled to discover, as an adult, that one reason the military moved my family around so much was because my father once had a superior who bluntly told him he didn't like Black people and my dad would never be promoted as long as he had anything to say about it.

In my elementary school years, I recall my mother regularly crying while recounting mistreatment at various businesses that my parents subsequently vowed we would no longer frequent. While we used to refer to these occasions broadly as racism in those days, we now describe them as microaggressions—things like waiting three times as long as white counterparts to be served in businesses or being talked down to when it's necessary to speak to a supervisor. My mother used to smile politely through tears as her naive little boy suggested she report her mistreatment to the police. The frequency of events like this, and a visceral need to thwart the injustice of them, are core memories for me. Scenes like these caused me to resolve at the age of eleven that I would become a lawyer. I never considered any other profession. I reasoned that our society should be able to talk openly about these things and correct them.

Because I was a military brat, my high school education was spread across Louisiana, Oklahoma, and Ohio. As difficult as my upbringing in Louisiana was, Oklahoma was the most difficult place I've *ever* lived. I had classmates who were openly white supremacists—we're talking white-laced black combat boots and homemade swastika tattoos. These kids were never confronted on their beliefs or behavior. Rather, minorities were expected to give them a wide berth. Racism wasn't something we were encouraged to discuss openly in school. While Oklahoma history was mandatory,

I didn't learn about the Tulsa Race Massacre of 1921 until I was thirty-seven years old. It somehow never came up in my predominantly white school. Not even during my junior year, when the shock waves from the 1995 bombing of the Murrah Federal Building physically rocked our school and our lessons turned to terrorism in the wake of our community's mourning. In hindsight, terrorism was a perfect opening to discussions of racism in our state's history. But it was never discussed.

During my senior year of high school I moved to a suburb of Dayton, Ohio. The proximity to Wright-Patterson Air Force Base made the city ideal for military families, and my high school was surprisingly diverse. Consequently, I convinced myself that the chill of northern winters killed off the racism I'd experienced in the South. It was a welcome reprieve. After graduation, I followed my parents to Spokane, Washington, and enrolled at Gonzaga University.

Like most aspiring lawyers, I studied the musings of dead political philosophers while pursuing a liberal arts degree in political science. I tried (with mixed success) to get good grades and I stayed (completely) out of trouble. My parents never had to worry about me breaking the law; the Reagan-era D.A.R.E. campaign messaging and 1980s *After School Specials* on TV did their work. I missed out on a lot of defining college experiences to ensure I maintained a pristine record for future law school applications.

When I arrived in Washington in 1997, I encountered a strange resistance to diversity—particularly to the deeply rooted Indigenous culture of that region—that didn't make sense in light of the experience I had in Ohio. This *is* the North, right? During my sophomore year, I served in student government and was privy to the details of many complaints made by minorities on campus. Again, I found myself in an environment where people weren't warm to the idea of discussing race when inequities revealed themselves in grading and treatment by fellow students. Gonzaga struggled with diversity. Less than 1 percent of the student body was Black at that time. Spokane County was only slightly better, boasting a Black (non-Hispanic) population of 1.8 percent.[7]

In hindsight, it probably had to do with the fact that our neighbor, Northern Idaho, was a notorious breeding ground for white supremacy—which I was blissfully unaware of while submitting my admission application. In 1973, Richard Butler, cofounder of the Aryan Nations, moved to Hayden Lake, Idaho, claiming twenty acres of wooded beauty that he subsequently marred with the construction of a white supremacist compound and "church," all less than an hour's drive from my alma mater. Looking back, the micro-aggressions make a lot more sense.

Northern Idaho was beautiful. A pristine lake, tons of outdoor activities, and thriving nightlife made Spokane's neighbor Coeur d'Alene a favorite getaway for college students. Yet I'll always remember it as the place I was nearly killed by the police. That night, I'd driven with four of my white friends to the North Idaho State Fair. As I started the car to head back to Spokane, no fewer than four officers surrounded the vehicle and ordered me to step out. Prior to this night, I'd been pulled over more than once for bogus reasons on my way to and from Idaho, and each time I was released without a ticket. Up to this point, racial profiling had never been more than an annoyance. It was kind of a running joke.* I'd never been ordered out of a car before. This was different.

Flashlights, headlights, spotlights, and takedown lights nearly blinded me. Maybe ten feet away, the primary officer barked commands. He was little more than a silhouette to me, but I could see his gun. I can still see it, drawn and aimed at my body, center mass. Years later, as a prosecutor, I would learn that blinding a suspect (referred to as the "wall of light") is a tactic used by the police to help disorient and incapacitate suspects, increasing officer safety. My questions were ignored but they had lots for me: "What's your name?" "Got any ID?" "Says here, you're a student [i.e., we don't believe you]. What are you studying?" "Got any *other* forms of ID?" "Where are you all coming from?" "Where are you going?"

---

*One of the Black friends I later made in Spokane was pulled over so often that none of his friends would ride with him because they were afraid of being late to their destinations.

The questions came all at once from multiple backlit voices. One officer stepped away, talking into a radio. There was a long period of silence.

Maybe only ten minutes passed while I waited at gunpoint, but it felt like thirty. Hands still raised, palms facing forward, my arms quivered. It was already late when we left the fair and arrived at my car; I was exhausted. But I felt like if my hands dropped, I would die. My body demanded a physical response of me: fight or flight. The uncertainty and injustice of the situation screamed fight, but I was too afraid to move. Tears came. I was going to jail or going to die, and I had no idea why. Finally, the head officer holstered his weapon and handed back my ID cards. The lights dimmed, though afterimages still blinded me. One of the cop-shaped shadows explained that I had fit the description of an escaped convict: Black guy, five feet ten, braided hair. Just a misunderstanding. Good luck in school. Have a good night.

That was it.

After gathering my cards, I collapsed in the driver's seat. In the car, my white friends tried to console me but lacked the words. We were all astonished. The drive home was quiet, save for our combined sobs. Deep, convulsing, sanity-unraveling tears. We all knew what had just happened. For my friends, this was the first time they got to see what living in Black skin looked like. I often think about what happened that night, but it's taken more than twenty years for me to articulate what so enraged me about this event, which some would dismiss as standard police work. Something was stripped from me that evening outside the fairgrounds in Coeur d'Alene, Idaho. What was taken in that moment wasn't life, property, or just time. It was liberty—not just my physical liberty in that moment but feeling the freedom to move about the world without racial barriers. My dignity as a human being was stolen. Without recourse.

Were my experiences in Spokane and North Idaho misinterpreted? Not likely. As testament to my encounters in the Pacific Northwest, the University of Utah's women's basketball team reported they were harassed by racists during their stay in Coeur d'Alene, Idaho, for the 2024 NCAA Tournament.[8]

Some canines can be trained to stay within the invisible borders of a yard with an electric fence buried beneath the ground that transmits a shock to their collars if they move too close. Anyone standing in the yard would see nothing but ample territory to roam freely, but the canine knows where the invisible barriers are. Similarly, there are ways in which minorities experience our nation that have fitted us with a type of psychological restraint alerting us to where we are and are not wanted. These are the kinds of experiences that do so blatantly. Others are more subtle. Either way, we're not supposed to talk about it. God forbid these experiences upset us and make white people uncomfortable.

I'm Speaking

A few years back, these rules were reinforced for me on a playground, of all places.

During my wife's tour of duty as a stay-at-home mom, our children had a knack for undoing the good work she accomplished throughout the day twice over. By the time I got home, she was practically standing at the curb ready to hand the kids off to me. Apparently, it's not funny if I keep driving and go around the block. *The more you know.* So one time, when I took our two youngest kids off my wife's hands for a sanity break, I walked with them to a nearby church with a playground that's open to the public. A woman was at the playground with a little girl about the same age as my daughter. Playing rodeo clown on a playground for a nine- and a four-year-old gets exhausting, so I was excited that one of the kids would have someone there to play with.

As we entered the playground, I gave a friendly hello to the woman. As hoped, our daughters began to play, and I made polite conversation with the mom. She informed me that she worked there at the church, and we figured out that one of her coworkers was a mutual friend. There weren't any other kids on the playground, but several other adults associated with the church were milling around the church entrance nearby. While the woman was congenial, there was a tension that eschewed small talk, so I gave her space. Within two minutes of our arrival, she gathered up her daughter and ushered her inside the church as though a storm was coming.

I thought her abrupt exit was a little awkward, but I assumed she had a good reason for it. It couldn't have been my appearance—I was wearing my finest dad attire: faded T-shirt, athletic shorts permanently stained by a smidge of paint, and my "good" sneakers. I put aside what happened and assumed the role of rodeo clown. Fifteen minutes and a sore back later, we began to leave. As we cleared the playground and made our way down the street, I saw the mom and daughter exit the church and resume playing on the playground. At that moment, I knew why they'd originally left.

Initially I was stricken by the conspicuousness of her motivations, but I quickly turned my attention to escorting our children back home on a public street without sidewalks. Within a half hour, I'd completely forgotten it. I didn't even think to tell my wife about it. Another in a long line of microaggressions. The experience didn't come to mind again until I saw an ad for that church online two weeks later. A young woman with a warm smile sat in her car, greeting me through the front-facing camera of her smartphone. She invited me to come worship with her and her fellow congregants in the family-friendly environment of the church she serves. It was the woman from the playground. And she was a pastor at the church. (It's important to note that not every congregation is egalitarian enough in their beliefs to permit women in ministry. This only emphasizes that these issues can arise in more progressive congregations as well as conservative ones.) The hypocrisy of it unearthed what I'd buried and forgotten two weeks earlier. I tried to let it go, I really did, but frustration punched through the doors and windows of my mind like zombies in Michael Jackson's "Thriller" video.

I made the mistake of sharing my frustration about the playground incident with some of my white evangelical friends. You would have thought my friends were defending a thesis. Excuses abounded:

"Maybe she had to go somewhere really quickly."
Me: *And return just as quickly when I left?*

"You can't say that woman is a racist because you don't
know her."
Me: *I don't know Richard Spencer either, but I think I know
what he's about.*

"Maybe she wasn't comfortable being around men."
Me: *So, she ran from me to the safety of the men gathered
at the church door who were already in eyesight?*

Somehow sharing my experience as a person of color morphed
into a trial in which I had to present my strongest case to justify
feeling hurt by someone else's racism. I wasn't supposed to talk
about it. On and on it went until one person intervened with reason: "How sad is it that as your Black friend is sharing his experience with you, you're disbelieving *him* and giving the benefit of
the doubt to a woman you've never met." The room went quiet.
The indictment had been read aloud.

A few grumblings later, the debate died. In that moment, I realized how succinctly my advocate had articulated the problem. I
couldn't see the forest for the trees. The issue at hand had never
been this woman's motives. I knew what I felt. I saw what I saw.
Forty-plus years on planet Earth as a Black male has more than
adequately equipped me to interpret context clues and nonverbal
communication in the context of prejudice. Yet, to my colleagues,
my credibility in discerning racism was pitted against the presumed
integrity of this stranger or against my colleagues' comfort. Either
way, they related more to the woman in my account who committed the wrong against me—a person they'd never seen or met—
than they did to me.

Knowing this is not an experience unique to me, I think it is
important that minorities know that we are, in fact, qualified to provide an accurate description of our experience. When we find ourselves debating with others about our lived experience, what we
are really arguing over is credibility. While I understand that we're

butting up against their ability to empathize and accept a disturbing reality that contradicts their own experience, I have no sympathy for this dissonance. If nowhere else, in the face of doubt, our credibility among those we live in community with should be enough to persuade them that our lived experience is legitimate. Our testimony is evidence.[9] As minorities on the receiving end of such irrational doubts, our most important takeaway is not that we stop speaking, but that we may be speaking to the wrong audience.

> Somehow sharing my experience as a person of color morphed into a trial in which I had to present my strongest case to justify feeling hurt by someone else's racism. I wasn't supposed to talk about it.

For many American minorities, particularly those living in the South, awareness and interpretation of discreet prejudices is a learned survival skill. We become quite good at it early in life. Yet our ability to make common-sense deductions is constantly questioned.

I recall several occasions in my adolescence, and even college and grad school, where a classmate let a slur fly and our mutual friends tried to convince me, "I know him. He's not a racist; he's a Christian." In these instances, not only was *my* testimony insufficient, but their biases against acknowledging racism defied the evidence provided by their *own* observations. I learned from this that the discomfort of our detractors is more important to them than our firsthand attestations. Even when clear language demonstrates prejudicial intent, whiteness gives greater credibility to an offender claiming they're not racist than to a minority calling them out. And if *overtly* racist remarks are so easily dismissed, what hope have we of holding white Christianity accountable when more subtle mechanisms of racism are employed?

Learning that our input is unwelcome in environments such as these, we are conditioned to believe our silence is golden.

As minorities, we also know the goalposts have legs. While there is a myriad of examples I could cite, and many that are more notable, some will always stick with me. In 2006, actor and comedian Michael Richards (best known as Kramer from the television show *Seinfeld*) famously shocked the world when he was recorded hurling racial slurs at Black hecklers in the middle of a stand-up comedy routine. The camera missed nothing: "Fifty years ago, we'd have you upside down with a fucking fork up your ass. . . .You can talk, you can talk, you're brave now, motherfucker. Throw his ass out. He's a nigger! He's a nigger! He's a nigger! A nigger, look, there's a nigger!" Despite the clearest view of the evidence, Richards appeared on the David Letterman show quibbling, "I'm not a racist, that's what's so insane about this."[10]

In December 2020, the owner of Moorhead Auto Center in Fairfield, California, ran a promotion for free smog checks for "families negatively affected by the China virus epidemic." In an interview (fittingly conducted by Asian American news anchor Dion Lim), Jeff Moorhead tried to assure viewers that his Christian faith was a talisman against xenophobia and argued that the same rhetoric was utilized by former president Trump and various news agencies, which exonerated him. In the interview, Moorhead said, "We have to evolve and become better people. . . . The term 'racism' used to really mean something, and it's used so much now where there's not actual racism going on and it's diluting—taking away from the actual focus." Then, in closing, "Thank you, and God bless."[11]

In the days leading up to the heated 2020 Georgia senatorial election between former senator Kelly Loeffler and the Rev. Dr. Raphael G. Warnock, Loeffler (a white candidate) appealed strongly to conservative Georgians in her attempt to defeat her Black opponent. Loeffler was photographed at a campaign event wearing an American flag hat and standing with Chester Doles, a former Ku Klux Klan leader who had been imprisoned for beating a Black man. Notwithstanding, Loeffler asserted during a debate, "There is not a racist bone in my body." However, in January 2021, Yahoo! News revealed that Loeffler spent close to $50,000 for a Facebook ad titled "Beyond Radical Raphael" in which an image of Warnock was drastically digitally altered to change his caramel, light-skinned appearance to scarcely more visible than that of a shadow.[12]

In March 2021, basketball sports announcer and former youth pastor Matt Rowan was caught using racial slurs while covering a game at Norman High School in Oklahoma. As the national anthem began, the girls' team assembled to kneel in protest. Rowan did not know that an open mic broadcast his comments to the TV audience: "They're kneeling? I hope Norman gets their ass kicked. Fucking niggers." Rowan and his supporters asserted the "good person" defense, denying that he is racist. Instead, Rowan issued a half apology that included the following defense: "I will state that I suffer Type 1 Diabetes and during the game my sugar was spiking. While not excusing my remarks it is not unusual when my sugar spikes that I become disoriented and often say things that are not appropriate as well as hurtful. I do not believe that I would have made such horrible statements absent my sugar spiking."[13]

These are but a few examples of many in America's recent history. However, these examples live in my mind rent-free as exemplars when debates about a post-racial America arise. Some people will never be convinced that the testimony of minorities to their own experience is valid.

As Robin DiAngelo explains in her book *White Fragility,* racism, in all its variegated facets, is easy to deny—even to ourselves—because Americans are convinced that racism is what we believe in the privacy of our heart, not what we do. Likewise, many Christians are somehow convinced that Christianity is what we believe, not what we do—our core convictions, but not how those ideas are enacted in addition to what we believe.[14] Astoundingly, these mental somersaults also overlook one of the most foundational adages of America's individualistic society, built from our Protestant work ethic: actions speak louder than words. Similarly, Jesus told us that a tree is known by its fruit (Matt. 12:33; Luke 6:44).

The friction we're encountering when we expose racism within white Christianity is not derived from misperception. We are eyewitnesses, and our testimony is direct evidence. When we speak of our experiences in the boiler room of the white evangelical machine, we do so with the confidence of knowing we are the only ones who have been there to see it. Thus we are more qualified than any to speak of it. The problem isn't us; we haven't lost our grasp of reality. The point of all of this is to say, there is no shortage of examples of racism at work in America generally, or white Christians specifically. However, even when racism displays itself prominently, white Christianity is, historically, the last to publicly recognize it for what it is. As such, it cannot be up to white Christianity to properly classify it.

When vice presidential candidates Kamala Harris and Mike Pence debated in October 2020, several times Pence interrupted Harris or continued talking well after the expiration of his time. Political candidates who find themselves in this situation—especially women—have a difficult tightrope to walk. The need to be heard and desire to be assertive are pitted against the risk of being perceived as *too* assertive or, God forbid, angry. Famously, after being interrupted numerous times, Senator Harris spoke over the vice president and reasserted her place in the conversation by stating, "I'm speaking. Mr. Vice President, I'm speaking." The admonition became a rallying cry for Black people—especially Black women—who are accustomed to being spoken over in society: You can't diminish my voice. I'm speaking.

We know that our experiences are valid. We have perceived the state of white Christianity accurately. And our stories are worth being told even when others try to speak over us. And so, we will not be silent. We're speaking.

Runaway Jury

One of the professors who taught me trial advocacy at Baylor Law School said that picking a jury is the most important part of a case. As a law student, that baffled me. *More important than presenting compelling evidence? More important than preparing witnesses? More important than dissecting the opponent's arguments on cross-examination?* Once I started trying cases, I understood. Yes, choosing who decides your case is the most important part of a legal contest. The quality of the evidence doesn't matter if the right people aren't listening.

In hindsight, some of my best closing arguments were in the trials I lost. Not always, but several times, it was because I was talking to the wrong audience. Sometimes, revisiting my cases with juries after the trials revealed that the decision to allow certain people on the jury sabotaged my efforts. Often, I discovered some jurors had made up their minds before even hearing the evidence. Personal experiences created biases against, or toward, law enforcement. Someone's family was impacted by a similar situation. In those instances, there was nothing that I could have possibly said to change their minds. They just weren't going to be persuaded.

Our nation's civil rights jurisprudence is replete with examples of how this plays out in courtrooms. Historically, the reason white men who lynched Black folks walked on those charges for so long is because minorities weren't allowed to serve on juries. Likewise, in domestic abuse cases, men who abused their partners were hardly ever convicted until women were allowed to serve on juries. Further, one reason that wrongful convictions, sometimes overturned decades later, land so frequently on minorities is because of juries that look so different from the accused. You can have the most righteous cause in the world, with the best evidence, but if the wrong people hear the case, you won't win. In fact, they'd rather not hear what you have to say.

In the Bible, we're given examples of this in the teachings of Jesus. Speaking of John the Baptist, who was imprisoned for offending the conscience of the king, Jesus vents his frustration at the disdain of John's audience:

> "And if you are willing to accept it, he [John] is the Elijah who was to come. Whoever has ears, let them hear.
> "To what can I compare this generation? They are like children sitting in the marketplaces and calling out to others:
>
> 'We played the pipe for you,
>   and you did not dance;
> we sang a dirge,
>   and you did not mourn.'

For John came neither eating nor drinking, and they say, 'He has a demon.' The Son of Man came eating and drinking, and they say, 'Here is a glutton and a drunkard, a friend of tax collectors and sinners.' But wisdom is proved right by her deeds." (Matt. 11:14–19).

I found more encouraging insight on this passage through the most unlikely of places: Facebook. Pastor Kelsey Payton, an acquaintance I love following on social media, volunteers her time at Healing Waters Outreach Center offering tangible resources for the community—serving single mothers and people recovering from addiction, and providing food for those needing assistance. Her reading of Matthew 11 reminds us that the institutional church doesn't have the best track history in recognizing the teachings of Jesus in real time:

> (1) "if you are willing to accept it" is Jesus letting us know there will be people who just are not willing to accept truth
> (2) "whoever has ears let them hear" is Jesus letting us know that some people just won't have ears to hear truth—whether truth is presented privately or publicly, it doesn't matter, they won't hear it [because] they simply do not have ears.
> (3) even in Jesus' day, the generation was dead set on measuring the actions of others to their own set of rules. A chronic addiction to "us versus them"
> (4) that generation created whatever reality they wanted to about JESUS CHRIST THE MESSIAH because they just didn't like what he said or did. They spread rumors he was a drunkard and a glutton . . . but we NOW know the truth about him. That he was NOT that . . . two thousand years later.
> (5) Jesus assured us that wisdom will be proven right by her deeds. That we must be holy since He is holy and just trust it'll all come to light in the presence of the resurrected Christ when we die.
>
> So be slow to believe when religious institutions declare a person as an enemy—after all, they have a history of crucifying the wrong guy.[15]

Whew.

The very frustrating fact of the matter is that wisdom is often not recognized in real time and, by some folks, not at all. This feels like a good reminder for those of us accustomed to being disbelieved, those whose arms have tired from reaching back, waiting for those seduced by racism to come to their senses and join us. It's very possible that the problem isn't you; you've got the wrong jury listening. And no amount of evidence matters if you're talking to the wrong people. In fact, they're not listening. They don't want to hear it. For them, you might as well be suggesting we sail off the edge of a flat earth. Be encouraged; the problem isn't you.

Speak No Evil

In my view, one of the most powerful scenes in all of Hollywood's history is the whipping scene from *Glory*. Denzel Washington plays a runaway slave, Private Silas Trip, who joined the Union army during the American Civil War. Having been caught leaving post, Trip is ordered to be whipped in front of troops for desertion. When time to receive the punishment begins, Trip audaciously removes his top, revealing a back so full of scars that it resembles the complex root system of a tree. This man has clearly been abused. As the beating begins, Trip takes each lash in cold defiance, hardly reacting as he stares directly at the colonel who ordered him whipped. At first, no pain is betrayed in his eyes. Eventually, the torture is too great, and Private Trip's pain, both physical and emotional, is betrayed not in screams or wincing, but by a solitary tear. Later, we learn the only reason Trip even left post was to find adequate shoes because his fellow Black soldiers were denied supplies by the racist quartermaster.

As an African American, as I watch this scene, Trip takes on a kind of messianic role, absorbing ferocious torment willingly. Yet I also suffer with him, discerning the injustice of undeserved mistreatment. At a visceral level I comprehend the cruelty inflicted upon him. The horrendous crack of leather breaking the sound barrier against human flesh—each lash splitting skin—feels demonstrative of how we are misunderstood in this world. And yet, like Trip, we dare not holler. To complain only demonstrates weakness and invites the next lash to land all the harder. We are told that we are imagining it all. We're expected to keep going, dig deeper, suck it up, do whatever you have to do—*but stop talking about it.*

What I would love for people, especially people of color, to understand is that we who have been wounded by white Christianity are *eminently* qualified to recognize spiritual abuse and its conspiracy with racism when we see it—despite all we are asked or told to believe. We recognize the whip when it is brought to bear by the church because we have felt its sting in every other facet of society. We have every right to call it by name in our faith, and it is holy in the eyes of God to do so. Going a step further, because our experience has imbued us with ears to hear and eyes to see the misuse of God's name, we have the moral obligation to do so.

We may have an ethical obligation to call our siblings in Christ into repentance. But more urgently, we survivors owe a duty to one another to affirm our collective sanity. Perhaps most importantly, we owe a duty to *ourselves* to give voice to the truth that would otherwise eat us alive in silence. In this respect, we can relate to the prophet Jeremiah, who cries out in frustration with the untenable predicament of burning up inside when he remains silent or being attacked aggressively for speaking the truth of who God is and what is expected of God's people.

> Whenever I speak, I cry out
>   proclaiming violence and destruction.
> So the word of the LORD has brought me
>   insult and reproach all day long.
> But if I say, "I will not mention his word
>   or speak anymore in his name,"
> his word is in my heart like a fire,
>   a fire shut up in my bones.
> I am weary of holding it in;
>   indeed, I cannot.
>   Jer. 20:8–9

We can't keep it in. We have to break the silence.

My encouragement for those who can relate to this feeling is this: God does not expect us to suffer in silence. We recall that Moses, Esther, Isaiah, Jeremiah, Nathan, Stephen, and even Paul are among many whom Scripture exhibits speaking the truth when society—indeed, those who claim to be followers of God—wants them to be quiet. And we are not unaware of the methods used to silence them.

Ostracization is no prize to be won in the arena. We do not protest because it is fun or fashionable to do so. We speak because we can do no other. Brothers and sisters, we deserve to be loved and believed. We deserve to speak and to be heard. And no one has the right to silence us. My colleague in the practice of law, Scarlet Petrucci, says of the ways white Christianity has sought to silence minorities, "People like you quiet. They like you when you're half of yourself. They don't like the real you; they like your presence." It seems hard for them to conceive anything beyond the ice-rimmed wall at the edge of the flat earth. Race remains the final frontier.

While the congregation that met in that building where the pastor hurriedly ushered her child off the playground no longer operates there, the building remains. Other congregations have come and gone since then, but every time I drive by that church, our subtle run-in with racism comes screaming back to memory. Along with it, the argument in which I had to defend my experience to overcome the disbelief of my white acquaintances. In a way, that church building has become a monument in my mind. It commemorates not just the ongoing difficulty for minorities to be accepted for who we are in the white church, but also society's refusal to accept our perceptions of reality as valid. But most importantly, it reminds me that our perceptions and experiences are worth discussing—even when we're told to shut up.

Chapter 7

We Wear the Mask (No Longer)

I don't *like* discussing race. America seems burnt out on it. In my experience, most minorities develop a kind of muscle memory from constantly warring to have our point of view heard and understood that causes us to brace every time we discuss our cultural differences in mixed company. Conversely, it feels as though most Americans have been trained to stop listening when race is discussed openly. As a result, we have moved to something worse than a color-blind society. We are a nation full of colors, blind to seeing people. I'm not sure when it happened, but somewhere we departed from "I have a dream" to "I don't wanna hear it."

For most of my life, I've inhabited predominantly white settings, attempting to fit in. I grew up in a time and place where it was not socially acceptable to be Black: Bossier City, northern Louisiana, circa 1985. All my neighbors, classmates, teachers, and community leaders were white. I was, as Zora Neale Hurston described it, the Black dot thrown against the stark contrast of a white background. For years, ours was the only Black family in a neighborhood actually named Green Acres.* It felt like Bossier learned about desegregation two days before we moved there. And that may

---

*For those who missed the Easter egg, *Green Acres* was a TV sitcom we Gen Xers grew up watching on reruns. The show follows a wealthy couple from Manhattan who move to rural America to run a dilapidated farm where they can live out the husband's idea of the American dream—working the land with his hand, in a suit. Hijinks ensue.

not be far from the truth. Bossier was finally integrated during the 1969–70 school year because of litigation that began in 1964 in the case of *Ura Lemon et al. v. Bossier Parish School Board.* The city remembered. According to one website, the Shreveport-Bossier area ranked sixteenth among the most segregated cities in America as recently as 2020.[1]

Shopping malls were the backdrop of most of my adolescent social life. Our community had a white mall and a Black mall. There was an unspoken, yet clearly understood, rule that Pierre Bossier Mall was where the white people shopped. Mall St. Vincent was for the Black folks. The most obvious, and most important, evidence of this rule was the astonishing lack of Black shoppers in the Pierre Bossier Mall. This unspoken rule was enforced by withering stares, ill treatment within the individual shops, and constant monitoring of Black patrons by mall security. We lived barely ten minutes away from the white mall. But if a movie prominently featured a Black actor, we had to drive forty-five minutes to Mall St. Vincent because those movies, no matter how popular, were not typically shown at Pierre Bossier.

Being Black in the wrong mall was problematic. Best-case scenario, you got served cold looks and cold food because the people in the mall restaurants didn't want to wait on you. Nevertheless, we shopped at the Pierre Bossier Mall because the alternative was too inconvenient and my parents were not going to easily concede that there was yet another place they were not allowed to frequent due to the color of their skin. For reasons that make no sense in hindsight, one of our favorite post-church lunch spots was El Chico, a Mexican-food chain restaurant in the mall. Almost every experience we had there was negative and culminated in my parents giving the manager an earful. It was not uncommon to wait thirty to forty-five minutes for our party of four to be seated as we watched larger parties of Caucasians claim their tables. With the addition of servers who ignored us or forgot our orders, we were lucky to get our meals at all, much less get them warm. As frustrating as the experience was, I think that we repeated this pattern because our parents wanted to teach us to insist on our right to belong. I certainly don't think it was about the quality of the food.

My parents worked tirelessly to ensure we had quality education, opportunities, and safety—a by-product of previously having been run out of a white neighborhood when a cross was burned in our front yard. I didn't really appreciate the lessons we were learning at the time. The regular fight for equality at the front lines of El Chico just felt like a spectacle. As a result, as far back as I can remember, my goal was just to fit in to the world around me. It wasn't easy. I recall waiting outside a friend's house, drinking from a hose on a sweltering Louisiana summer day while all my friends took turns using the bathroom and getting ice water inside. This was because, as my friend explained to me, his daddy told him that he didn't "want niggers sitting on his toilet." Today, if my son came home and informed me that he'd had this sort of experience among friends, I would insist that he find new friends. But for me, where else could I go? In an exclusively white context, where prejudice was normalized, with which of my peers could I seek shelter? This dilemma epitomized my upbringing in the South. The best I could do was to take it in stride.

Adapting to Survive

Particularly for minority children constrained by social dynamics they cannot control, an inability to develop the necessary tolerance can be catastrophic. I remember running out of a very nice restaurant during Sunday brunch, screaming, "I don't want to be Black!" because my eight-year-old heart couldn't take it anymore. Today, as a forty-something father of three, I don't recall exactly what my parents said to console their hurting son; neither can I comprehend how they mustered the strength to say it. But I know it involved accepting what couldn't be changed and pushing through the pain. Said another way: adaptation.

Perhaps there was even something caught or misinterpreted from

the dogged persistence embodied by my parents which communi-
cated that there's no reprieve for emotions when there's work to
be done. This may be a holdover from generations of Black ancestors who quickly learned that America doesn't play fair and that,
in a society that constantly undercut their efforts, they had to be
exceptional just to be seen as capable. Combined with the aggressive individualism promoted by the conservative evangelical industrial complex, there is simply no room left to tolerate minority
complaints. There's no time to mourn.

A. D. Thomason, author of *Permission to Be Black* (2021), candidly recounts a conversation with his sister that explained the
intense drive and adaptive instincts he and his siblings developed
in youth:

> She goes, "Adam, you remember when mom got shot, we went
> to the hospital?"
> So my mom was shot five times, so we go to the hospital,
> and we see her, right? I'm twelve at the time, and [my sister is]
> fourteen, and my brother is fifteen. We see her . . . traumatic situ-
> ation, right? But that ain't even the point. I know it's crazy, me
> saying that ain't even the point. But that's not even the point.
> The point is this:
> I said, "Ang, didn't we have to go to school pretty soon?"
> She was like, "No, Adam. We had to go to school *the* next
> day."
> I go, "Angie, why did we go to school the next day?"
> She goes, "'Cause our uncle said, 'You should not put your
> life on hold because something bad happens.'"
> Now think about that, bro. That's why my counselor was
> saying, "I'm surprised you're alive." I didn't even get to process
> my mom's shooting, my dad's leaving, like to this day, there
> was never—outside of talking to my counselor recently—there
> was never, like (someone asking), "Man, how did you feel about
> seeing your mom like that?" We had to go to school the next day
> and that's the reason why. So, lay that reality on all the Black
> folks from 1619 that didn't get to put their life on hold because
> their child was taken, their husband was castrated, because
> she was raped . . . I mean, you just go down the list. And I'm

thinking like, *Oh no! We have never processed our humanity; our emotions.*[2]

The ability to keep going, to endure, to persist, to suit up in camouflage allowing us to blend into the social framework has become, for people of color, a truly crucial learned defense mechanism. We don't get time to process what we're feeling.

One of the hardest things in mourning is how the world keeps turning. There's an indignity to the kind of loss that feels like it should kill you but leaves you living but emotionally disfigured. For example, when someone you love deeply passes, it feels that it's the end of the story or, at least, should be. We can't picture life without them, so when they're gone, what is life? How is it supposed to work without them? Everything seems wrong. The story is supposed to end here. We're not supposed to see beyond the pages of the last chapter. The audacity of the sun to shine when your world ends. People shopping, laughing, eating, going to church, living life without regard of the nuclear holocaust we're walking through. No pomp or circumstance will suffice. A seven-gun salute is insufficient. This is particularly true of Black and Brown people living with a sense of loss from racial trauma—even more so in the church.

We're never allowed to mourn the coordinated efforts to erase everything this nation forced our grandparents, parents, and us to endure. Every law fashioned and passed to limit the social space we can move in. Every slur and stereotype eagerly consumed and parroted by our white acquaintances. The recorded lynching of Black folks at the hands of law enforcement that is quickly relativized as we're admonished: "Just move on. No one wants to hear what you people have to say. Stop talking about it. Stop complaining. Stop preaching that woke theology. Stop singing. Stop kneeling. Shut up and dribble. Stop wearing T-shirts. Stop marching. Stop protesting. Stop hashtagging. Stop teaching about it in schools. Stop putting those books in school libraries. #CriticalRaceTheory. #DEI. Stop. STOP. *STOP!* Shut up. You don't get to mourn. Adapt."

Therefore, I say this to my fellow minorities and allies: because expressionless persistence is what is expected of us, stopping to seek our own healing is rebellion. In environments where we have never been allowed to pause, mourn, heal, or grow, removing the mask and refusing to say "I'm fine" is defiance. Stopping to mourn is an act of resistance. Our tears are an act of worship.

Our nation conveys a constant message of "otherness" to people of color. Yet, somehow, without cognitive dissonance, it also communicates another message: "You can transcend race (or, more specifically, the alienating effects of racism), gain wealth, and even *earn* respect in society by assimilating into, and occupying, the white stratosphere." This messaging was particularly loud in the 1980s and 1990s when prime examples of successful conformists included Clarence Thomas, Bill Cosby, and O. J. Simpson—Lord, have mercy. Presented with what appeared to be a cheat code to achieving the American dream, assimilation seems all but a foregone conclusion. As a result, African Americans learn to despise our Blackness because it is an impediment to blending in, a brightly hued stripe ruining the effect of the camouflage.

> Because expressionless persistence is what is expected of us, stopping to seek our own healing is rebellion. Stopping to mourn is an act of resistance. Our tears are an act of worship.

I find this instinct follows Christians of color into white Christianity, where we are expected to be ever winsome. We're taught there's glory to be had in our suffering and the subsequent power of our testimony. This even becomes justification for perpetuating the status quo. Just soldier on. Persevere. Overcome. Smile. Adapt.

I think we talk about adaptation far too flippantly. We don't consider all its nuances. It's certainly true of society generally, but especially true of Christianity. We tend to see personal transformation as a prophylactic to prevent adversity rather than something that happens as a result of it. Consider how adaptation works in nature. For example, the mimic octopus (*Thaumoctopus mimicus*, for those easily fooled into believing I didn't just learn the scientific name thirty seconds ago on Google), when pursued by prey, can change color to camouflage itself. Clinging to objects like coral, it contorts itself using its tentacles to replicate even the *texture* of its environment. No matter how narrow or abrasive the environment, this creature appears to belong. This adaptation isn't passive. It is a comprehensive, prolonged distortion for the sake of survival, a defense mechanism that is nothing short of an evolutionary miracle, nature's version of deepfake technology, so thorough in application that it can convince the most observant onlooker of its authenticity.

For minorities, our alienation within white Christianity comes with the somber realization that we have unconsciously adopted similar survival techniques in the church, losing ourselves in the process. From the outside, we seem to blend effortlessly into hostile environments. It might appear as though the exercise of enduring prolonged discomfort—adapting to harsh environments—eliminates the discomfort or even that we're built to endure it.*

However, acclimation and comfort are not the same thing. We make adaptation look easy because we have extensive experience. At some point it becomes second nature. When we conform to white culture's expectations, we do it instinctively *despite* the pain because our choice, as the adage goes, is adapt or die. Churches that require this of us teach us a deepfake *theology*. This religion promotes a sort of cultural schizophrenia where we navigate between our own culture and that of the church, able to let our guards down in the first environment but having to be hypervigilant in the latter. We realize this comprehensive code-switching is the currency of the realm, and so we learn to "speak the King's English to the Queen's taste."[3] More often, however, we burn out from valiant yet doomed efforts to pour the fullness of our identities into the stricture of a vase shaped like Christo-Americanism. The cumulative

*We would be remiss not to consider how this same rhetoric was deployed to defend enslaving Black people ("Their dark skin enables them to withstand the sun and heat") or continues to lead to higher morbidity and mortality rates in Black women ("They're stronger. They can endure more pain. They're probably exaggerating what they're feeling").

effect that such long-term mimicry demands leaves us exhausted and emotionally gnarled from the effort.

In their book *Burnout: The Secret to Unlocking the Stress Cycle,* Emily and Amelia Nagoski provide an apt illustration:[4]

> White men grow on an open, level field. White women grow on far steeper and rougher terrain because the field wasn't made for them. Women of color grow not just on a hill, but on a cliff-side over the ocean, battered by wind and waves. None of us chooses the landscape in which we're planted. If you find your-self on an ocean-battered cliff, your only choice is to grow there, or fall into the ocean. So, if we transplant a survivor of the steep hill and cliff to the level field, natives of the field may look at that survivor and wonder why she has so much trouble trusting people, systems, and even her own bodily sensations. Why is this tree so bent and gnarled?
>
> It's because that is what it took to survive in the place where she grew. A tree that's fought wind and gravity and erosion to grow strong and green on a steep cliff is going to look strange and out of place when moved to the level playing field. The gnarled, wind-blown tree from an oceanside cliff might not conform with our ideas of what a tree should look like, but it works well in the context where it grew. And that tall straight tree wouldn't stand a chance if it was transplanted to the cliffside.

Evangelical church culture, often baiting its disciples with the lure of prosperity, maximized potential for Christian manhood/womanhood, flawless parenting skills, and *coolness*, particularly promotes the assuefaction of adversity for minorities. Without regard to the inflicted injuries that cause our souls to have taken the shape of the gnarled tree, whiteness expects—no, demands—an Instagrammable, abundant life of victory, without considering the ways it thwarts our effort. "Do more," "work harder," "why are you like this?" They may give no consideration of the fallout the church has caused, but children born in the irradiated shadow of a nuclear reactor will understand why they glow in the dark centuries after the disaster.

I didn't realize I was wearing camouflage until it was no longer necessary. Once I finally found a body of believers that allowed me to be my full, authentic self, I unconsciously relaxed, and for the first time, I realized how hard I had been working to adapt. It was as though my body released a breath I was unaware I had been holding. We need to experience genuine Christianity to recognize the counterfeit. We need to live in freedom to realize we've been adapting to avoid predators.

In the documentary "Who We Are: A Chronicle of Racism in America,"[5] the ACLU's deputy legal director, Jeffery Robinson, uses interviews, documents, and legal history to draw a straight line from slavery to modern manifestations of racism in the United States. As an example, Robinson highlights disparities between the law and the lived reality of minorities exemplified in the mixed success of the Montgomery bus boycott (December 1955–December 1956). To make his case, the documentary examines a pamphlet circulated in the Black community by Dr. Martin Luther King Jr. and white ally Glenn Smiley the night before the integration they'd fought so hard for took effect in the city of Montgomery—more than a year after the campaign began and two years *after* the landmark case of *Brown v. Board of Education* was decided.[6] The instructions (with Robinson's takeaways) included these items:

- The bus driver is in charge of the bus and has been instructed to obey the law. Assume that he will cooperate in helping you occupy any vacant seat.
- Do not deliberately sit by a white person, unless there is no other seat.

    (Takeaway) Where did this come from? This is the difference that every Black person knows. It's the slip between the law and living. Yeah, the law says you can ride that bus and sit wherever you want, but don't go getting yourself killed over it.

- In case of an incident, talk as little as possible, and always in a quiet tone. Do not get up from your seat! Report all serious incidents to the bus driver.

> *(Takeaway) Talk as little as possible and always in a quiet tone. Don't make white people uncomfortable because the cost of that could be your life.*

- If another person is being molested, do not arise to go to his defense, but pray for the oppressor and use moral and spiritual force to carry on the struggle for Justice.

  > *(Takeaway) And I don't know what to say about that one and I definitely don't know what to say about this one:*

- If you feel you cannot take it, walk for another week or two.

  > *(Takeaway) This is the difference between the law and living when you're Black in America.*

Even in victory, we are trained to temper our embrace of freedom. Whereas our white brothers and sisters live without the invisible boundaries, minorities have been taught not to look too free. Stay humble in the presence of white supremacy. Don't get uppity. Know your place. Be content with your plight. Wear the mask.

The Body/Soul Dilemma

Often, when people of color want to discuss race and issues of justice in the church, we're accustomed to hearing all kinds of excuses:

- "It's a sin problem, not a skin problem."
- "We're all the same in God's eyes (so we don't need to talk about how you're being treated like you're not the same)."
- "We don't want to talk about politics."

These platitudes and excuses allow believers who are uncomfortable facing the truth to turn the conversation away from tangible ways that we can fight inequities in the world we live in. Of all these mantras, the last bothers me most—the suggestion that racial identity is "political." Set aside for a moment that the American evangelical church has no qualms discussing politics from the pulpit when it benefits their agenda (even if it jeopardizes their

501(c)(3) tax-exempt status). Never mind that when the need is urgent, refusing to take a position *is* itself taking a position if it maintains the status quo. Reframing biblical concepts like equality and justice as political allows essentials of Christianity to be fashioned into something that belongs to "the world." Here's how bad the situation is: even though overt racism seems to be gaining legitimacy in our culture by the day, if a white pastor were to say as much from the pulpit—or point out specific examples found among white Christians in most congregations— that pastor would be in danger of losing a job. Meanwhile, the need for Christianity to face the problem head-on is beyond desperate.

If we label these discussions as political, we have a reason to avoid the issue altogether. We've heard many pastors decry distinctions between the sacred and secular when blending the two serves to turn out Republicans at the polling booth. But the separation is firm when it's time to discuss believers' duties to the marginalized. The propensity of Christianity to separate sacred and secular as it applies to minorities isn't just misguided—there's an insidious origin to intentionally looking past the cultural value of souls inhabiting minority skin.

> Reframing biblical concepts like equality and justice as political allows essentials of Christianity to be fashioned into something that belongs to "the world."

I was fortunate enough to hear biblical scholar and author Esau McCaulley discuss scholarship on "the body/soul dilemma" during his visit to Truett Seminary in 2023. The dilemma postulates that in America, Black people have historically been viewed as either bodies without souls, or souls without bodies. The gross implication of this history is as follows:

If Black people are simply bodies, deprived of souls, then we are something less than human. This thesis worked well for the traffickers of enslaved people who needed some moral basis for their behavior. When we're seen as less than human, Black people do not fully embody the *imago Dei* when compared to the "more civilized" standard of white culture. Therefore, Black people become feral animals to be traded, mortgaged, whipped, and violated in any number of ways without triggering the culprit's empathy. This philosophy makes us nothing more than chattel.

Conversely, if society disregards Black bodies, giving concern only to the condition of the Negro's soul, then white Christians have license to concern themselves strictly with the spiritual formation of Black people while completely disregarding what's being done to our bodies. I believe this ideology explains the disregard, if not contempt, that white Christianity has had toward societal injustices protested by minorities.

The modern obstacle to the church seeing Black people in the fullness of humanity (both spirit and flesh) is not that we are seen as soulless, feral animals but that our bodies are commodities that can be used, mistreated, or disregarded so long as the church ministers to our souls. To be accepted in white Christianity, minorities are asked to adopt the view that only the eternal care of our immortal souls after death is important in the divine plan of the universe. The condition of a Black soul in the present life, housed within a mistreated body, is morally and theologically unimportant to white supremacy. An apt example provided by Jemar Tisby in his 2019 book *The Color of Compromise,* and by Michael O. Emerson and Christian Smith in *Divided by Faith* (2000), is found in the rituals surrounding the baptism of enslaved people in the American South by Frances Le Jau, a European missionary to South Carolina. Le Jau required enslaved Blacks to agree to the following declaration before they could be baptized as Christians:

> You declare in the presence of God and before this congregation that you do not ask for holy baptism out of any design to free yourself from the Duty and Obedience you owe to your master while you live, but merely for the good of your soul and to partake of the Grace and Blessings promised to Members of the Church of Jesus Christ.[7]

The message was clear: entering the faith does not make Black people brothers and sisters in Christ such that they are on equal footing with white believers. Because white people remain superior to Black people, the theory goes, faith in Christ has no effect on how Black bodies should be treated. Thus, again, Black bodies could be physically abused by their slave masters without regard to the spirit within. Rather, the Negro should be content in Paul's assurance that the sufferings of the present are not worthy to be compared with the glory that shall be revealed.

From this, we see that white Christianity has, from the foundations of our nation's history, dangled a promise of paradise for our eternal souls in front of Black believers, while clearly communicating to us that our faith offered no promises regarding freedom in the present life. If we revere pastors holding these views as genuine representatives of Christ, the message to minorities is that this theology reflects that *God*—not just the church—is indifferent to injustice. Such an indifference would signify that God is also unloving. For how can a loving, all-powerful God ignore the plight of God's creation?

I just can't help but think that this same dilemma is at play in how white Christianity continues to view the social plight of Black folks in our nation today. The body/soul dilemma reveals itself in the vocabulary adopted by conservative Christians critiquing minorities over social issues. As a lawyer, I'm most attuned to this rhetoric in the context of law enforcement and the legal system. In response to police brutality in particular, this racialized gnosticism births talking points that completely look past the violence to victim-blame:

Obey the law of the land.
Submit to those in authority.
Should have just complied.
Shouldn't have been breaking the law.
I guess she'll stand for the pledge of allegiance next time.[8]

For believers to adopt language that blames victims of racism for the abuse they've suffered is profoundly unlike Christ. Yet from chattel slavery to scapegoating the marginalized, the body/soul dilemma has remained present in the makeup of America. To be clear, Christians who believe that God is unconcerned with the protection of our bodies or the condition of our souls are not only misrepresenting Christ to minorities but also attempting to absolve themselves of the indifference displayed in their convictions. With such a philosophy comes a tireless commitment to remind Black people that the expectations inherent in our spiritual abuse include our ongoing commitment to observe the niceties. To wear a mask. To adapt and endure. As Nat King Cole sang:

> Smile though your heart is aching.
> Smile even though it's breaking.[9]

Long before the phrase "code-switching" was coined to depict the social demands on Black Americans weaving in and out of predominantly white environments, to their own cultural contexts, then back again, Paul Laurence Dunbar encapsulated the experience in a poem titled "We Wear the Mask."

> We wear the mask that grins and lies,
> It hides our cheeks and shades our eyes,—
> This debt we pay to human guile;
> With torn and bleeding hearts we smile,
> And mouth with myriad subtleties.
>
> Why should the world be over-wise,
> In counting all our tears and sighs?
> Nay, let them only see us, while
>   We wear the mask.
>
> We smile, but, O great Christ, our cries
> To thee from tortured souls arise.
> We sing, but oh the clay is vile
> Beneath our feet, and long the mile;
> But let the world dream otherwise,
>   We wear the mask!

Dunbar's prose is an anthem for minorities oft admonished to shut up and accept the inequities that distinguish our cultures with a smile. But it's past time to declare that something's wrong when adaptive countermeasures are needed, and encouraged, for minorities to endure in the *church*. With the perspective that comes from exiting these inhospitable conditions, we realize we have not just deceived those around us in order to survive, but we also deceived ourselves. We have so closely embraced the beliefs of patriarchal, evangelical, Christian nationalism that its dogma became indistinguishable from the teachings of Jesus. When we finally detach ourselves from the decaying coral, we recognize it as an unhealthy misrepresentation of who God is. Only then can we rightfully see ourselves for who we are in the eyes of God.

And so, brothers and sisters, it is time we release ourselves from harmful, performative deceptions of white Christianity. Instead, we remove the masks that prevent us from being our full, authentic, genuine selves in every cultural context and resolve never to don them again.

We confess our deeply felt need to adapt for survival—not to create waves, to fit in.

We believe that God has something more for us than staying under the radar—something more than survival.

We acknowledge the potential for idolatry in acceptance.

We seek release not just from the bondage that others have placed us in but also the bondage that we have placed ourselves in as a coping mechanism.

At the base of this fire, as at the base of an altar, we lay down the mask.

Chapter 8

The New Jim Crow Theology

*I*n her book, *The New Jim Crow*, Michelle Alexander makes a compelling case that the blatant caste system which excluded Black Americans from participating in the promises of American democracy in the Jim Crow South has been replaced by a comprehensive, but less overt, form of systemic discrimination that evolved vis-à-vis the American legal system. Alexander's insights emanate from her experience as an attorney with the American Civil Liberties Union (ACLU). Her intimate knowledge of the machinery of the legal system enables her to speak to the bankrolling of increasingly militarized police forces, the abuses of racial profiling, and misuse of prosecutorial discretion, all of which reinforce that original caste system in a way that we hardly recognize exists in the law.

But where one social system operates to degrade minorities, it is rarely the *only* system at work to accomplish those ends. Rather, America is so replete with the effects of white supremacy that the degradation is comprehensive—even affecting the church. Said more bluntly, if racial biases play a role in one's work, they likely infect one's faith as well. As minorities, we find this out the hard way. Therefore we would do well to consider parallels between Alexander's insights of social division in the legal system and white Christianity.

In 2019, Amber Guyger was convicted by a Texas jury for the murder of twenty-six-year-old Botham Jean. Jean, a Black male, was a beloved worship leader and youth pastor at Dallas West

Church of Christ. Guyger, a thirty-year-old white woman, had been a Dallas police officer for nearly five years at the time of the shooting. The evidence at trial matched what the general public had been told for months since Jean's death made national news. Guyger was returning to her apartment complex after a long shift. Guyger told law enforcement that she was so exhausted that she failed to realize that she was on the wrong floor of her apartment complex when she entered the identically situated unit owned and occupied by Botham Jean one floor above hers. Having somehow gained entry into Jean's apartment, Guyger found a Black man sitting in the dark, watching television, and mistook him for a burglar in her own residence. Officer Guyger shot Jean dead. The jury found Guyger guilty of murder and, before assessing her punishment of ten years, the jury was informed of text messages and social media posts that the prosecutors believed depicted Guyger's racist attitudes toward minorities.

In Texas, the family of the deceased is given the opportunity to publicly address the defendant in the courtroom after sentence has been pronounced. The victim impact statement made by Botham's mother displayed all of the grief you would expect from a woman who had lost her son, coupled with stunning and unexpected poise. The portion of this case that made the most ripples in the evangelical world was Botham's eighteen-year-old brother, Brandt, using part of his victim impact statement to tell Guyger that he forgave her for killing his brother:

> If you truly are sorry, I know I can speak for myself, I forgive you. And I know if you go to God and ask him, he will forgive you. And I don't think anyone can say it—again I'm speaking for myself and not on behalf of my family—but I love you just like anyone else. And I'm not going to say I hope you rot and die, just like my brother did, but I personally want the best for you. And I wasn't going to ever say this in front of my family or anyone, but I don't even want you to go to jail. I want the best for you, because I know that's exactly what Botham would want you to do. And the best would be: give your life to Christ. I'm not going to say anything else. I think giving your life to

Christ would be the best thing that Botham would want you to do. Again, I love you as a person. And I don't wish anything bad on you.[1]

Brandt went a step further, securing permission from the judge to give Guyger a hug in the courtroom at the end of his statement. The moment was unusual not just because of his posture toward Guyger, but also because it allowed a criminal defendant to have physical contact with a person involved in the trial in a way that usurped the security concerns that bailiffs and judges typically have in criminal trials. The courtroom's solemnity was filled with audible sobs, mixed with the clicks of dozens of camera shutters as the media pounced on the rare sighting. In addition, Judge Tammy Kemp, an African American woman, took the unusual step of hugging Guyger and handing her a Bible after the sentence was pronounced.

These images were touted throughout the conservative white Christian world at breakneck speed as a model for how Black people should respond as victims of racial injustice. Seemingly every white evangelical pastor, media outlet, social media post, and blog had something to say about the example that Brandt Jean had provided for how oppressed minorities should extend grace to their oppressors. Overlooked in the rush to wield Brandt's statement was his own admonishment that he spoke only on his own behalf, not even that of his family. Shortly after Brandt delivered his statement in the courtroom, Botham's mother, Allison Jean, delivered her own impassioned statement for the media, expressing anger and demanding accountability in police reform. Addressing her son's statement to Guyger, she told one media outlet, "What he did today was remarkable, and he did it all on his own."[2] But Allison also made clear that Brandt's expression of grief differed from that of the rest of the family.

No matter. The "hug felt 'round the world" was quickly weaponized. A clip of the event shared by Fox News rapidly garnered over 168,000 likes and 122,000 shares on Facebook. It was largely my white acquaintances who ensured the story overwhelmed my news feed for days. The story was highlighted in the Baptist Press.[3] The Acton Institute labeled it an "ultimate act of love,"[4] language that feels strangely misplaced, echoing the way we view Jesus's death on the cross. The *National Catholic Register* opined, "Brandt Jean's extraordinary actions show the ordinary demands of what it means to be a disciple of Jesus Christ."[5] Edward J. Burns, a white bishop who heads the Catholic Diocese of Dallas, said in a public statement, "I pray we can all follow the example of this outstanding young man. Let us pray for peace in our community and around the world."[6] The Institute for Law Enforcement Administration in Dallas honored Brandt with its 2019 Ethical Courage Award.[7]

In Waco, the emerald jewel centered on the rodeo buckle of the Bible Belt, white church leaders used social media posts and Sunday sermons to seize the opportunity to emphasize Brandt as the model of what racial reconciliation looks like in the church. To believers immersed in white Christianity, Brandt's forgiveness epitomized what righteousness looks like for Black people—in stark contrast to the rest of his family's perspective. Racial bias reveals itself in conservative Christianity not just in its politics, but also in the deputization of particular Black individuals against the whole of Black culture in theological contexts.

In 2020, conservative white Christians flocked to the internet again to fight Black people with Black people. Orlando Magic basketball player Jonathan Isaac made news when he stood, wearing his jersey, during the national anthem while his teammates knelt, arms interlocked, while wearing Black Lives Matter T-shirts. The media was particularly interested in Isaac's counterprotest because he is a Black athlete. To the delight of many white evangelicals, Jonathan replied:

> For me Black lives are supported through the gospel. All lives are supported through the gospel. We all have things that we do wrong and sometimes it gets to a place that we're pointing fingers about whose wrong is worst. Or whose wrong is seen, so I feel like the Bible tells us that we all fall short of God's glory. . . . That will help bring us closer together and get past skin color.

And get past anything that's on the surface and doesn't really deal with the hearts of men and women.[8]

Did you catch the talking points?

- All lives matter.
- It's a sin problem, not a skin problem.
- Police brutality is an individual sin issue, not a systemic racial issue.
- We shouldn't point fingers because there's wrong on "both sides."
- Let's not talk about race.

For weeks, Isaac's narrative was served up to me in direct messages unprovoked, as well as in response to completely unrelated posts, and the posts of white colleagues appearing in my newsfeed. "*This*" the narrative went, "is the messaging you should be using your platform for. This is what Black people need to hear." It's certainly what the traditionalist white Christian contingent is comfortable hearing. However, by this time, I'd already left behind TFI, and, with it, the urge to ensure that white believers remained comfortable as we speak honestly about race. That inner work was a process; it didn't happen overnight.

Friendships Forged in Fire

By 2016, Toxic Fellowship Inc. (TFI) had become so unrecognizable to the minorities attending that many of us began, instinctively, to seek each other out in and among the crowd of approximately four thousand members. We learned each other's stories; we networked. We created a smaller church within the church in order to vulnerably share our feelings with one another without fear of being labeled *divisive*. From this collection, a core group formed. We created a private page on social media to support one another and even shared a Friendsgiving meal in my home. In that time together we processed our bewilderment with the church's unrecognizability and affirmed each other's frustrations:

"Why don't they see it?"

"So, it's not just me?"

"No. It's not just you."

"You're not alone."

"What's it going to take to change them?"

Despite the size of this congregation, and the significant number of minorities attending, we had each been siloed in such a way that our experience within the congregation caused us to question the validity of our feelings.

> One problem was that the *culture* of the church made discussion of things that were important to us as people of color taboo.

Yet the problem wasn't easy to put a finger on at first. For instance, we largely agreed that it wasn't that the individuals in our separate small groups were racist toward us. Nor were there (usually) noticeably large gaffes made from the pulpit.[9] So where were these feelings of isolation and alienation emanating from? It was in the air we breathed. One problem was that the *culture* of the church made discussion of things that were important to us as people of color taboo. Most often, race matters were waved away with spiritual bypassing: "We're all one in God's eyes," or "The only color that matters to God is the red blood that covers all our sins." Yet this sentiment was also paired with subtle affronts that made the environment noxious: We watched church leaders relay QAnon conspiracies and racially tinged propaganda on social media. We endured the complete refusal of the pastors to call out this behavior within the congregation from the pulpit when asked to. All of this made TFI a hard place to feel at liberty to enter the presence of God. I will never cease to be perplexed by the irony that when minorities asked the church to address its community's shortcomings to facilitate unity, the church labeled us divisive.

Before the Friendsgiving meal in our house came to a close, we created a plan of action. We committed to utilize our influence to lobby the leadership and report back to one another in the days ahead. All of us had been long-term members of the church with unique relationships with folks in leadership: the senior pastor, his family, assistant pastors, elders, you name it. We were inspired. This was a rescue mission for the soul of the church. We decided to do what evangelical high school and college ministry had taught us to do: target the people with influence in the church to change their hearts and start a revival.* Having identified key figures, we learned we were all within one degree of separation from those we needed to reach. These were people who had gone on mission trips together; had previously served or were still serving together on staff; were attending small groups together; and were lifelong family friends. These were relationships that should have mattered.

We soon learned that they didn't.

Over the weeks to come, one by one, each of us returned with our tails tucked between our legs to report that our concern with how racism had crept into the church had been dismissed. In some cases, the leaders had specifically named the worldly influence of the social gospel, Marxism, or critical race theory as the basis of their rejecting minority concerns. Some pastors saw denouncing racism in church as an either-or proposition. They feared that by speaking up for minorities, they would alienate the majority. Of course, my response to such fears is *Good! If your mission is to educate people how God's love should work in the world around us, addressing how God's image-bearers are mistreated seems like an important step. Let those offended by that notion go elsewhere.*

---

*For the uninitiated, one of the popular strategies to increase the size of a church youth group in the 1990s was relationship evangelism. Youth pastors instructed the children in their charge to invite the "cool kids" from school to youth group. This strategy reasoned that if the quarterback or the head cheerleader came to youth group and gave their life to Christ, they would soon leverage their influence to invite all their friends to church. Soon, all the kids on campus would feel as if church is where the cool people are. Of course, this strategy offered nothing for the youth who were social outcasts at school who felt a sense of belonging at church. Worse, if the strategy worked, it deprived the outcasts of one of the rare safe communities they had as the social pecking order was transferred from the classroom to the pews.

Another frequently cited obstacle to moving in the right direction was that the pastors weren't sure how to transition the congregation into discussing race-related issues openly. Indeed, how do we know if the time is right to openly discuss race in our churches? I have a theory that the time is right if (1) you are in church and (2) you have discussions. The people who are enraged when the pastor applies the Scriptures to our modern social settings to combat racism are not upset because the pastor dipped a toe in the water. They're upset because the pastor approached the pond at all. To them, a toe in the water is just as reprehensible as diving in completely. Nor do they want any water from the splash to touch them.

The most common response from those in leadership to whom we brought our concerns was, "Wow. I've never heard this before. I didn't realize this was a problem." However, I was aware that multiple minorities were meeting with these same leaders to express similar thoughts—sometimes on the same day. It was this consistent lie that sobered me to the reality that we were being patronized. The ambivalence of our church leaders toward our pain revealed the incursion of white supremacy in their theology.

Up to this point, I was driving myself mad asking why the church didn't see the problem. Did they not have access to the right books, theologians, or podcasts? Did I need to introduce my pastors to minority pastors in the community with whom they were unacquainted? What could I do to change the concerning internal culture growing in our congregation? In hindsight, I realize I was wrong to assume the leaders were acting in ignorance. We hadn't arrived at this place by accident. Coming to this realization was a turning point for me.

Though we all returned from our strategic meetings with the church leaders empty-handed, I walked away with an important insight: Our efforts were not being thwarted by communication problems with white believers. The obstacle is not a lack of understanding. The trouble is that certain brands of Christianity are guided by philosophies that conflict with any orthopraxy that dignifies Black and Brown bodies. It's not that they don't understand why addressing race is important; they disagree with the premise of saying so publicly. In their minds, there is no need to address race in church.

Said another way, minorities are not being overlooked in the white church by negligence. The alienation of minorities, and the simultaneous investment in the comfort of white believers, is a calculated decision. When this paradigm took root in white Christianity at large, the net effect was not just a perversion of the gospel. It is a subtle, yet comprehensive, estrangement of all cultural relevance (save that of a white, male, conservative, nationalistic, cisgendered point of view) from orthodoxy that produces the disenfranchisement of minorities from the church. Culture war is just another part of the ministry meta-objective. This is spiritualized discrimination that evolved vis-à-vis white Christian religion. The new Jim Crow theology.

Sins of Commission and Omission

There's an important distinction to be made here. The problem we run into as minorities attempting to transform (or even just inform) the culture of a white-minded church congregation is not necessarily that its leadership consciously resents minorities. Rest assured, that may be true in some instances. However, animus is not a necessary cognitive requirement for these spaces to become toxic to marginalized communities. Hatred is not a necessary active ingredient. Willful indifference—paired with patriarchy, questionable theology, Christian nationalism, or a craving for political influence (particularly right-leaning influence)—has the same effect. Likewise, we are arrogant to believe that our presence, which has already been taken for granted and looked over, is capable of changing the momentum of such a large ship. No, not every offense visited on minorities in predominantly white congregations is an intentional slight. But neither does it have to be to achieve the desired effect.

In criminal law, when a person steps outside the norms that society enshrines in the law, that violation of the law is frequently referred to as an "offense."* When an offense is committed, the document that charges the accused with the offense must specifically include a phrase alleging that this crime was committed "against the peace and dignity of the state." This recital is so common that prosecutors, judges, and defense attorneys typically take the language for granted without any real consideration. However, what the law communicates with this phrase is that the very reason the alleged behavior *is* an offense is because it violates the peace and dignity of the community. Let me say that again: *the reason that the alleged behavior is offensive is because we have been deprived of peace and dignity.*

In criminal law, there are generally two types of crimes: offenses of *commission* and offenses of *omission*. Offenses of commission are *committed* with distinct action (an *actus reus*) coupled with criminal intent (*mens rea*). On the other hand, some behaviors are criminalized due to a *failure* to act where there is a duty to do so. We refer to these as *omissions*. So the law recognizes that you can cause offense by something that is done wrong or by a failure to do something when there is a duty to act. Whether by act or omission, criminal law recognizes that offenses may be conduct-oriented or result-oriented in their nature. An offense that is conduct-oriented is criminalized because the law focuses on the *action* of the accused, rather than on the resulting harm. The *actus reus* is the primary element of the offense. In comparison, result-oriented offenses are primarily *mens rea* crimes; they focus on the *intent* rather than the actions of the accused. This will become relevant in a moment.

As an example, a child (we'll just name him Scotty) who intentionally throws a baseball at a window is responsible for the damage to the window if it breaks and, in Texas, could be charged with criminal mischief. Scotty's bad intentions (*mens rea*), coupled with unlawful action of throwing the baseball at a window (*actus reus*), caused harm to the home owner's property, against the peace and dignity of the state, forming an offense of commission. The crime

---

*While offenses are synonymous with crimes, in the everyday setting of the courtroom, legal professionals typically use the word *offense*.

is a conduct-oriented crime of commission because the primary element of the offense is the action of throwing the baseball, not the resulting damage to the window. *The offense is caused by problematic behavior.* Still with me?

Now, suppose Scotty slips into his stepfather's study and removes his stepfather's prize possession: a baseball autographed by Babe Ruth. Further, Scotty's intention in doing so is to keep the ball for-e-ver because he doesn't believe his stepfather will notice that it's gone. Scotty has committed the offense of theft. There is an unlawful act, coupled with the intent to permanently deprive the owner. The offense is a result-oriented crime of commission. Scotty's mind-set at the time he took the baseball is the primary element at issue because his intent was not just to relocate the baseball but to permanently dispossess his stepfather of ownership. Therefore, *the offense is caused by the resulting harm, not so much by problematic behavior.* OK, one more hypothetical.

Suppose Scotty wasn't the one who went into his stepfather's study to take the ball. Suppose his friend Ham was the bad actor and stole the ball with no intention of returning it. He did this with Scotty's full knowledge, and Scotty didn't object despite having been told that his friends weren't allowed in the study. Minutes later, Scotty, Ham, and all their friends are playing baseball at the local sandlot* when the ball is hit over the fence of a neighboring yard, forever lost to the jowls of a two-story-tall mastiff named The Beast. In this instance, Scotty would be responsible for the theft of the ball due to an omission (the failure to intervene when he had a duty to do so) rather than by commission (taking the ball himself). In fact, a prosecutor could argue that, in failing to act, Scotty aided Ham's actions and adopted Ham's criminal mind-set as his own, becoming an accomplice to the offense. The first bad actor's intentions and actions (commission) combined with the second actor's failure to act (omission), causing harm to the owner, against the peace and dignity of the state.

---

*Honestly, I don't care how old you are, you should have gotten this reference by now. But, for those who missed it, see *The Sandlot* (20th Century Fox, 1993). Please, try to keep up. You're killing me, Smalls.

You didn't hear me: when there is a bad actor in the community, and someone with the responsibility to act fails to act to protect the peace and dignity of its citizenry, the person who failed to act is just as responsible as the bad actor for the harm caused to the community, and that responsibility may exist directly due to bad behavior or indirectly from the resulting harm that was done.

Applying these legal concepts to the context of white Christianity, I've found that most church leaders want to choose what sort of offenses they are held accountable for. They want to be evaluated by overt actions (commissions) rather than failure to act when they know there is a duty to do so (omissions). When a spiritual leader (who otherwise has no aversion to discussing political issues) declines to address the myriad of derogatory comments made by the president that affect how believers perceive women and minorities, that is an offense of omission. Especially when women and minorities are sitting in the pews. These same spiritual leaders want to be lauded for the collective good that their church does while shirking responsibility for those in their charge. They will launch a sermon series on the fruit of the Spirit while turning a blind eye to the abhorrent behavior of their associate pastors in the comment sections online. Because they don't recognize the concept of collective culpability, they take no ownership of the behavior of their collaborators. Nevertheless, a better view of Christianity acknowledges that pastors are principals who bear equal responsibility to their agents.

Delving further, the lens of whiteness typically only sees a duty to accept responsibility for conduct-oriented behavior, rather than also taking responsibility for result-oriented transgressions. Such a view neglects the fact that the choice *not* to act is not just an internal cognitive calculation but is, itself, an action. The decision is conduct. So while a pastor may want to believe that their hands are clean, if an omission produces a result-oriented offense, harming minorities in their congregation, the lens through which those minorities assess the situation holds them just as responsible as it would for the commission of a conduct-oriented offense. In fact, there's an argument to be made that it is far more insidious to blithely whistle by the concentration camp, pretending not to see the chain-link fence, the barbed wire, the guard towers, and the emaciated victims standing on the other side. All while fancying, "I didn't do it. It's not my problem to fix. It's probably not even all that bad."

As I reflect on the impact that the new Jim Crow theology has had on me, I consider an observation that my friend and fellow lawyer Cyndia Hammond has often made. Everyone, she hypothesizes, wants to be judged by their subjective, internal intent, not their impact.* One of many problems with this standard is the cover it provides for bad-faith actors who are well aware that their actions and omissions have a negative impact on minorities. It allows them to feign ignorance and surprise when held to account by claiming that their track record should evince that their hearts are in the right place. "Oh, wow. I've never heard this complaint before. I'm sorry that situation made you feel that way," they would argue, "but judge me by my intentions (not the incidental result that was caused)." Taking things a step further, they would attempt to divert any effort to hold them accountable by quickly requesting forgiveness for the pain ignorantly/innocently caused by their actions (or inaction), yet failing to acknowledge or understand that a duty is equally owed to anticipate the result of their conduct. From their point of view, no duty of foresight is owed. Therefore, this mistake is capable of constant repetition, yet consistent evasion of responsibility. But as we have established, a judicious view of ministry demonstrates that result-oriented offenses are just as problematic as conduct-oriented ones. When these precepts are not appreciated, the church is no longer a safe place for those who look different from the majority culture.

---

*To be discussed further in chapter 8.

Taking Ownership

Throughout my life as a Christian, I've found that the larger the congregation, and the more charismatic the leaders are, the more likely they are to struggle with the humility that is necessary to fulfill the roles required to minister to a diverse body of believers. When pastors strive to appeal to a large audience (that is, the majority culture) rather than to shepherd a flock intimately—to know and be known—history has proved that they typically draw from skills that translate better in corporate management roles than ministry. Of course, ministries are not meant to function as corporations. This sounds like common sense, yet the American evangelical and nondenominational church tradition in particular is steeped in consumerism, worship "experiences" with lights and fog machines, easy three-step formulas to a better life packaged in sermon form, lobby kiosks selling the worship team's latest LP and/or the pastor's newest book on parenting, dating, and an awesome prayer life. What you will likely never see in these lobbies are resources teaching evangelicals how to incorporate their faith in the conversation about race, justice, and equity.

As someone who embraced this model of church for decades, I will be the first to confess that it's challenging as a believer to recognize the point at which a church loses its focus and begins to veer off course. But I know that when the church begins to see congregants as commodities, clients, or even investors, it infers a very different relationship and duty than when they see the body as sheep to be protected. And when minorities whose presence in the congregation primarily serves as window dressing are already being utilized as a type of commodity, it can only go downhill from there.

In an example that seems too spectacularly on the nose to be true, TFI exemplified this in a campaign seemingly designed to replenish its post-COVID attendees' commitment by unironically referring to its most devoted participants as owners rather than members or congregants. "Are you an owner?" one social media post read.

If you have decided to make [TFI] your church home, we encourage you to become an Owner! People typically think of the word "member" when considering joining a church. At [TFI], people who join the church are called owners. Membership often implies becoming a part of an organization and receiving certain benefits while ownership implies taking responsibility for the organization. To learn more about [TFI] and what it means to be an owner, you are invited to attend our [TFI] Ownership Night. You will learn more about our history, our beliefs and the ways you can get connected at [TFI]. Whether you're ready to make [TFI] your church home or you just want to learn more, we'd love for you to join us.

Whew.

Listen, there are times when a cultural variance necessitates deviation in how the gospel is presented. For example, in her book, *An Untidy Faith*, author Kate Boyd explains how it would be unhelpful for readers abroad, in cultures that don't have bread, to read Jesus describing himself as the "bread of life" in John 6. "Using that word," Boyd writes, "would put up more barriers than lower them, which is the point of using the people group's language in the first place. Bread is sustenance in the Bible, and this people group had something that they consider a chief part of their sustenance—the sweet potato. In their Bible, Jesus is the sweet potato of life."[10] Cultural variances like these make complete sense when they're necessary to *expand* the availability of the gospel to people whose cultures are different from ours in the West. After all, Western Christianity has a history of claiming a monopoly on biblical interpretation even though evidence demonstrates the adoption of Christianity in Egypt as early as the third century AD and Ethiopia as early as the fourth century during the reign of the Askumite emperor Ezana.[11]

But there are myriad problems with viewing church members (either overtly or subconsciously) as "owners." Perhaps there is a fitting irony to framing an American evangelical church's membership in economic, capitalistic terms that the American public understands. But in doing so, aren't we *narrowing* the scope of those to whom the gospel ministers? When the church begins to see congregants as commodities, the marginalized are easily disregarded or exploited. Conversely, when the church sees the majority culture as clients, or even investors, there is a constituency that expects a return from their investment. Implicitly, a duty of loyalty is created toward the investors, to the detriment of the *minority* stakeholders. Pun intended. This all infers a very different relationship and duty than when we see the body of Christ as a vulnerable flock of sheep in need of protection. So, no wonder white Christianity panders to one group to the exclusion of another.

Notice again that the conscious, explicit motive of the leadership in an environment defined in mercantile terms can appear to be race-neutral. The disparity in treatment is not due to a disdain for one group but rather a bias toward the other, the investors.[12] Nevertheless, a market-driven approach to our faith that contemplates dividends for some and nothing for those who don't "invest" is inescapably exploitive. Every person created in the image of God becomes a resource—a connection, a target for a pitch, stock to be counted, something that somehow serves our needs. There's a reason that multilevel marketing businesses work so well in evangelical circles. When this commercialized ideology lands on already marginalized Black and Brown populations in the church, the inevitable exploitation demonstrates yet another facet of the new Jim Crow theology.

Another problem with the appearance of religious profiteering in the church is that even the most generous interpretation of "ownership" proves deceptive in spaces that are already toxic for people of color. In a corporate context, owners have invested time and resources in exchange for a level of access or input in the company's direction. While the ownership metaphor seems to promise an all-access backstage pass to every member, minorities who are longing for the church to speak out on issues of social justice often find that white Christianity apparently still doesn't view them as full-fledged church members endowed with all the rights and privileges pertaining thereto.

Despite how much I loved the ministry and ministers at TFI, I had to reckon with the fact that it was neither a hospital for healing the spiritually wounded nor the multicultural family pointing each other to Christ that it claimed to be. It was what too many evangelical congregations have become: a superficially diverse, multilevel marketing scheme turning Jesus into a commodity easily traded for status, cultural influence, and power. There was a specific itinerary to facilitate *that* vision and it did *not* include deviating from the mission to engage the myriad of ways the church could tend to the specific wounds of BIPOC (Black, Indigenous, and people of color) members. To use Mike Kelsey's analogy:

> Oftentimes we can feel like welcomed guests in predominately white churches, I think sometimes we feel like this in predominately white spaces in general. But it's kind of like being at a bed and breakfast, right? Everybody is nice, you can use all the amenities, you get a seat at the dinner table, you can eat the food, you even get a bed, you get a room, but the menu is already predetermined. Your pictures are not up on the wall. You don't get to decide what paint color goes on the wall. You can't move (the furniture).[13]

I couldn't possibly have said it better. If there is to be ownership taken within the body of Christ, it should be for the vices that mar the picture of Christ presented to the world.

Throughout 2020, I made a point of thanking white Christians who discussed race at any level. While speaking may have been the bare minimum that they could have done in most instances, I wanted to commend them for doing even that much in light of how little it felt white Christians of influence were saying on the whole. "Thank you for speaking" or "thank you for your bravery," I said. Sometimes it felt like the perfunctory greetings we give military veterans as we pass by in public: "We appreciate you. Thank you for your service." Even so, I wanted to honor them, in particular, for the courage it took them to speak up as white Christians. Perhaps seeing these examples would inspire others.

Since that time, I have found truly multicultural churches that have no qualms about addressing the ways that God's view on racism and misogyny is integral to the gospel. Finally becoming part of a congregation where confronting racism, misogyny, and all forms of discrimination is commonplace made me realize: Truth-telling isn't brave. It's a standard kingdom ethic. It's not fear keeping white Christianity from truth-telling. It's a lack of integrity.

> **Truth-telling isn't brave. It's a standard kingdom ethic. It's not fear keeping white Christianity from truth-telling. It's a lack of integrity.**

No matter how beloved the church claims we are, no matter how close to the inner circle we may be, when a church's leadership has an unhealthy agenda, nothing will overcome it, and the fact that minorities may not be flourishing under such an agenda is considered by them to be an acceptable loss. Regardless of how noble the goal that distracts them may be, pastors have an affirmative duty to protect, serve, and act in the best interests of their flock. Not just the "investors." This is the most basic and important role a pastor has. If that duty is overlooked in view of loftier goals—if the shepherd ignores an attack on their sheep while examining greener grass—then the point is lost. Neglect is as much an implement of destruction as avarice or contempt.

By contrast, when we recognize that in caring for our souls, our clergy have much greater responsibilities than those who owe us a fiduciary duty, it's clear that we need to hold them to a higher standard of inclusivity. I think that for this reason, the Bible admonishes those who would enter ministry to do so with an appropriate level of trepidation:

> Not many [of you] should become teachers [serving in an official teaching capacity], my brothers and sisters, for you know that we [who are teachers] will be judged by a higher standard [because we have assumed greater accountability and more condemnation if we teach incorrectly]. (Jas. 3:1, Amplified Bible)

Simply put, if you're not willing to take on the responsibility of sacrificially loving, in words and actions, all image-bearers as yourself, don't take on the role.

So, how do we break free of the new Jim Crow theology? The first step has to be recognizing that the ostracization and marginalization of minorities as image-bearers is not an accident. As you reflect on what went wrong in the congregations you've inhabited, do you really believe that the leaders within white Christianity just don't understand what they are doing? Or is feigning ignorance simply providing cover for a litany of abuses? Beloved, these are not isolated instances but a pattern and practice—an operational scheme. Take time, in this moment, to reflect. Consider all of the wasted opportunities the church has had. Name it for what it is.

Pause and lament what the church could have been. Acknowledge that white Christianity is not God's plan for the body of Christ and commit to divest yourself from it. Say it out loud: this is not the vision of the church that Christ had for us, and I'm not going to be a part of a congregation that is unwilling to say so loudly, clearly, and often. Acknowledge the grief of accepting that we are not going to receive the care that we have waited so long to receive in these spaces. Say it out loud: I won't be strung along; it's time to leave. We declare that God has better for us than living under a multitiered caste system.

At the base of this fire, as at the base of an altar, we lay down our denials of the harm caused to us. As our fire grows, we admit that, regardless of their intentions, the impact of whiteness has, in fact, wounded us. We admit that these blows were, at some level, intentional and therefore free ourselves of giving the benefit of the doubt and subjecting ourselves to further abuse.

Chapter 9

Angry Gets S*** Done

*W*hat will it take for you to get angry?

According to Dr. Elisabeth Kübler-Ross, there are five stages of grief that those in mourning may experience at various times, in no particular linear order.[1] I've found that these apply to all of us who have mourned our departure from white Christianity. No matter how our individual emotional journeys ebb and flow, the common goal is to move to acceptance through these stages:

- denial
- bargaining
- depression
- anger
- acceptance

In a vacuum, these stages appear to be straightforward. But when the church, the place that you typically go for spiritual healing, is also the implement used to wound you, how do you process your grief? When we are in this predicament, it's hard to know where to find answers. Sermons seem hollow. Worship songs don't inspire. God feels too distant for prayer to have effect. And somehow, every Scripture we read speaks to the situation and makes us want to scream, "How could they possibly miss this?"

How do the stages of grief help us recognize where we are as we process spiritual betrayal? For me, the inner dialogue looked something like the following.

Denial. There's no complicity with racism at our church. Our congregation is too diverse to have a problem with diversity. Isn't it? Look at all the good work we do in the minority community surrounding the church. In fact, they intentionally opened this church in a disenfranchised community.* It must be the case that my friends and the leadership just don't *see* what's wrong.

Bargaining. Let's compromise. Maybe I should pour my efforts into educating my white Christian friends. They'll listen to me. Maybe I can sit down with Pastor Khakipants. Talk to him. Share a meal with him. If I just explain it clearly enough, he'll understand. If I show him how *I* read these Scriptures, it could open his eyes. Maybe they'll let me start a special program or ministry to get the point across. Maybe I was placed in this position "for such a time as this"? Besides, if I stay, maybe I can change the institution from the inside out.

Depression. Why is no one getting it? Who can be trusted? Who are my friends? I feel isolated. Why am I shaking hands with these people who are smiling in my face every Sunday, only to perpetuate stereotypes, false information, and low-key racism during the week online? And if they are willing to say these things publicly, what are they saying privately? Why are my "friends" telling me they saw my protracted attempts to educate bigoted folks on social media, yet refused to chime in as they saw me fighting tooth-and-nail for my sanity?

Anger. Now I'm just mad. There is no lack of information at play. I've already spoken to John about this. I gave Candace that book. I spent two hours talking with Matthew last week. Why aren't they getting it? Now that Chad says he gets it, why isn't he saying anything or working to educate the folks around him? Why are so many people in this church saying the things they do online when they know how hurtful they are? Why are they doing the things they do, or failing to do what needs to be done? *Why isn't the pastor prioritizing teaching the flock how to love their neighbor?*

*But now I wonder, did they open this evangelical church here to minister to the surrounding community or because the building costs were lower in this part of town?

Acceptance. The problem isn't me. The issue isn't a lack of understanding. There's no shortage of information or resources available. They just aren't listening. They don't care. The things they want are more important than the reality in front of them. This place isn't safe anymore. I can't pour any more of my time, energy, or sanity into this black hole. It's time to leave.

Does this sound familiar?

Everyone processes their grief differently. Some get stuck in anger. Some live in depression. My default coping strategy is a form of denial—pushing everything down inside because lived experience has taught me that there may not be a safe place or time to talk about feelings.* In the meantime, if I can just get over the next hill, there will be time to mourn and process my feelings later. Just keep pushing on. This is, of course, just a macho method of running from the problem. The way that white Christianity glorifies toxic masculinity, insisting that biblical manhood looks less like the meekness of Jesus and more like the strength of Samson, does nothing to help men like myself process this grief. After all, men would rather kill a lion bare-handed than go to therapy.

But eventually, we have to reckon with the irony that this form of church has become ungodly and has caused us great harm. We have to accept that we have worshiped in, financially supported, and labored for congregations that have forsaken the work of the gospel and given themselves over to the seduction of political power and societal influence. There is no circumventing our fall through the stages of grief, but one aspect of the five stages is more helpful than others: anger.

Most minorities and their allies partnered with believers within white Christianity precisely *because they told us* that we all want the same thing: to see the Lord's kingdom come and will be done on earth as it is in heaven. We now know we were deceived. Skillfully. There is no shame in this confession, and it's a confession worth making. How can we not be angry grappling with the revelation that the church has become a killing field for the marginalized? This is

*"I'm fine."

a jarring message for Christians who have been taught that anger can only be evil. Every stage of grief has psychological import. But this understanding is essential to moving from the less productive stages of grief into something useful. Our theological imaginations need something more than a vision of reconciliation that requires us to snuggle under the same blanket with our abusers.[2]

Our theological imaginations need something more than a vision of reconciliation that requires us to snuggle under the same blanket with our abusers.

Personally, I have moved from the depressive state of "woe is me" to a point now where it's time to do something. I no longer accept living in the paralyzing despair that overshadowed precious moments that cannot be relived. I am no longer content to hope for a better day as we deny the predicament we find ourselves in today. I will not come to the negotiating table to bargain for a fraction of the respect, courtesy, or fullness of life in Christ that is intended for me. As an Enneagram 8 with a 9 wing, I can appreciate the instinctive reflex that bids us to stay in these congregations in hopes of reconciliation. What I need you to understand is that our instinct for self-preservation is reliable and we must trust that instinct to lead us out of these unhealthy relationships.

Anger Is Underappreciated

Over the past several years I have concluded that anger is underappreciated. To the point, I often think about a scene from the show *American Gods* in which Orlando Jones portrays the spirit of an African deity named Anansi—the king of stories and a known mischief maker. In one episode, Anansi appears to a group of Black African men who are doomed to enslavement, chained hand and foot within the hold of a transatlantic slave ship. True to form, Anansi incites a revolt wherein the enslaved Africans choose to break their chains, slaughter their captors, and burn the ship, all the while knowing they will all perish in the process.

Initially the captives are hesitant to act. So as a motivator, Anansi reveals to them the future that awaits them in the New World: violence, cruelty, disease, and hopelessness that will continue for more than three hundred years after their arrival. His speech taps into the heart of the outrage understood by so many BIPOC, and in the show, it dispels any notions of compromise or false hope. In the shadowy bowels of the Dutch slave ship, one enslaved man shakes visibly as he begins to comprehend the bottomless horror of his predicament. Reading his expression, Anansi's speech culminates with a whispered declaration to the group, "This guy gets it. I like him. He's getting angry. Angry is good. Angry. Gets. S***. Done."[3]

In the context of reclaiming our faith, this point cannot be overlooked: anger is a powerful motivator for liberation. Bargaining, denial, and depression are paralyzing, but angry gets stuff done. Undoubtedly there is a dark side to anger that can be ungodly. Yet there is great validity to the believer's righteous indignation with the parasitic sins that are plaguing God's church. To quote my friend Emily Snook, "The God of the Bible takes seriously the harm done in the name of Jesus."[4]

Christians wounded by the church's complicity with racism have every right to be angry and plenty to be angry about. We should be angry at the dominant misrepresentation of Christ in white Christianity, birthed from an unholy alliance with Trumpism, alt-right politics before that, and conservative Christian nationalism before that. We should be infuriated by allegations that hundreds of sexual abusers have found safe haven in the Southern Baptist Convention.[5] We're right to be enraged when Christian institutions of higher learning invite a renowned Black scholar to their campus to speak, praise his work, then publicly demean him as a symbol of society's ills once he leaves campus.[6] We should be furious that one of the most popular books sold in 2022 made the case that Christian nationalism is virtuous. We ought to be irate when pastors ignore the concerns we raise for the spiritual health of their congregations where red flags abound.

Those who can sit peacefully at a Thanksgiving table with extended family and silently agree to disagree about all the things that have real-world, daily effects on so many have a privilege. Good for them. But their experience is not ours. Therefore, they have no right to demand the rest of us not be angry. We are processing the fact that our childhoods, our friendships, our health, and our joy have been torn from us—by those who should know better because they taught us better. We are reevaluating formative memories and our entire worldview. Realizing those we deemed to be faithful may not actually be Christ-followers, we are trying to figure out what to do with these nonbelievers. We don't want to live in this anger, but we should be willing to camp out in the discomfort of it long enough to do what we can to change what the church is doing wrong or to escape with our sanity intact.

As my family joined the caravan of departures from TFI, I frequently wondered how hundreds could leave a congregation without the exodus having any effect on how the church conducts itself. Who would have to leave TFI in order for them to take responsibility and change? Were there any persons of influence significant enough to change the culture? It turns out there were not. Not because people of significant influence weren't leaving. Some were. But no matter how many congregants (many of whom were minorities), volunteers, ministers, or elders left, nothing could take this politicized, commercialized form of Christianity off mission. This was driven home for me when TFI published numbers revealing that the average weekly attendance in 2016 during the school year was 3,273. After the pandemic and the political fallout of 2020, those numbers changed dramatically. In 2022, TFI reported the average in-person attendance during the school year was 1,716. You would think that the absence of so many members would be felt within a body of believers and prompt change within the leadership, especially if negligence on the part of the leadership prompted the desolation. And yet, no substantive change for minorities could be seen. No one who shared the same values as BIPOC Christians could be so inept as to miss this exodus, or so naive as to reject the need for introspection. This awareness caused me to realize that the offenses—the acts and omissions which divided our congregation and the church at large—were intentional. And that revelation prompted my anger.

After years of processing my experience and helping many others to process their own stories of church trauma, I am convinced that we cannot begin to heal until we recognize that white Christianity didn't hurt us by accident. The institution's objectives require that minorities conform, acquiesce, or leave. Said another way, they have to change us, wear us down, or kick us out. In the infamous words of Mark Driscoll, "You either get on the bus or you get run over by the bus. Those are the options. But the bus ain't gonna stop."[7]

Should I Stay or Should I Go?

The analysis of deciding whether to stay in a church that is comfortable alienating minorities is not that dissimilar to the decision for those in unhealthy relationships. We have to consider the time invested in the relationship, the likelihood of change, the recurring pattern of wooing and hurting with promises of improvement. We have to weigh the potential loss of communal support from those in shared circles. We are told that we're loved, needed, and valued. That we belong here. We may be sprinkled with public praise and tokens of affection, but there is seldom a commitment to substantive reform. Ultimately, we have to consider whether the bad outweighs the good. In the immortal words of the English punk band the Clash, "Should I stay or should I go?" This cannot be overstated: If you find yourself pondering these questions, or relate to anything I have to share, it's because some part of you recognizes your frustration is justified and it's already time to leave.

It is a common misconception that in order for a relationship to be abusive, it has to feel abusive 100 percent of the time. A relationship that is abusive even 50 percent of the time can still be accurately defined as abusive because it is predictably and reliably harmful. The same could be said if it were true only 25 percent of the time. There is no magic formula for the quantity. It's a matter of *quality* of life. We will live with as much as we're willing to put up with. We wouldn't expect a person who is being abused 100 percent of the time to willfully remain in that relationship when there's no benefit in doing so.* There usually has to be something of perceived value in the relationship to entice someone to willfully remain in a toxic relationship. The good is what entices us to stay despite the harm perpetrated against us. Often what is good or wholesome in the relationship is very good, though what is ugly may be very ugly. So which defines the relationship? Is it the good, despite the bad, or the bad, despite the good?

What I need you to understand is that just having to do that calculus at all is probably evidence that the relationship has become problematic. Good partners and good churches don't make us perform complex math. Despite logic or even our gut feelings, there will always be a perceived benefit in staying because what we get out of being there is the lure that entices our presence and enables the abuse. "A devil's bargain always has a carrot to it; it's not all hook."[8]

> There will always be a perceived benefit in staying because what we get out of being there is the lure that entices our presence and enables the abuse.

Anger may not be sustainable forever, but it serves a purpose. When we are tempted to freeze or fawn, anger can enable us to move from analysis paralysis or servility into fight or flight. Anger emboldens us to stop giving the benefit of the doubt to those intent on keeping us in a cycle of abuse facilitated by constant gaslighting. Importantly, this includes spiritual abuse. Those unaffected by, or responsible for, the ruse that white Christianity has pulled on God's children are quick to admonish us not to be angry. And for the longest time, I bought it. I once believed that "angry Black people" were in sin. This is because I was discipled to believe it. Therefore, once I became an angry Black person, I thought that I was broken—rebelling against God. However,

---

*Though in some instances, the nature of manipulation and abuse may be so extreme that it does happen.

when I saw the way that white Christianity partners with patriarchy and bigotry, bruising minorities, women, and the LGBTQIA+ community alike, I realized that it's not just me. We're not broken. We're not just angry minorities in rebellion from God.

So why are we being treated, and spoken down to, as though we are? In a word: control. Once we realize that we're not broken or imagining what we feel, the next helpful realization is that the people striving to make us believe such are doing so on purpose.

One way that the effort to control minorities who question white Christianity manifests is by pointing a finger back at its accusers. In my observation, even when offenders are willing to acknowledge a fault, they still attribute at least partial blame to the victims of their abuse or find a way to center themselves. Feeling pressure from minorities to address the state of our nation in 2020, TFI issued a ten-page position paper on race that provides an example. Authored by four of the church's leaders from various campuses, two white and two Black, the paper advises that white congregants listen humbly to the frustrations expressed by people of color, and then apologize *for the parts they can agree are valid.* In response, minorities should affirm white people for their good intentions. People of color should respond with grace for white people's racially insensitive comments or actions, the paper says, because such "mistakes" are just like any other sin.

But the church's complicity with racism is not just any sin. It undermines Christ's selfless examples of compassion, which confer dignity on those whom society hardly wanted to recognize. Racism is antithetical to the redeeming work of the cross, which seeks to equalize all humanity and reconcile them to God. As University of Notre Dame law professor Thomas Shaffer wrote, "If the three crosses on Calvary mean anything, they mean that no one is so repulsive, or so condemned, that he is not entitled to have a companion in his misery, and that none of us—not even the Son of God—is too good to be chosen as the companion."[9] Therefore, asking the marginalized to willingly submit themselves to a cycle of emotional abuse in order to prevent their abusers from feeling the sting of accountability for their institutional harm is ungodly.

Furthermore, if we talk about the work of making the church a place that is welcoming and hospitable to minorities who have been assaulted by the church as something that "both sides" have responsibility for doing, we are completely ignoring the dynamics of power that make the relationship unsustainable. Another problem lies in asking minorities who have been subjected to racialized spiritual abuse to meet "halfway" those who harmed them. In principle, what is being asked is that minorities make efforts to support the relationship as the offending party (ostensibly) does the same. But in reality, if the offender is unwilling to make sincere and significant efforts toward rehabilitation and restoration, expecting instead to be given grace for repeated mistakes and affirmation for any small acknowledgment of wrongdoing, what is really asked of minorities in this situation is to continue enduring the abuse. The church should not view the work of divesting itself of racism as something to be balanced like weights distributed across a triple-beam scale. A better analogy would be to view racism as a dangerous cancer that, while widespread, may still be effectively removed from the body if we act quickly. As it would be imprudent to consider tolerating such an illness in our physical body, so too would it be to consider requests for compromise with racism in the body of Christ.

But What If They Didn't Intend to Cause Harm?

This question, or some form of it, is the most common response to efforts to hold religious leaders responsible for spiritual abuse. In legal jargon, what role should a bad actor's subjective intent play in their culpability? None.

Let me be clear: I feel strongly that those who claim to be ignorant actors are only *feigning* ignorance because our world has changed too much for anyone to pretend they haven't noticed. The issue presented has been clearly outlined.* Anyone with access to

---

*Remember, we discussed this in chapter 2.

a television, a newspaper, or the internet lacks an alibi for identifying the problem and appreciating a need to address it. We live in an era often referred to as the "information age." In an age when most of us carry pocket-sized supercomputers capable of sending a signal requesting information about literally any topic within the repository of human history to the nearest cell phone tower and then to the nearest satellite (in space!), then almost instantaneously receiving the information in any known language, there is no excuse for ignorance.

Likewise, they say that a picture is worth a thousand words. But what about video? If seeing Black people lynched in 4K Ultra High Definition, as we all did in 2020, didn't change someone's heart, what words could minorities possibly add that could? What adult living on planet Earth these last few years can legitimately claim ignorance of the racial divisions in America, or how failing to recognize the struggles of the marginalized has contributed to said division in the church?

There is no shortage of resources available to help those who want to learn how to decolonize their faith and ensure that minorities are seen, heard, and valued in their congregations. That's not to say that the church's response has to be perfect. The response just has to *be*. As people of color, we would much rather see white Christianity genuinely attempt to address the problem of racism in the church but do it imperfectly than to do nothing at all. Notice that I said *genuinely*. We can tell when pastors are doing the bare minimum in order to string minorities along without committing to the renewal of their minds. In those instances, it would be better for us to see white Christian congregations for what they truly are so that we can govern ourselves accordingly—by leaving.

So no, those who have chosen to function in church leadership aren't absolved of bad leadership in the area of social justice simply because they claim they didn't know any better. In terms of the church's complicity with racism, *any* level of cognizance, coupled with bad action, or a failure to act, can rightly be fully recognized as sin against the body of Christ. We are, all of us, utterly without excuse.

Having said that, it's important to recognize that bad actors rarely admit to acting with actual malice. Even within our modern political hellscape where white supremacy is gaining legitimacy, it is the rare bad actor that would take full accountability for overtly racist behavior and admit intending to cause offense. We can clearly discern that any religious leader who would admit intending to cause harm is a bad person. But good luck securing such a confession. Here again, the law provides us with guidance.

In chapter 8, we established that to be found guilty of an offense, almost all crimes require a *mens rea* (guilty mind) and an *actus rea* (guilty act). We learned that there are some instances in which conduct is an essential element of transgression against the peace and dignity of those wounded by the church. In other instances, it's not the *conduct* but the *resulting damage* that is at issue. The offense may be committed by specific actions or by the *failure* to act when a duty to act exists. For example, a failure to love neighbor unconditionally, a failure to speak against racism, or a failure to acknowledge the many ways racial bias manifests among congregants has led to offenses committed against image-bearers and our holy God.

In law there are varying levels of mental culpability (*mens rea*) with which an offense can be committed, and the severity of the offense differs based on whether the actions were performed intentionally, knowingly, negligently, or recklessly. On opposite ends of the spectrum, an offense is intentional if it was the conscious objective or desire, but reckless, even if it was not intended, if the offender *should have* been aware of a substantial and unjustifiable risk that the harm would occur regardless of whether they actually knew of the risk. Notice that responsibility is placed on all types of offenders using this standard, regardless of their subjective mental state. The reason is because the intent that this perspective evaluates is not the intended impact, but the intent of action. With few exceptions, if the action is voluntarily taken, and the actor could appreciate right from wrong, the actor bears some level of responsibility for the offense, regardless of their subjective mental state, and regardless of whether their intended action matches the impact on those affected. Responsibility can be attributed regardless of whether the offender intended the transgression or simply should have known better. This is the standard I propose that we hold white Christianity to. Precisely because there is no excuse for our spiritual leaders to remain ignorant concerning race and justice, we can hold them accountable for their offenses because they *should* know better.

For those harmed in white Christian spaces, there is no need to attempt to distinguish what level of mental culpability the offenders acted with. Clearly, we should be angry if the offense was intended. However, we also have the right to be angry if the offenders should have known better. I see a lot of the latter being used to keep people who are being manipulated in unhealthy situations. But there is no excuse for those who accept the high calling of caring for the health of the human soul. Rather, they are to be held to the highest of standards (Jas. 3). Yet, to adopt a commonly used Christian definition for sin, many have "missed the mark." There's just no rational basis for racism in Christianity, yet somehow it endures. Not to put too fine a point on it, there are people whose *job* in ministry—and I'm talking the occupation that enables them to pay for their housing, groceries, electricity, water, heat, and air—is to love God, love their neighbors, and teach others to do the same . . . and they still can't do it.

WWJD?

For those hesitant to apply such strict standards to those in ministry, allow me to rephrase the issue this way: Is it fair to hold pastors accountable to the high calling they have chosen, which has such unique influence that they bear the ability to strengthen, corrupt, or grieve the souls of others? Remember, when you articulate the issue clearly enough, the question answers itself. But, for good measure, the answer is yes. While I've never attended seminary or pursued a religion degree, it feels like this should literally be the first concept that such students are taught on their first day of their studies. In fact, it is likely the most important truth to remind them of throughout all their years of study. Granted, this lesson would be missed by pastors without formal religious training and those who endeavor to build huge ministries equipped with nothing more than their audacity. But ideally, it could create a new standard of care that would permeate the field of ministry.

Perhaps such an attempt at an objective standard of care for believers was best exemplified in, of all places, the 1990s fad of wearing bracelets that read, WWJD? (What would Jesus do?). My sincerest apologies to all the folks that I made fun of back then for wearing those bracelets. I had no idea how much some people truly needed the regular reminder to ask themselves that question. Our church leaders would do well to ask themselves this question a little more often. While it is hard to say with certainty what the Son of the living God would do if he walked the earth today, we have pretty good guidance in remembering that all the law and the prophets are dependent on the instruction to love (Matt. 22:40). So it would be worthwhile to ask ourselves the question.

> **We can no longer continue to give the benefit of ignorance to those responsible for our pain, even if they claim the harm was unintentional.**

Considering the urgency of our present situation, we can no longer continue to give the benefit of ignorance to those responsible for our pain, even if they claim the harm was unintentional. Again, Cyndia Hammond, a fellow lawyer and colleague, has wisdom to share on this point:

> Our country needs a big lesson in intent versus impact. My intent matters less the more harmful the impact is. . . . We have to stop hiding behind intent when the evidence is overwhelming that the impact is going to be harmful. Intent is quickly becoming a shield behind which we hide our unrighteousness—including a refusal to confess while repenting. We do not get to abuse our fellow humans just because we claim we are not intending to. . . . We want all the grace flowing from a person of color, and none of it coming out of our mouths. When we look at the life of David

in whole, we see early on that those in power extend grace, but it is never God's intention for those in power to demand (grace) of the ones they have harmed. On the contrary, those in power who are godly, humble themselves before God and men when they have acted wrongly. To flip the script is a form of spiritual abuse.[10]

A minority friend who confided that he had one foot in, and one foot out of, his predominantly white congregation said it this way: "Whether it's intentional, First-Degree Murder, or Reckless Manslaughter, the impact is the same. There are bodies left on the ground and justice needs to be done. Accordingly, you have every reason to be angry."

So now we know that we are not insane. But if we're not crazy, then why is the church doing this to us? Because so many churches, run like businesses, enamored with the consistency of viewing life from the driver's seat without regard to others in the car (much less on the side of the road), believe that their mission is more important than serving God or loving the people God calls them to serve. The plot is lost. They've forgotten the work of God in doing the work of God. Said bluntly, their priority is gaining and maintaining power in politics and culture. As discussed in the previous chapter, if we are not contributing to that objective, we are of no value. In comparison to that mission, we were *never* of value. We were always a tool to be utilized, another set of hands on the assembly line. Having seen the machine for what it is, there is no longer a place for us if we are not going to continue to serve its purpose. Hopefully, when we understand *that* reality, we can begin to understand where anger serves its purpose: to liberate us from mourning long enough to find the freedom and space to move through the other stages of grief properly, into acceptance and healing.

The stages of grief are not unlike the body's response to the stress cycle. Again, Amelia and Emily Nagoski, coauthors of *Burnout: The Secret to Unlocking the Stress Cycle,* offer us much wisdom here. In their speaking engagements,[11] as well as their book, the Nagoski sisters explain that humans have evolved our stress response in order to negotiate immediate dangers. For example, a human on the ancient plains who encountered a lion had to choose whether to respond to that threat in fight or flight. In response to the stressor (the lion) the body begins the stress cycle. Fear sends adrenaline into the body, elevating the heart rate and blood pressure and supplying the body with energy to prepare for the task ahead. Cortisol increases glucose in the bloodstream for the benefit of the brain and substances that are beneficial for tissue repair. Nonessential functions are stifled to prioritize the essential functions like blood flow to the legs to facilitate escape. The human outruns the lion, entering into the safety of a dwelling, and, eventually, the lion gives up and walks away.

Now, while the mind may be aware that the stressor (the lion) has departed, the Nagoskis teach us that our bodies are still experiencing responses to the stress that are no longer beneficial because they were only meant to aid our survival in the short term. Although the stressor is gone, the *stress* must still be dealt with. Therefore, we have to consciously adopt behaviors (like exercise or meditation, for example) to help signal to our mind and body that we are no longer in the fight-or-flight dilemma to allow the body to complete the stress cycle and return to a relaxed state. Absent these efforts, we get stuck in one part of the cycle, without an outlet for our stress. Our body will continue responding as though the stressor remains, and, eventually, we experience burnout.

Similarly, the stages of grief present us with inescapable elements that must be addressed for our emotional and spiritual health. In the modern era we have many different types of stressors that are more likely than encountering a lion. Imagine, for the moment, how these psychological and physiological dynamics are applied to our situation.

We would quickly implore any loved one exposed to an emotionally abusive relationship to leave the situation immediately. Why, then, would we reject our own advice? Why do we hesitate to recognize the same psychological trauma visited upon minorities in toxic religious environments as its own form of abuse? White Christianity has become an ecosystem in which inhabitants are conditioned to believe that we are not allowed to get angry and, therefore, not allowed to get free. The one emotion among the stages of grief that would help us to achieve the escape velocity necessary to free ourselves from the pull of spiritual abuse is the one we are not afforded. In the same way that the Nagoskis teach us how important it is to complete the stress cycle, so too we must complete our cycle through the stages of grief, using anger to propel us free.

God has gifted our corporeal physiology with the emotion of anger along with joy, sadness, and confusion—all of which have their proper time and place. As our emotions are divinely integrated, we must recognize anger as a necessary part of the grieving process that can't be circumvented. As we reflect on the intentionality with which the church has harmed us, we declare that *this* is the proper time and the proper place for anger. Our anger is not one of vengeance or hatred but of disdain for the marred re-presentation of God's image. Our anger is, therefore, shared by God. We choose to be angry.

Chapter 10

Burn It All (Take Nothing with You)

*T*he division caused by racism in American Christianity reminds me of the novel *Lord of the Flies*. The story goes like this (spoiler alert—seriously, you've had more than sixty years): Marooned on an island without adult guidance, prim and proper British boys turn nearly feral. They create a tribalistic civilization normalizing cruelty, savagery, and murder.

The story concludes when a hunting party, and the peer they're chasing, run into a naval officer on the beach. They've been rescued. The adult surveys the pack of spear-wielding children adorned in loincloths and war paint emerging from a jungle engulfed in flames and asks, "What are you doing?" The question prompts tears and long-overdue introspection. The officer's presence brings an objective truth that defies the distorted reality the children constructed for themselves.

Similarly, Black people know that when Jesus returns, the American church will be forced to confront an undeniable reality that exhumes our true but buried identities as he asks us, *What are you doing?* However, the American church does not have to wait until the end to begin that introspection. Nor should it. We need to shed the lies with which we have adorned ourselves. First among these lies is that our faith demands our continued presence in spiritually abusive relationships.

Today there are many calls for unity in the church and in politics. Yet, after so many years of estrangement—most recently due

167

to Trumpism, gaslighting, and erasure—how can minorities hope to build relationships with our spiritual siblings in white Christianity? Should we? Without a commitment to holistic application of the *imago Dei* (the image of God), calls for unity remain a pretense for conformity under the banner of cultural Christianity. Such unity, a "negative peace," as the Rev. Martin Luther King Jr. wrote, cannot be our aim. Unity is a mechanism—the manner and means of achievement. Not the product. Those who would look at the state of the Western church today and say that there is no problem are, themselves, the problem.

After all we have recently seen and been traumatized by, we must be leery of congregations that are still afraid to sully their brand with the controversy of dignifying Black and Brown lives. In his book *When to Walk Away,* Gary Thomas highlights the story of the rich young ruler to emphasize that in the Bible "one thing we don't see when others walk away is Jesus giving chase." Thomas reminds us that not everyone who heard Jesus changed or followed him. Letting go of others can be a lonely path to walk, but Thomas insists:

> As powerful as Jesus was, as brilliant as Jesus was, as pure as Jesus was, and as surrendered to God as Jesus was, not everyone he interacted with "changed," repented, or agreed with him. Here's the principle that comes from that: Sometimes to follow in the footsteps of Jesus is to walk away from others or to let them walk away from us.[1]

So be it. Where we are unwelcome or unheard, let us shake the dust from our feet and move on, as Jesus instructed in Matthew 10:14.

Jesus spoke clearly of how we are to honor him by loving our neighbors. Therefore, the disingenuousness of assigning blame to "both sides," claiming ignorance in understanding that our actions can disproportionately impact the marginalized or feigning uncertainty of Christ's expectations of us, is rebellion. As ambassadors of Christ, we must remain committed to equity, inclusion, and defending the cause of the poor, the widow, the orphan, and the oppressed. The prophet Isaiah spells it out clearly: "Learn to do right; seek justice. Defend the oppressed. Take up the cause of the fatherless; plead the case of the widow" (Isa. 1:17).

If we sense ourselves walking further from cultural Christianity as we pursue these goals, it is only because they fell behind. A chasm exists between us because whitewashed cultural Christianity has cut the bridge's rope from the other side of the ravine. It is, therefore, up to the white church to rebuild the bridge and find its way across as we turn to face the path God has called us to.

I cringe in conversations about race when I hear believers call for "unity" among the body of Christ and admonish minorities for expressing their frustrations with the state of our union. Let us be unified, yes. Let us be unified in God's understanding of what justice demands. Let us be unified in love for our neighbors, compassion, and empathy. Let us be united in truth. It *is* possible. We will achieve unity when white Christianity joins Black and Brown believers in our commitment to equity, inclusion, and defending the cause of the oppressed.

We have a tough road ahead, saints. But for those willing to hear it, there is a road ahead. Our hope will not be realized in politics or cultural Christianity but by our willingness to be transformed by the renewing of our minds. In a time when "the world" (through politics) and the church are hell-bent on gaslighting us, I can't overstate the import of reminding each other we're not crazy. We know what we saw. They said what they said. They're not ignorant. It wasn't an accident. The pain is real. Our trepidation is justified. Let the revelation that each and every one of these offenses was perpetrated against us with purpose intensify the fire in the whole of who we are—a fire that burns hot enough to consume our tether to the toxicity of white Christianity. Given no options, it's time to drop the match and walk away.

If you're processing trauma from white supremacist theology or spiritual abuse, weighing which long-term relationships need to be severed or maintained, or wondering how on earth the body of Christ can function together correctly after so much bias has been revealed in its members, you're not crazy. You're not alone.

And you're not wrong to believe that it cannot be done until those who have caused this division are removed or repent. Friends, I say this in love but also with conviction: We do not need to reconcile with white Christianity. White Christianity needs to be reconciled to Christ.

Time to Leave

Take this moment to visualize yourself literally leaving white Christianity. Picture the building where you worshiped or the religious institution where you worked. Envision yourself physically turning away from that church and those people. You have waited long enough for them to change, and you know they don't intend to. You have seen enough to know there is nothing of substance behind the facade of that building. You know enough to appreciate that none of your words can influence the hearts of those left behind. Imagine yourself walking away from that place. See your feet and legs moving as you place distance between yourself and those people.

We do not need to reconcile with white Christianity. White Christianity needs to be reconciled to Christ.

Previously, the imagery of fire has served as a campfire—an impromptu altar where we have laid the burdens that white Christianity has placed on our souls. Now, let us imagine that fire inside of us as it burns away everything that ties us to the dysfunction of white Christianity. See the colors of the flames as they flicker within you: red, orange, yellow, white, red again. Like heat energy for a steam engine, this fire will drive us forward. Picture the flames growing brighter with each deepening revelation of betrayal. Feel the heat it produces. Watch it consume every doubt that you have toward your own judgment and the decisions you've had to make to liberate yourself from spiritual abuse.

See the faces of the pastors who mistreated you. The people who diminished your pain. Take a mental snapshot of every person or event that you associate with your pain from this spiritual trauma and imagine those pictures falling, drifting like snowflakes, until they're caught by the flames inside you. Visualize them falling to the base of your fire. Watch as the heat browns these photographs—bubbling and warping. Tearing open as the fire penetrates then withers each one. Until what little remains are pieces of fragile, crumbled, ashen paper all but consumed as the heat of the fire lifts it like sparks above the flames, where it flickers and disappears.

Take the time to do this for every thought that you associate with your pain from white Christianity. Call to mind every conversation, every argument, every place, every person, even the music that you associate with the places we're walking away from. Commit to allowing this fire to consume everything that comes to mind. Nothing escapes the flames. If you later recall something you missed, you can come back here and add it to the fire again, because this fire is yours. It will always be yours. Soon we will break camp, leave this place, and begin the journey ahead. When we do, we will take nothing with us but the fire that burns within.

Part 3

A Light to Our Path

Chapter 11

The Cavalry's Not Coming

*O*ne of Hollywood's most popular action movie tropes is the Cavalry Refusal. Cold, hungry, injured, exhausted, facing a hostile force, a small band of underqualified protagonists call for help in an hour of desperate need. Soon they realize they're in over their heads and no one is coming to their aid. The cavalry's not coming.

In that moment, the protagonists dig deep within themselves to muster the stamina necessary to face the end with dignity. They try to become their own rescuers—knowing it will likely cost them their lives. Nevertheless, finding a strength born from necessity, somehow the heroes find the fortitude to make a good show of their final stand, go down fighting, or face unconquerable odds. Cue the metaphorical montage of grit and self-determination wherein mortal wounds get bound up with duct tape and spit, psychological demons are finally faced by remembering a guru's words of wisdom, and the indomitable spirit of Western ingenuity comes to the fore. While the good guys ride out with every expectation of certain doom, salvation appears from unexpected allies at the last possible moment.[1]

Examples of this device are more common in literature and media than we realize. (Spoiler alerts ahead but, honestly, if you haven't seen these movies by now, shame on you. Do better.) We see it in *Avengers: Endgame,* when Steve Rogers (Captain America) is alone on the battlefield, facing Thanos, "the mad titan" who acquired the ultimate bling and snapped half of all life into oblivion (an occurrence survivors refer to as "the blip"). Captain America's trademark shield—made of the strongest metal in our galaxy—has been broken by the antagonist's sword and there is no reasonable expectation of help from any corner. No matter. He will fight. With shallow breaths, Rogers is staggering toward inevitable demise when he hears a voice over his comm that he hasn't heard since the blip five years ago. "Cap, it's Sam. Can you hear me? On your left." A sling-ring portal opens and three long-fallen heroes arrive on the battlefield. Sam flies onto the scene through the opening as more portals appear. Soon thousands of warriors who were previously "blipped" away appear at Rogers's side in battle formation. The cavalry has arrived.

We see it in *Return of the Jedi,* when Luke Skywalker refuses to kill Darth Vader though he clearly has the upper hand. He won't do it. But the emperor is clear: if he won't join the empire, he must die. Luke refuses. "So be it, *Jedi.* You will be destroyed." Suddenly bolts of blue lightning shoot from the emperor's hands. Not in short bursts either. They wrap around Luke like electric tentacles as the emperor laughs maniacally. The emperor gloats over Luke mercilessly, "And now, young Skywalker, you will die." This is the end. But wait! The emperor was unaware that Vader had been disarmed by empathy toward Luke. Vader attacks his master from behind, throwing him into a bottomless pit inexplicably situated directly below the throne room. Somewhere below, the emperor's force lightning contacts the ship's reactor core and triggers a chain reaction that will destroy the ship after Luke escapes. Again, in the unlikely form of Darth Vader, the cavalry has arrived.

Those examples are my favorites, but there are others you'll recognize. In *Lord of the Rings,* Gandalf arrives with the Riders of Rohan when all seems lost at the battle of Helm's Deep. In *The Chronicles of Narnia,* a resurrected Aslan appears with reanimated soldiers to save Peter and the Narnian army from the White Witch. In *It's a Wonderful Life,* Mary and Billy rally the townsfolk to the Bailey home to donate what little money they have to the Baileys. Miraculously, it all adds up to more than is needed.

Despite its entertainment value, the Cavalry Refusal trope is difficult for me because it touches deep emotional scars earned from standing alone discussing matters of race in the church, hoping for support to arrive but coming to the dismal realization that the cavalry's not coming.

Perhaps this feels relatable. Here's another analogy from the relational realm. Imagine that your romantic partner was seduced by another lover, moved out of your home, and spent days . . . months . . . years in the embrace of the paramour. Then one day, your partner appears at the door to tell you that they want reconciliation. Suppose you let your partner inside the door, sit down with them, and ask them to commit to leaving their lover. Given every opportunity to do so, they simply won't say the words. "Will you leave them and recommit to me, forsaking all others?" Instead of answering, your partner changes the subject. They say things like "I love you," "I need more time to address it correctly," "You're priceless to me," "I need you," "Let me make it up to you."

> Are you ready to forsake white supremacy? Lack of a clear answer is itself an answer.

BUT ARE YOU DONE WITH THAT HOME-WRECKER?

. . . silence . . .

I believe this is the proper way to view our struggle with white Christianity's noncommittal disposition toward us. The church says things like "We love you," "We need you," "Be patient with us," "We're working on ways to improve our communication and involvement in conversations surrounding race." But they never seem quite able to carry their vision through to completion. *Are you ready to forsake white supremacy?* Lack of a clear answer is itself an answer. The reality is that things aren't going to change, so we must move on in order to walk in wholeness.

I see this same heartbreaking awareness come to spouses going through the devastation of divorce. In my capacity as an attorney, numerous times I have been in court with a mistreated spouse waiting to finalize a divorce. The scene is almost always the same: our client (most often the woman) sits stoically next to me waiting for the judge to take that imposing seat behind the bench. At the other end of the counsel table, her soon-to-be ex-husband sits beside his lawyer, trading whispers, stealing side glances at my client. In the back of the courtroom sits his new lover, who is likely the reason we're here in the first place. The mistress is usually a younger approximation of the woman beside me—a version that has not yet given birth to children or endured sickness and health together with him. She's here in a form-fitting dress as a twist of the knife in my client's back. In two years, I'll receive a call from her looking for an attorney once they've also separated.

Husband and lover exchange knowing smirks. The wife pretends she doesn't notice, but she does. My client's hands tremble as we review the paperwork, a document titled "Final Decree of Divorce." As we go through the provisions concerning their children's summer visitation schedule, she begins to understand that this is really happening. She's angry. She's exhausted. She just wants it all to be done. Yet, every time, I also observe something else: a brief, wistful longing. If he would just come back. Who knows how it would work, but if he would just repent, they could have everything they vowed to have together. The clouds could still part and the cavalry could still arrive. As we reach the signature page, she turns to me with tears in her eyes. This is it. She knows she can't be whole as long as there's one foot in the past. But she has to ask, "Am I doing the right thing?" Each time, my assurance is the same: This was always up to him. Things only turned bad because of him; there was nothing else she could do. So, she squeezes my hand, takes a deep breath, and signs her name.

I believe that as we wrest free of our idealized projection of white Christianity, we are experiencing a separation that can be just as crushing as divorce. The deeper our roots in this faith community have reached, the harder it is to extricate them from the earth. It is impossible to do so without losing parts of ourselves. Artist and former pastor David Hayward puts it astutely: "the reason your deconstruction affects everything is because your religion did."[2]

In hindsight, I realize that my continued presence in a white evangelical congregation after 2015 was the most naive, and ill-fated, quest cognizable—an attempt to church the church and reclaim the soul of white Christianity. In the face of burgeoning hate-filled rhetoric among believers, I truly thought I could bring my white siblings in the faith back to a genuine relationship with Christ by just reminding them what the Bible said. My impossible aspirations were buoyed by years of patriarchal Christian nationalism that hyped up young men to believe each of us was the next David, a warrior uniquely qualified and exclusively called by God to bring his kingdom come and his will be done on earth. Serious main-character energy. Somehow this resonated despite the obvious fact that every other young man in the room was simultaneously receiving the same *rhema* word of prophecy to single-handedly achieve the same goal in the full hearing of his peers. You guys, there can be only one. Still, I went for it. I wanted to believe it. I was the chosen one. After all, John Eldridge assured me that every man longs for a battle to fight, an adventure to live, and a beauty to rescue.[3] Perhaps I was chosen for such a time as this. If you know, you know. But here I could have used a piece of wisdom shared by author Kaitlin B. Curtice: "A relationship to the church that consists of 'maybe if I stay things will change/I'll find community' is an abusive relationship. I lived it for over 2 decades of my life. Get outta there, please."[4]

Here was the flaw in my reasoning. I thought that once my co-religionists had the right information, they would respond accordingly by repenting for being led astray by alt-right politics. Revival would break out. Jesus could heal our land. It was all up to me. I chose to stay with TFI, and white Christianity, to be the change I wanted to see. This undertaking led to the Friendsgiving meal I mentioned in chapter 8 and the objectives defined thereafter. Our strategy to reach the hearts and minds of wayward Christians was the same tactic that the church utilized with the youth of the 1990s: relationship evangelism. Make friends and tell them the good news they've never heard. There were only two weaknesses in that plan: (1) relationship evangelism itself and (2) assuming lack of information was the problem.

If you are like me, you once believed that since we Christians share the same biblical morals, if we simply *point out* the apparently overlooked presence of white supremacy in our midst, everyone will see it, agree that it is a problem, and desire to see it changed. We never considered the possibility that white supremacy is a welcomed guest in some churches rather than an unseen trespasser. This is not a notion that is accepted quickly or easily. It is precisely because I realize that white Christianity has become an environment where racist rhetoric and behavior can flourish that I can testify that what is being taught within its walls is not the life-transforming gospel of Jesus Christ.

While the travesties of 2020 in particular (Ahmaud Arbery, George Floyd, Breonna Taylor, Andre Hill, Manuel Ellis, Rayshard Brooks) brought enlightenment to so many, there are still those who somehow still require more evidence, need further convincing, still see "both sides." They don't get it because they don't want to get it. There is nothing that we could have done or said to prevent this separation. It's time to finalize our separation. This is really happening. They're not going to change. The cavalry is not coming.

Breaking Camp

There is a form of Christianity that values societal equity and is willing to address topics like police brutality. Conversely, there is a more individualistic form of Christianity that requires nothing of us. As believers, we are charged with choosing which theology is that of Christ. How do we work to stir those who refuse to be stirred to adopt the correct theology? *We don't.* Those who have not responded to our calls for aid at this point have made it clear that they have adopted a Christianity that requires nothing of them and are completely unwilling to engage in the dialogue. As mind-boggling as it is, it's really true that for one shining moment in 2020, the church momentarily opened its eyes to see what minorities have said for so long, then rolled over in bed, mumbled that we were "woke," and returned to its slumber.

If the issue we were up against was simply a matter of ignorance, a lack of education, then knowledge would be enough to combat it effectively. The knowledge that minorities who are learning and serving within white Christianity are pained by the way the church operates is insufficient because our pain has to be weighed against other priorities and considerations. All we've asked for is equality within what Josiah Royce and Dr. Martin Luther King Jr. called the Beloved Community. These are not romanticized, abstract, impossible goals. It's just a matter of prioritizing the love of neighbor.

For those of us who have left the evangelical church, the Cavalry Refusal presents a story arc with which we are uniquely acquainted. We've pleaded with our parents, met with our pastors, had coffee meetings with colleagues, cried over lost friends, prayed for revelation on behalf of our church leaders, fasted for insight into the spiritual warfare that seduced our communities, and longed for revival. We reasoned that if we spoke loud enough often enough and presented enough evidence of correct orthodoxy, other leaders would step forward and preach a gospel untainted by Christian nationalism. But nothing changed.

Once I realized that the cavalry wasn't coming, I decided to close the door on white Christianity. It's only *because* of that decision that I've been able to continue clasping my sanity and belief in God. I can believe in God, and his faithfulness, because I know that it is completely other from all that I have seen in white Christianity. Having journeyed through this process personally, I know the joy of healing that comes on the other side of walking away. There's only so much that we can do. With that assurance, I can guide those who stand in the same place I once stood, and I can tell you—you can afford to wait no longer. Reinforcements are not coming. There's no point in defending this outpost. It's time to break camp.

Beloved, we deserve better. We deserve more than the dregs of love in the faith community. We deserve more than trickle-down orthopraxy. We deserve more than to sit by the window, pining for our ex to realize the mistake they've made and come running back into our arms.

I do have encouragement for those who find themselves in this place.

In my moments of desperation, clinging to little more than diminishing certainty that I am walking in obedience to God, I found a different Jesus from the one I worshiped for so many years. To affirm that I had a sound grasp on reality, I had to scour Scripture with new purpose to fully explore what God tells us about himself. I had to dissect my convictions to separate what Christ has said from what well-intentioned but misguided believers have taught for so long. And good news: I found out I'm not crazy. You're not crazy. You haven't lost your mind. If you're measuring yourself against the white patriarchal toxic Christian nationalistic evangelical industrial machine, take refuge in knowing the problem isn't you.

> There is community among the poor in spirit if we're not too prideful to be counted among their number.

Walking away from white Christianity was lonely and painful, but it has been the best thing I could do for my faith. And forging a new path has brought me into community with others who were also looking for a way forward. There is community among the poor in spirit if we're not too prideful to be counted among their number. Perhaps we've grown too accustomed to living in a perpetual state of spiritual plenty. It's much harder to live with joy in a state of spiritual suffering. But I'm learning how to do it. As a result, I have been radicalized by the most authentic form of Christianity that I've ever known. Further, at the risk of sounding judgmental, I now realize that many within the machine of white Christianity who claim to be Christians have never actually met Christ. To quote James Cone again, "Oppressed and oppressors cannot possibly mean the same thing when they speak of God."[5] As such, we can't expect reinforcements to correctly respond to simply having heard the call. A trumpet sounding for help is strange music in their ears.

Dr. Michael Gorman, a New Testament scholar and professor of biblical studies and theology at St. Mary's Seminary in Baltimore, makes the same observation of the religious leaders who criticized the apostle Paul:

> All [their] criticisms, directly or indirectly, call into question the legitimacy of Paul's apostleship. From Paul's perspective, however, the fundamental problem of these self-styled ministers of Christ is not that they criticize him. Rather, it is that their criticisms of him belie an understanding of Christ, the Spirit, and the gospel (11:4) that is *so thoroughly antithetical to the message of Christ crucified as to be demonic* (11:13–15).[6]

We need to accept that it is completely possible for people we worshiped with, who have vast knowledge of Scripture, to be so deeply wrong about their complicity with racism and hatred that they may not actually know God. We should all have a healthy dose of introspection when we read Matthew 7, but I can't help but think white Christianity is missing something. Jesus tells us:

> Not everyone who says to me, "Lord, Lord," will enter the kingdom of heaven, but only the one who does the will of my Father who is in heaven. Many will say to me on that day, "Lord, Lord, did we not prophesy in your name and in your name drive out demons and in your name perform many miracles?" Then I will tell them plainly, "I never knew you. Away from me, you evildoers!" (Matt. 7:21–23)

We don't talk enough about the fact that the people described as having this conversation of tragic reckoning with Jesus are people who identified themselves as believers. For all purposes, they looked like believers on the outside. But worse, these people *thought* that they were believers on the inside too! They prophesied in Jesus's name (v. 22). Remember here what we discussed in chapter 3 about taking the name of the Lord in vain (Exod. 20:7). These people cast out demons, which throughout Scripture usually signified a healing. They attempted to do miracles in the name of Jesus, *and it worked.* They had all the evidence of fruitful

Christian ministry. But they never knew Jesus. And the way that Jesus saw them was not as mostly good or only 50 percent abusive. Jesus calls them "evildoers."

So what's the path forward?

In Psalm 119:105, the psalmist writes, "Thy word is a lamp unto my feet, and a light unto my path" (KJV). When I consider this verse, I think about the difference between old-fashioned oil lamps and modern flashlights. While the psalmist never had the benefit of flashlights in their time, I think it's fair to draw a comparison. Flashlights cut a path through the dark that broadly reveals the terrain far ahead. Hand-held lamps, by contrast, illuminate a small radius. They only allow you to see your immediate surroundings and the next few steps ahead. Said another way: walking in unfamiliar territory by lamplight requires more courage, more faith than if you could see the terrain all at once. In this path ahead we may not see the full scope of the work God will do, but we can trust our next steps to God. We have solidarity in our sufferings. And together, gathered in community, our lamps produce much greater light. As a person of color in particular, I take much solace in knowing that the same grace God gave to our ancestors, and to us, accompanies us as we set out on this course like the children of Israel who followed the spirit of God as a pillar of cloud by day and a pillar of fire by night.

Our once-esteemed friendships may fail, but we are not alone. The cavalry's not coming, but God is already with us.

Chapter 12

Permission to Leave

*W*hile I believe that it's important for those of us who have been harmed by racialized spiritual abuse to accept that the cavalry is not coming, that's not to say that all is lost. And if you've made it this far, I think it's important to acknowledge that we've done a lot of work throughout this book to arrive at this point. Uncovering all the painful aspects of divorcing ourselves from white Christianity is difficult, emotionally taxing, spiritually exhausting work. But, in a way, everything we've covered so far has been prelude to the most important work to be done: we need to decolonize our faith, resolve not to look back, and commit to our healing. It's time to leave and leave it all behind.

Just as unhealthy relationships don't have to be problematic 100 percent of the time to be abusive, so too a toxic church may still have beautiful aspects that, nevertheless, cannot justify our continued presence there. People whom we love may continue to attend because they don't yet fully appreciate the scope of the blight. Spiritual leaders whom we admire may continue to work there due to financial dependence or naive aspirations of reforming the institution from the inside out. Leaving may mean that ministry opportunities unique to that congregation may be lost. But we have to leave for our own spiritual and emotional health.

As a parallel for knowing when to leave spiritually abusive environments, one of my good friends, Dr. T. J. Webb, shares this advice about toxic workplaces:

I don't know who needs to hear this, but this can be true:

- My job is abusive/exploitive, and I need to leave immediately.

Even if the these are true too:

- I love the people I work with.
- I respect the people I work for.
- I believe in the mission of the organization.

My advice: leave anyway. Unless you know it's imminently going to get better, make a plan to leave. You can maintain friendships with your coworkers. You can support the mission from the outside if you choose. You can choose to forgive, even build-up, its leaders—from a distance. But even a great organization with great people and a great mission doesn't have the right to expend your well-being. It can be a great organization for the community, for clients or patients, for the whole human race—and not be a great organization for you, the employee. So leave. Leave as quietly or as loudly as your conscience demands on behalf of your coworkers, the mission, and the person who will have your job next. There are other organizations with great people and great missions; go to one of those instead. And when you get there, look around to figure out who in your new great organization is on the brink of leaving and only hasn't because they believe in the people and the mission so much. Then work to create change and make a way that they can stay and thrive instead.[1]

One of the first lessons that the Bible has to teach us is that it is completely possible for an oasis—a place that was once beautiful, wholesome, and nurturing—to become polluted. And just like Eden, we know it's possible for humanity to be the reason for that contamination. So it is with the church.

While it is important for believers to walk out their faith with the support and accountability of community, it is no failure on our part that a place that once fulfilled those needs has become hostile to our flourishing. I imagine that ours is not the only generation to wrestle with these realities. Faithful believers objecting to the institution of slavery, bans on women in ministry, the vices of segregation, and

LGBTQIA+ exclusion have all likely found the American church as unrecognizable as we do today. History is on our side.

It's important to understand that leaving doesn't mean we lost. It doesn't mean that all hope is forever lost for those we walk away from. Leaving is recognition that our emotional and spiritual resources are better spent elsewhere, and so we choose to be loving to ourselves. My wife explains it this way:

> My letting go and walking away doesn't mean that *God* walks away. He may still work in those who hurt me and they have a journey to walk to know Him. It is not selfish of me to let go. It's not just about me. It's also about our children and anyone else in our lives that we invest in who wants and needs the love I have to give.
>
> My sincere, long-held desire to follow Jesus and be right with Him may have been manipulated by toxic theology and left me wondering if I'll ever be enough. But to be manipulated, my sincere desires to follow Jesus had to be there first.
>
> I still love Jesus. The problem is not my faith; it's not God. The problem is God's people.

Here's the deal: I don't know how to end racism. I'm pretty sure that it can't actually be done. We can regulate, to some extent, racist behavior. We can dismantle racist institutions. We can't regulate racist thought. The local church, where people congregate with the specific purpose of understanding what our sovereign creator has to say, should be the most reliable venue for neutralizing the effects of racism in our society. Having refused to undertake that responsibility, the church can no longer rightly be seen as the church. I laughed out loud when I watched pastors online in 2020 crying out to God, asking for a fresh word for our nation, standing in congregations that should have been closed due to COVID-19.

> **It's important to understand that leaving doesn't mean we lost. It doesn't mean that all hope is forever lost for those we walk away from. Leaving is recognition that our emotional and spiritual resources are better spent elsewhere.**

What if God's message to America in 2020 was, "Stop killing Black folks; love the Lord with all your heart, soul, and mind; love your neighbor as yourself by wearing a damn mask"? I imagine Jesus in heaven, tapping a microphone like "Is this thing on?" while his every word is ignored by the church.

God's will for humanity has not been hidden. And what the Lord has to say to us remains the same as it has ever been: "He has shown you, O mortal, what is good. And what does the Lord require of you? To act justly and to love mercy and to walk humbly with your God" (Mic. 6:8). It's been the same word now for twenty-eight centuries and counting. Therefore, I ascribe great fault to a church that teaches any other doctrine or emphasizes any other role in society.

A congregation set on seeing God's kingdom come and God's will be done but ignoring the greatest commandments—love of God and love of neighbor—is not the Lord's church. And in our current climate, love of neighbor has a very specific application in fighting the specific evil of racism in every facet of society in which it rears its ugly head, particularly when its members operate locally in those realms: law enforcement, education, politics, medicine, theology, law, real estate, employment, finance, and so on. To be clear, love of God and love of neighbor does NOT look like a political pep rally, has no relation to nationalistic sentiment, and likely has more to say about what we're missing than explaining why we're right. This is the great work of our time. If the church wants to be mobilized to act in society, look before you: the harvest is plentiful.

Ignorance, Inaction, or Apathy

Sometimes when I think about the apparent indifference of Christianity to the way that white supremacy lands on minorities in its churches, I'm reminded of a scene from the movie *Boyz n the Hood.* After his brother, Ricky, is killed in an unprovoked act of gang violence, Doughboy (played by rapper Ice Cube) laments the societal erasure of Ricky's life demonstrated by the fact that the local news reported on affairs in the world abroad but had nothing to share about the death of his brother. He sums it up by saying, "Either they don't know, don't show, or don't care about what's going on in the hood." Ignorance, inaction, or apathy.[2]

What enabled me to definitively cut all ties to white Christianity and its people was the revelation that there are only three possible explanations as to why these churches neither change, nor seem to care:

1. they don't have the information (ignorance);
2. they have the information but don't see fit to act on it (inaction); or
3. they don't care (apathy).

As to the first possibility, we live in the age of information. The wisdom of nearly every culture that has ever existed from the beginning of time is available to us free of charge in digital format on devices that most of us carry in our pockets. No one with an IQ greater than 60 is deprived of the knowledge, or resources, to learn the information. The accessibility of data is too great. This is especially true when we, believers of color sitting in their congregations, are the best resources available and they refuse to listen to us. They have radar, but it's not turned on. So they don't see the dangers minorities are warning of.

As to the second possibility, I've learned it is completely possible for Christians to believe everything that we have to tell them about how we are *all* negatively impacted by the influence of white supremacy in the body of Christ, and even to feel concern, but to take no action toward rooting it out of our faith. There are a number of reasons this may occur: they believe that their busy lives can't accommodate another cause; they're intimidated by the magnitude of the problem and don't know where to begin; they don't want to commit their resources to the cause; or they're afraid that speaking out will lead to their own ostracization. Whatever the reason, their concern just isn't great enough to act upon.

For some of these white believers that we've lived in community with, however, it's entirely reasonable to think that they believe everything we share with them—including the heartache we've endured—and simply don't care. They just don't see our plight as their own. At its core, this is a lack of empathy. Our problem just doesn't affect them. Meanwhile, we're negotiating the rubble of wrecked lives, bleeding and bandaged, as the church watches indifferently. Here there is *no* concern. They see the bogeys on their radar. They recognize that there is a clear and present danger. But they will not deploy resources to aid us because we are considered acceptable losses in their eyes. In these settings, pastors will smile to our faces but privately label our issues as part of a social gospel and actively subvert our efforts behind closed doors.

We'll recognize that our congregations fall in this category when we recognize ourselves as victims of gaslighting. At TFI, for example, there was a consistent refrain when minorities expressed a need for the church to discuss race publicly: "we'll get back to you" coupled with full-fledged ghosting while every action taken in the meantime displays complicity with white supremacy. When we're in institutions that refuse to change, it's vital that we have an accurate understanding of who we are in their eyes and why they're not responding. Either they don't know, don't show, or don't care.

In March 2018, the *New York Times* published an article titled "A Quiet Exodus: Why Black Worshipers Are Leaving White Evangelical Churches,"[3] which reports examples of the deep wounds felt by minorities in toxic churches. Tamice Namae Spencer reflected on her disappointment in the response of her predominantly white church after the killing of Trayvon Martin. When white members said she was being "divisive" when she brought it up, Spencer thought, "It's not even on your radar and I can't sleep over it. . . . And now that I'm being vocal, you think I've changed."

The same article also mentions the efforts of the Rev. Dwight McKissic, one of my African American acquaintances and senior pastor of Cornerstone Baptist Church in Dallas, to address racism in the Southern Baptist Convention (SBC). In 2017, McKissic proposed a resolution for the SBC to condemn the burgeoning racism of the alt-right movement that was definitively shot down. "Pastor McKissic was told that racism had already been adequately addressed by the Southern Baptists," reported the *Times*. He was further admonished "that the resolution was inflammatory and that sympathy for the alt-right was not an issue in the church." However, the SBC was reportedly embarrassed by the optics of their decision after their rejection of the resolution became public knowledge. Thereafter, a modified version of McKissic's proposal was passed. Despite his experience in 2017, McKissic continued to be a faithful, active member of the SBC in the following years. But minorities can hold on only so long. Fast-forward six years.

In June 2023, Dwight McKissic attended the annual convention for the SBC, as he had done many times before. However, that year, he and his executive staff members attending the meeting recognized it would be their last one as they departed the convention floor after the vote to place unbiblical restrictions on women.

Responding to one of my social media posts regarding the three paradigms listed above influencing white Christianity (ignorance, inaction, and apathy), McKissic warns nonminority pastors that these three perspectives create questions that minorities in their churches or organizations will "inevitably ask—personally, privately, or publicly. . . . Those [minorities] who leave cannot make peace with [these questions] unanswered," McKissic concludes.[4]

Here, I find it important to reemphasize that malicious intent in the form of actual hatred toward minorities is not a necessary ingredient of racially inhospitable churches. I'm not arguing that the white church is composed exclusively of racists. I'm just saying there are other ways for believers to warm themselves than standing beside burning crosses set ablaze by the folks with the pointy hoods. The wealth of knowledge available concerning the experiences of minorities in the modern church precludes their ability to claim ignorance. They're not misinformed. They're uninterested. And those who continue to joyfully attend and serve these churches do so with full knowledge of their complicity. Meanwhile, the news media daily presents us with evidence that those tasked with the great responsibility of guiding believers are increasingly unqualified to do so.

"Hey, Brother"

In her book, *Untidy Faith,* Kate Boyd discusses the involuntary response that millennial women feel when they receive private messages that start with the phrase "Hey girl." The initiated know the message will come with some pitch for a multilevel marketing ~~scheme~~ vision selling the idea of a #Blessed life.

Most Black Christians have a similar, visceral reaction to reading the phrase "Hey, brother" or "Hey, sister." To some, it's just a greeting. But we Red Tails, veterans of the religious culture war, recognize this seemingly innocuous salutation as the first salvo in a battle with the "all lives matter" crowd.

- "Hey, brother. I saw what you wrote on your wall. I just wanted to tell you that I love you, though I don't agree with you that . . ."
- "Hey, sister. I saw your post about white supremacy. Would you be willing to meet for ~~covfefe~~ coffee or lunch to talk about it? I just want to hear your heart on this topic. My treat!"

Those who agree to these meet-ups believing they're going to converse with an open-minded acquaintance soon find themselves in heated battles to defend their ideological position. Worse, they're often admonished that their perceptions are somehow unbiblical, or even demonic.

I have a radical suggestion: let's stop giving spiritually abusive people access to our hearts and minds. No more coffee meetings. No more lunches. Those who are truly interested in learning about our experiences need to demonstrate their commitment to learning about antiracism by doing their own work rather than asking us to give the Cliff Notes. For our own sanity's sake, I propose we stop agreeing to teach 100-level classes about what the church needs to fix about racism. We're well beyond that now. If our white colleagues want access to our thoughts and emotions, they need the prerequisites to that course:

101—Understanding God Is Real and Has a Lot to Say about Love and Justice in the Bible
201—Slavery Was Bad and There's No Way around That
301—Racism Really Exists, in Forms Both Overt and Subtle, throughout Society
350—Racism Is Bad and Black Lives Really Do Matter
401—There Is No Room for Racism in the Body of Christ nor in American Society

We can't afford to wait for believers to abandon white supremacy and join us on this side of the ravine. A tree is known by its fruit. Therefore, the value they ascribed to us who are suffering emotional, spiritual, and even physical violence due to racism will be made known by their actions. By how quickly they make the journey. But stagnation—neutrality—is hardly an option.

If your spouse walks out of the dressing room and asks, "Do these clothes make me look fat?" you'd better have *some* response. You will not get away with declaring you don't want to be involved. Of course, you *could* say you don't want to be involved, and that answer is going to land you in the office of a counselor or a divorce lawyer. At some point, the refusal to provide honest feedback is, itself, unloving. There are some circumstances in which neutrality just cannot be afforded. There is no middle ground. No one is neutral on a moving train.[5] Similarly, we have permission to shed ourselves of the lie that "both sides" have work to do, or that "neither side" (the first cousin of "both sides") is doing things the way it should.

It is beyond time for white Christianity to repair the damage it has intentionally inflicted upon minority image-bearers. If the church can't take ownership of its sins, it's time to go. You have permission to leave. Nor should we settle for a cheap form of reconciliation that costs nothing of those who want to move past "the race thing" and get to the business of being a church. We can recognize cut-rate attempts at harmony:

- It costs little or nothing of the perpetrator.
- It comes at great emotional or other cost to the victim.
- The burden to facilitate learning or healing rests on the victim.
- The efforts to facilitate learning or healing are tempered; for example, "Whoa, hold on a minute," "Slow down there," and the like.
- There is unwillingness to empower the voices of the marginalized with positions of leadership equal to or greater than those serving at the highest levels.
- There is unwillingness to publicly and unreservedly repent, seek forgiveness, and repair the harm done.
- There is unwillingness to publicly take a backseat in order to amplify the voices of the marginalized and learn from them.
- Tranquility within the congregation is more important than providing justice for the disenfranchised.

Anything less than full dedication to the objective of closing the rift that separates us is a half measure that will only delay or thwart the healing that is so desperately needed in the church. The objective cannot be unity for the sake of unity. Rather, it has to be solidarity—unity and agreement of thought and action, specifically in a theologically correct, fully inclusive, sleeves-rolled-up, hands-get-dirty application of the gospel. In that context, we have to understand that there is a biblical way to view sin and a nonbiblical way, then correctly locate ourselves in the context of that view.

Let's be clear: in an abusive relationship, the abuser is in sin. This is true of all abuse, including spiritual abuse. It's the abuser who is responsible for the condition of their sinful heart. There are no "sides" to consider. If the abuser goes to church, they should be confronted with their sin. They should be counseled and guided through the process of abandoning that sin. By contrast, the abused should find the church to be a refuge for healing, validation, and protection.

But when the church is the abuser, where do the abused go? Who watches the watchmen? As an aside, the reason religious trauma wounds so uniquely is because the source of healing and the instrument of pain are the same. Now, we can pray for our abusers. We can speak truth to the abuser. But the abuser is responsible for the posture of their own heart. For this reason, our abusers have the grave responsibility, as we all do, to seek and know and understand Christ for themselves because the local church may not be equipped, or appropriate, to guide them in their understanding. And in a vacuum, the world will disciple them instead. For this reason, Christians need to be quick to listen to minorities, quick to repent, and quick to rectify so that there is hope of repairing the emotional damage as the believer is working through their crisis of fellowship, if not faith. We can't skip acknowledgment of the problem and go straight to happily ever after.

> Let's be clear: in an abusive relationship, the abuser is in sin. This is true of all abuse, including spiritual abuse. There are no "sides" to consider.

Getting to Unity

Six concepts frequently get conflated and misapplied within Christianity when it comes to unity in race relations: repentance, forgiveness, reconciliation, restitution, reparations, and restoration. It's vital to understand each concept in order for us to give *ourselves* permission to leave. Otherwise, we can be manipulated into believing that the healthy Christians' relationship to Christ and neighbor require our continued presence and participation in abusive spaces.

Repentance

The easiest concept to begin with is repentance, because repentance is about your *vertical* relationship with God. That's it.

Repentance (Greek *metanoia*, "change of mind") involves "turning with contrition from sin to God; the repentant sinner is in the proper condition to accept the divine forgiveness."[6] Repentance deals with the condition of our souls—an inquiry that only God is ultimately qualified to decide. Repentance requires us to ask, "Have I properly humbled myself before God in recognition of my sin?" For Protestant Christians, no works are required in repentance.* God may yet require more of us as a matter of discipline, repair, reconciliation, and so on. But those additional actions are not prerequisites to God's absolution of our sin. The additional efforts we make toward those goals (discipline, repair, reconciliation, etc.) may provide evidence to the outside world that we have, in fact, repented. However, only God sees our heart.

Forgiveness

Forgiveness is about your *horizontal* relationship with other people and requires no action by others. Forgiveness may be triggered by an act of repentance, but forgiveness does not require repentance as a prerequisite. Likewise, the repentance of another person does not automatically trigger our forgiveness. This is because forgiveness and repentance are exclusive; they don't occupy the same plane.

We forgive to help our hearts move on. Forgiveness is executed unilaterally and done solely for the benefit of our own hearts and minds. Our act of forgiving our trespassers requires no action on their part. Therefore, *forgiveness does not require further relationship with the one who wronged us.* Nor does it require our continued

---

*Remember: every time a Christian talks about "works," a mosquito gets its wings. I know this is a subject filled with centuries of doctrinal debate. Let me simplify for our context: when I say "no works are required in repentance," I simply mean no other rituals or tasks are required.

trust in that person. Those who wronged us may not even know (or care) that we forgave them. As an example, we may find ourselves working to forgive our grandparents for wrongs they perpetrated against us decades ago, and working to do so long after they are deceased. Similarly, we may forgive someone who hurt us in a former romantic relationship, without ever telling them as much. Perhaps the ongoing nature of their toxicity makes such a conversation unwise. Yet it does not hinder us from lightening our hearts by forgiving them. Likewise, we may forgive someone with whom we have ongoing relationships, while knowing that continued vulnerability with that person would be unwise. In a book called *Soul Care,* Dr. Rob Reimer observes:

> There is a difference between forgiveness and trust. Forgiveness is a gift granted by the offended party. Trust is earned. And while forgiveness is unilateral, reconciliation is bilateral; it requires that both parties fully participate.
>
> In order for reconciliation to occur, the offended party must fully forgive to the level of the offense: if there is a five-gallon offense, there must be five gallons of forgiveness. And the offender must fully repent to the level of the offense: he or she must offer a five-gallon apology. Only then can trust be re-established and the relationship reconciled. When someone is unwilling to repent, you can still fully forgive them, but the relationship will be shallow at best.[7]

I've never heard an evangelical pastor preach that forgiveness does not mean giving our abusers continued access to us. But, in case it is unclear, forgiveness is not the same as reconciliation.

Reconciliation

Reconciliation is also about our horizontal relationship with other people, but whereas forgiveness is unilateral, reconciliation is bilateral; it needs cooperation from both sides to succeed. One cannot do it alone. Importantly, reconciliation is a noun, not a verb. It is a state of existence, the successful result of doing work to fix the harm committed—not the work itself. Victims of abuse often fall prey to cheap reconciliation that offers no repair of the damage but expects relationship all the same. This manipulation inevitably leads to further abuse.

In Christian spaces, it seems that we rarely have a healthy understanding of what forgiveness is and is not. When the language of forgiveness is manipulated by abusers to reverse the roles of victim and offender and coerce an unhealthy form of reconciliation, we call that abuse. If we choose to forgive, but the offender doesn't like subsequent boundaries that we create, they may chalk it up to a lack of forgiveness on our part. That's fine, so long as we know better.

Actions designed to facilitate healing reconciliation—at minimum—shouldn't create further harm. Feelings of guilt, or viewing reconciliation as something that *must* be achieved, rather than something we *get* to achieve, are clear indicators that our efforts toward reconciliation are misguided.

Restitution, Reparation, and Restoration

Restitution, reparation, and restoration are the *methods* by which we accomplish true reconciliation.

Restitution is replacement value paid for the thing stolen, lost, or broken, one for one. It is a legal term of art. Restitution asks, "How *much?*"

Reparation is also a legal term of art, literally meaning "repair." **Reparation is what is done to fix the problem.** It asks, "*How* do we fix it?" In contrast to restitution, reparation is completely unconcerned with the expense involved in repair. Therefore the cost of reparation may exceed the expectations of those responsible for the repair. This, of course, is why we shouldn't do something that we're aware may cause damage in the first place. Nevertheless, the party responsible for making reparations is not the party in the best position to determine what is necessary to repair what's damaged and, therefore, doesn't get to dictate the terms of the repairs.

As an example, our abusers don't get to say, "Stop complaining! It didn't hurt that bad." Because every person is unique, it may take more to repair the relationship with one person than it does for another. This may be true even though both persons were victims of the same offense. In the legal world, lawyers say, "You take your victims as you find them"—meaning that the offender is liable for the damage caused to their victim even though another person may not have been equally harmed.

Restoration is the final state of the thing after it has been repaired to its original condition. Restoration is the end goal and a necessary precedent to reconciliation, which may be accomplished by way of restitution and/or reparation. Restoration examines the finished product and determines whether all has been made right. Have we left things as we found them before the offense or (if we found them in disrepair) in their original, good-as-new condition? Visually, we can conceive of restoration as healing without a scar.

So when we consider how to go about reaching the goal of reconciliation, we consider these steps:

- Restitution asks, "How much does it cost to fix it?"
- Reparation asks, "How do we fix it?"
- Restoration asks, "Did we, in fact, fix it?"

You don't commit to restoration because it's cost effective. You do it pursuing the end result—to see the thing in its former glory. In the case of classic cars, for example, it may cost an absurd amount of money to locate and install an antique hood ornament. However, serious collectors are willing to pay more than the market price for a missing component because the end goal is to see the whole car restored to its former glory.

If nothing else, I hope these distinctions clarify that reconciliation is neither cheap, convenient, nor easy. Too often, I think white Christianity wants to skip over the work of reconciliation and go straight to "happily ever after." A crucial distinction between reconciliation and repentance is the public nature of the amends. The horizontal nature of reconciliation necessarily requires that the healing process be observable. Before we can even hope to move forward as a united body in Christ, we need the church to acknowledge its wrongs publicly—not just privately to God. Not in individual meetings among minorities. This needs to be done as often and in as public a fashion as possible. We need white Christianity to confess its complicity with racism as loudly as the untruths it touted from the pulpits.

Only by witnessing this done publicly will those who were complicit hear, see, and begin to reflect on their roles. And only then should we consider reoccupying their spaces. Only the most sincere, sustained efforts can assure minorities that white Christianity desires our whole selves in combined worship, build long-term reconciliation, and fortify our relationships against the future waves to come. Only after this work is done can we be made whole. And if a church is unwilling to produce fruit in furtherance of this work before asking us to rejoin, it is time to take our leave.

> **We need white Christianity to confess its complicity with racism as loudly as the untruths it touted from the pulpits.**

For all its talk of unity, white Christianity should be ecstatic to receive, and incorporate, feedback from us on its role in fighting racism. Is unity really the goal, or is unity just a euphemism for conformity with cultural Christianity? Are we pursuing a comprehensive vision of reconciliation that commits to discipling the church in how it missed its complicity with racism? Or is the goal that everyone plays nice together and no one rocks the boat? I recently heard someone say it in a way that should resonate with the church, "The end goal is not unity. Unity is a mechanism to the end goal. Gangs are united. The Nazis were united." Our goal, as believers, is unity under *Christ*.

Social Distance

During the early phases of the COVID-19 pandemic, one of the ways Americans were encouraged to view the necessity of quarantine was an image of a book of matches. If you strike the first match in a book of matches while it's still connected to the others, you've really lit the entire book. Because they're all connected, it's only a matter of time until the last one gets burned. But if one of the matches is removed from the middle of the book, the created space provides a buffer between the inflamed matches and the ones on the other side.

Let the reader understand: Sometimes the only thing we can do to protect ourselves and the ones we love is to remove ourselves from exposure. Sometimes we need to recognize that others are too far gone to be reformed. But we needn't sacrifice our sanity, our emotional health, or the well-being of those who stand behind us simply because we started off connected.

The same dynamics that are at play in emotionally abusive relationships can exist in toxic church environments as well. There are lots of valid reasons that people who are trapped in abusive relationships feel obligated to remain there: emotional dependence, reliance on a community of mutuals, deference to perceived spiritual authority, and so on. It's not the victim's fault; abusers understand these weaknesses and are prone to exploit them. It's one thing to deconstruct and realize that you've changed. It's something different to deconstruct when you realize that it's actually the church that's changed.

By remaining in these environments, we grant our abusers continued access to us—facilitating continued abuse. Meanwhile, we put on a good face, enduring suffering in seclusion under the misguided nobility of quiet martyrdom. At the same time, our continued presence assures those outside the relationship that this environment is safe—not just for us, but for them as well. In a sense, we provide cover for the abuse, inadvertently becoming accomplices in the process. When we think of the decision to remain in these terms, we can see that it is incompatible with the teachings and actions of Jesus. In fact, as the Rev. Dr. Malcolm B. Foley points out, leaving is a way of caring for our abusers by cutting off their ability to sin against us.[8]

In the same way that remaining in a toxic environment sends a message, so too does our departure. By leaving, we diminish the hold that our abusers have on us and their capacity to reproduce, and we provide warning for those who are unaware of the dangers that exist. Willfully subjecting ourselves to suffering for the sake of suffering is not part of God's plan for our lives. God doesn't want us living and worshiping in abusive spaces. Nor does God desire to use our presence as an endorsement, luring others to the same condemnation. It's important to have models of faithfulness that don't look like staying in abusive church settings or leaving faith altogether.

With this in mind, our path is clear: If your church doesn't understand the importance of dismantling racism head-on in this day and age, revelation isn't coming. You're not in a safe space. Leave. If you're not empowered to publicly tackle the issue of racism head-on, leave. If the shot-callers think you're too loud, leave. If the pastors who caused you offense aren't willing to take a backseat and learn from someone on the topic, leave. The longer we stay, the greater the effects of psychological manipulation will be. You have permission to leave.

Chapter 13

A Newer Hope

*W*hen the first installment of the *Star Wars* movie saga was released in movie theaters in 1977, the audience was unaware that they were viewing the middle of a much larger tale.* The film was actually the fourth part of the story line, though it was the first of the *Star Wars* movies to debut in theaters. Having been dropped in the middle of this tale, fans were spared viewing what had preceded: the fall of a once-thriving democracy within the Galactic Republic and the transformation of one of the galaxy's most revered heroes into a villain. Those events forced the few heroes who survived the transition into hiding across the stars without much hope that justice could ever be restored. For nineteen years, this was a dark, comprehensive reality. It was a bleak period in the story for an audience to peer into. The characters of this first movie could hardly appreciate that they were embarking on a journey of personal, and cosmic, redemption embedded within the embers of a rebellion.

In a similar fashion, the disciples who witnessed the wrongful arrest, prosecution, kangaroo-court trial, sentencing, and execution (if not lynching) of Jesus couldn't comprehend that Christ's victory would be built on the foundation of such tragedy. If we are discouraged by the place we find ourselves, there is some good news in

---

*Nor could they have imagined the legacy of the franchise culminating in a battle between Emperor Palpatine's clone and his granddaughter who had to have been conceived under very sketchy circumstances.

our journey away from white Christianity: what feels somber and fatal in this moment we may yet see as the turning point in our liberation. "Rebellions are built on hope."[1]

Our generation is not the first to struggle with the failures of the church and the ways its betrayals hurt real people. Yet God's people continue to endure. There is a faithful remnant in this small band of rebels. God is at work through God's people, even if we can't see the full picture. We may be on a long road. However, God's grace has brought us this far through deconstruction, and we remain in God's hands. Together, from this vantage, we can see the landscape more clearly than we once did and advocate for all to hold a better view of Christianity.

I don't want to diminish the importance of the question that we must all ask: Where can we find hope in our breakup with white Christianity? In our shared commitment to love God, love neighbor, and encourage each other as we walk from under the shadow of spiritual trauma together.

> I don't want to diminish the importance of the question that we must all ask: Where can we find hope in our breakup with white Christianity?

We know that we're here only because white Christianity dropped the ball. So, if the church is the problem, can the church be the answer? Well, it depends.* I think we need a broader understanding of who "the church" is. Yes, we can take some encouragement from the fact that American Christianity represents only a fraction of the body of Christ. But that's still not enough; that knowledge is little comfort when our experience is living surrounded by Americanized Christianity.

When we consider "the church," it's worth reassessing who God's people are and whether we want to continue sacrificing our sanity on the altar, investing in those hell-bent on convincing us that we're insane as they intentionally malign the image of God.

*Remember what we said about the way lawyers learn to answer questions?

As one acquaintance wrote, "Jesus couldn't do much with people from his own community who rejected His divinity. He eventually had to move on to others who would receive Him, who also were included in His Father's assignment FOR Him. Staying can prevent calling and obedience."[2]

Not everyone is in a place to recognize what the character of God looks like. If there is any hope of the church being the answer for broken hearts, it can only be after we get honest and specific enough to say that white Christianity is not the church that Christ envisioned us becoming. And we can hardly do so if we idolize a shadow of what we're meant to be.

One of the most common phrases heard in and around TFI was "the local church is the hope of the world." I recently learned this phrase was probably borrowed from Bill Hybels, pastor of Willow Creek Community Church, who likely coined the expression and was utilizing it at least as early as 2010. Of course, we might do well to question Hybels's view of the local church, since his credibility was called into question after his sudden resignation amid sexual harassment allegations at Willow Creek. Those accusations were bolstered by an independent report that found that the allegations were credible.[3] Even still, the motto sounds pretty sensical. But here's the thing: it's a lie.

There is a danger to Hybels's axiom when it is internalized by an assembly of people convinced that they have exclusive insight into the will of God, which just happens to align perfectly with one political party's platform. In such environments, clichés have a way of becoming doctrinal statements and tantamount to orthodoxy. While I get the idea, at no point does the Bible call the local gathering of believers the hope of humanity. Rather, our hope is in Christ and God's promise to make all things new.[4] As God's children, we have a part to play in that work, even if imperfectly, on this side of eternity if we'll only make the effort. This is a better hope than what amounts to a social club meeting weekly to reinforce ideals that exclude the very people God longs to love on. Are we worshiping Jesus or an institution?

She Deserves Better and So Do We

In their 2023 book, *She Deserves Better*, Sheila Wray Gregoire, Rebecca Gregoire Lindenback, and Joanna Sawatsky expose the ways that long-held, but misogynistic, teachings on sex, self, and speaking up commonly land on young women in evangelical church culture. Discussing their research with podcaster Johnna Harris, Sheila makes observations on the need to leave that could easily apply to racial toxicity as much as sexual toxicity:

> Let me take you back to grade four math: What we found is on *average*—remember when you learned averages in grade four?—on average, going to church and believing in Jesus is a helpful thing. Okay? It's good, so I'm not telling anyone don't go to church at all, all right? Going to church, having a community around you, you tend to end up with better marriages, better mental health, you know, all that stuff. *But,* if girls go to church and they believe these toxic teachings about modesty, about purity, about how they don't matter as much, then all of the benefits of church disappear. So, if we know that church, on the whole, is good, and we know that these toxic teachings bring the average down, there *has* to be something bringing the average up. And what I just want to encourage people to do is go find the churches that are bringing the average *up*. Because they are out there; they might be smaller churches, they're probably not glitzy, probably not megachurches. There might be some good megachurches but probably not as likely. But there are good places, but we need to give ourselves permission to not have to stay in places that are harmful.[5]

Again, it's important we rely on models of faithfulness that don't look like staying in a toxic church setting or leaving our faith altogether.

What are some practical ways to find hope after deconstructing from white Christianity? I'd like to share what has worked for me and brought me to a place where reconstruction is finally possible. I don't mean for this to be a checklist of five easy steps to living

your best life. Everyone's experiences are different, but I do think
these will help provide us with hope for the journey.

1. Create Your Own Community

Notice, I did not say *find* your community. Most of the people that
I've spoken to who have left white Christianity have expressed
how difficult it is to find a church that cherishes the same understanding of the gospel as they do. For some, leaving is easy enough,
but where can they land? It seems the farther south in the United
States you are, the harder it is to find a healthy post-evangelical
church community.

Of course, if you *can* find a congregation that feels like a safe
place to put down roots again, all the better. But I suggest you don't
spin your wheels for too long looking. If you can't find it, *create*
the community that you're looking for. In a period when healing is
our primary goal, I suggest that we have enough flexibility to adapt
in whatever ways necessary to regain fellowship. That may mean
doing home church for a while. That could mean gathering family or friends together to stream sermons from a church in another
state. It may look like developing a network of people online who
are safe and committed to being each other's biggest advocates and
encouragers. It might look like dedicating one evening to breaking bread with people whose friendships are highly valued without discussing our faith at all.

In 2013, our law firm began having a weekly meeting that, for
lack of originality, we labeled Jesus Time. The inspiration for this
practice came from the teachings at TFI which admonished the
congregation that living with "passion and purpose" meant considering how our identity in Christ could play a role in every area
of society—from medicine to law, education, business. How could
we incorporate our faith more intentionally into our law practice?
Several of us attended TFI at that point, so getting on the same page
was easy. At the same time each week, we closed down our office to
the public as many of our attorneys, staff, and even interns met to
read Scripture together, pray together, and/or discuss our faith. But

sometime around the point that white supremacists donned khaki pants and white polos, picked up tiki torches, and descended on Charlottesville, Virginia, chanting "blood and soil," our meetings started to feel . . . hollow. As our team met to discuss the practical application of Scripture to the work of justice, we had an increasing number of questions about what the church overall seemed to be missing. I was especially frustrated that the very exercise we learned in church—relating our faith to all areas of society—became heretical when minorities wanted to apply the same thought process to ways that every area of society is touched by racism (i.e., critical race theory), including the church. Acknowledging the interplay of faith and social structures was fine for evangelism but taboo in combating white supremacy.

> This miracle didn't come from a church congregation but the gathering of like-minded people that we created where stewarding our emotional health is a form of worship.

Soon, Jesus Time became less about Bible study and more about us discussing, and caring for, each other's emotional well-being. Today, we continue meeting as an office on a weekly basis for Jesus Time, but our time is decidedly focused on mental health. While we still open and close the meeting in prayer, we've shed nearly all of the religious aspects of our meetings because those things no longer serve us well. What does serve us well, however, is our time intentionally connecting with each other on a deep emotional level about things that we never would have felt the freedom to share when we were all deeply embedded in white Christianity. As a result, the community we've created has carried me through some of the most difficult times in my faith and personal life. This miracle didn't come from a church congregation but the gathering of like-minded people that we created where stewarding our emotional health is a form of worship.

I want to drive this point home: the focus of creating community should be on finding people conducive to our healing. This is essentially rehabilitation after significant injury. Take it slow.

What's important here is not necessarily that we're creating a *faith* community, but a community to live in faithfully.

2. Don't Should on Yourself

There's a turquoise coffee mug in our kitchen cabinet with white letters that spell out "Don't Should on Yourself." Besides the fact that it's one of the larger coffee mugs we own, the reason that my wife and I sometimes race to be the one who gets to use that mug is the inspiration it adds to our first cup of coffee in the morning. The phrase was apparently coined by psychologist Albert Ellis (who also referred to the attempt to conform to external expectations as "musterbation"[6]). I don't know much else about Ellis, but I'll be eternally grateful for this bit of wisdom that seeps into my spirit every morning like the warmth of the coffee that fills the mug. Having spent most of my life learning what white Christianity thinks I *should* be doing, it's a great relief to realize that I won't lose my salvation or be any less of a Christian if I don't continue those practices according to specifications.

I'm not a morning person. I never have been. During the school year, I'm lucky just to get up early enough do my part of the busy morning ritual of feeding the dogs, packing lunches for three kids, having coffee, bathing myself, getting dressed for work, and walking out the door in time to take the kids to school. I simply *cannot* add a morning quiet time to all of that.* My wife, on the other hand, thrives on waking up early. Somehow, she is able to do her part of getting everyone ready for the day, getting herself ready, and getting out the door on time without a problem. But more impressively, somehow she usually has room for quiet time in and among all the madness, despite waking up at the same time as I do.

---

*If you are among the uninitiated, "quiet time" is the evangelical name for a period of daily prayer and Bible reading, ideally in the morning, to prepare to face the day with a "biblical worldview" top of mind.

It would be easy to believe that my inability to practice having a quiet time first thing in the morning reflects a deficiency in my commitment to God. I have thought as much in the past. Even when I've had the opportunity to have a quiet moment of reflection on Scripture first thing in the morning, I usually find myself rereading the same sentence over and over for thirty minutes as I struggle to stay awake. It just doesn't work for me.

As insignificant as it may seem, getting beat over the head with an expectation to have a consistent morning quiet time is one of the most often-cited complaints I hear from those reevaluating their ties to white Christianity. Many people feel inadequate because they are not able to perform some of the daily details of their faith in the manner prescribed by their pastors. Conversations with single mothers, for example, showed me that the ability to practice a consistent quiet time in the mornings is a privilege that many people don't have. This is a marked contrast from married couples whose adult children have left the nest, stay-at-home parents with a quiet house to themselves after getting the kids to school, or couples without children. These have a luxury many lack. But it's unjust for the church to insinuate that Christians who are unable to do so are somehow less faithful. Seems like a no-brainer, but somehow the message is taught, or caught, that rituals such as these are integral parts of being a good Christian. As such, the guilt over our inability to conform to these expectations becomes an obstacle to our faith. Don't should on yourself.

As alluded to previously, I only recently regained the ability to read the Bible. For the better part of three years, I simply could not read Scripture—particularly the New Testament—without silently arguing with the memories and convictions of the ubiquitous "they," who lived rent-free in my mind. Reading the words of Jesus, I found myself asking, "How can they read the same Bible and argue that our nation has no responsibility toward the poor? Especially when evangelicals like Sean Feucht demand that America be known as a 'Christian nation'!" or "How can we read Paul's admonition to the Corinthian church that accommodation is fine when we discuss food sacrificed to idols but declare war on Harry Potter?"* If reading Scripture causes you more mental harm than spiritual good, it is completely fine to take a break from reading Scripture. You won't lose your salvation for taking a sabbatical. Don't should on yourself.

Because deconstruction was a radical endeavor for me, I started from the beginning theologically. Every aspect of my faith was fair game for reassessment. What I found to be incredibly helpful in this phase of my deconstruction was listening to what other

I developed a new love for Scripture when I was no longer expected to read it with a color-blind eye toward issues of social justice.

people have to say about Scripture. I binged podcasts and devoured audiobooks by Christians wrestling with the same kinds of theological questions I was: Where did the church go wrong? Why don't our white Christian friends see the same things I see? How can you look at the red letters of the New Testament and also see God as champion of discriminatory authoritarian capitalistic American ideologies?

These lifelines taught me how to read the Bible critically, showed how ancient cosmology influenced biblical writers, and exposed the cultural lens modern Western Christianity uses to interpret an ancient, foreign text. Listening to women perform biblical exegesis laid bare things in Scripture I'd never considered and revealed how valuable the voices of women are in Christian ministry. I gained vocabulary for my feelings of disenfranchisement and began to see that my experience wasn't unique to one congregation—it was endemic to white Christianity. In this process, I learned much more about Scripture than I had reading it in white Christianity. I developed a new love for Scripture when I was no longer expected to read it with a color-blind eye toward issues of social justice. While it was lonely leaving

*For that matter, how can we be fine with the use of magic in the Lord of the Rings franchise but (literally) preach that Harry Potter is demonic?

a church community we'd inhabited for a decade, I grew deeper spiritual roots during this period of turmoil than I had in a long time. And all of this happened by unconventional, it's-OK-not-to-go-to-church-every-Sunday, no-I'm-not-plugged-into-a-small-group means. Don't should on yourself.

3. Decolonize Your Faith

If white Christianity is the cause of our pain, expanding our horizons beyond white church traditions is one of the cures. Chances are that if you're burned out on the homogeneity of the evangelical tradition, you're probably reacting to the long line of dead white theologians upon which the tradition is based.

Which church fathers do the pastors of your church quote and venerate? Were they slaveholders? Does their theology require work-arounds to the moral contradiction of owning human beings in the real world while simultaneously espousing great wisdom about heady concepts like the Trinity? If your congregation is multicultural (or even just multiethnic), why does the music played by the worship team come mostly from white musicians? Is there room for Black gospel traditions in worship music? If members of the congregation are Spanish speakers, or bilingual, are the songs ever performed in Spanish? Is there opportunity for Scripture readings to be in the native languages of diverse congregants while the English translation is projected for others?

Practice envisioning what Christianity that is not presented exclusively in white American contexts could look like.

4. Don't Negotiate Your Dignity

On July 24, 2020, Tyler Burns, president of The Witness: A Black Christian Collective, presented a message that has changed my life. The message was titled "Don't Negotiate Your Dignity." The message was so powerful that when I conveyed its import to me, The Witness granted permission to include a QR code here that links to the full video of his message.[7] What follows here is a synopsis of the full video.

Tyler recalls attending an athletic event in high school and over-hearing a group of white students discussing their frustration with an interaction in class between a Black student and their conservative white teacher. "I don't get the big deal. We gave them their bathrooms," one of the white students opined. In this student's view, white people *gave* freedom to Black people (Black people didn't earn it by fighting for it) and, as a white person, he got to take credit for "giving" that freedom himself (although he was not alive at the time). Red flag.

"Don't Negotiate Your Dignity"

Today, Tyler continues, the conversation that Black people should be having is not whether we should be free. We've litigated that issue. But white Christianity tends to want to demand that we negotiate *how free we get to be.* As an example, most people would concede that the lynchings we saw in 2020 were heinous and that the perpetrators should be punished, though not all have. After widely reported killings of Black people, Burns observes, there's commonly a two- to three-week window in which leaders offer statements of sympathy and concern. The more public the discussion, the more momentum that calls for justice seem to gain. But then the negotiation starts. The conversation shifts away from the strongly worded statements, sympathies, and prayers to questioning how necessary the reforms proposed by minorities are. How committed should we be to taking steps toward change? How free do Black people really need to be?

Within five weeks of the event that sparked these conversations, there are pastors renewing conversations about topics that are irrelevant to the discussion. We hear them debating about Black Lives Matter as a slogan versus an organization. "We didn't ask you to support an organization," replies Burns. "All we asked was for you to arrest the cops that killed Breonna Taylor. Fight for justice in your communities. Listen. Learn. Lament. Legislate. But the negotiation has started." By asking for justice, Black people have infringed a little on the comfort of white people, and since it makes them uncomfortable, they want us to shift the conversation. This pattern justifiably frustrates, and angers, Black Christians, but we may not understand why. In response, Tyler asserts that it is because it is dehumanizing to watch someone else negotiate how much dignity our people deserve. It is dehumanizing to have people who have never spoken out against our oppression dictate to us the method, tone, and manner in which we're allowed to challenge them.

Essentially, Tyler opines, we are "trying to fit wholesale the things that we're talking about in a theological frame that wasn't created with us in mind." For people whose theological framework is standard American evangelical ethics, justice does not fit into the framework they're used to working from. If something doesn't fit in that narrow, anemic framework, the problem must be with us— we who are asking for change. Not with the system. "The problem is you just want a little bit too much. Calm it down." Then they make us feel bad for discussing the things that will make us whole, to which we are entitled as image-bearers of God: being treated well; being paid a fair wage; being protected from police brutality. These things may be basic, but they don't fit inside the framework of standard American evangelical theological ethics.

So what does white evangelicalism offer at the negotiating table? It offers a performative concession instead. It offers a sermon where the pastor washes the feet of the Black people in the congregation. It offers a worship set where the entire congregation holds hands and sings together. But it doesn't offer to repent and repair. Meanwhile, we're frustrated because we didn't ask for these gestures. We wanted something far more substantive. But performance fits in the framework of standard white American evangelical theological ethics. Change does not. So evangelicalism makes us feel bad for refusing to accept the negotiation terms. It's our fault for not accepting superficial efforts to resolve the issue.

Here, Tyler drives home the point so well that he must be quoted directly:

Don't negotiate about your dignity. Do *not* enter into the negotiation about that. Don't do it. Don't do it. It's tempting. So many of us have internalized the fear that we are not acting the right way because for years we were told that we were not supposed to protest. For years we were told it's not biblical for us to talk about justice this way. Not right for us to do this. Not right for us to consider these things. And we are feeling in our hearts the confliction that makes it seem like something must be wrong with *us*. That's why I speak to Black Christians. Because you have been told for so many years that something's *wrong* with you. Just because we want to be treated with dignity and respect. Just because you want to be loved and valued. Just because you don't want to be tokenized. . . . You're pleading and you're begging with the church just to see you and to recognize you and you deserve that. You deserve to be seen, and loved, and valued. And you deserve for people to do the hard work of educating themselves on the best way to treat you. On the way to treat you with dignity and respect and to lead you into wholeness.

Tyler's encouragement is so important that I frequently go back to listen to it again. In a world committed to making us believe that we have lost our reason, we need these reminders to anchor us in the reality that the problem is not with us. We're not insane. We deserve to be seen, loved, and valued for all of who we are. Don't negotiate your dignity.

5. Fight for Your Sanity

Hope is also found in the vehement, relentless defense of our sanity. With all of the references that I've made to *Star Wars,* it's only fair to employ an analogy from *Star Trek.* Good science fiction series are my guiltless pleasures in life. *Star Trek: The Next Generation* will always hold a special place in my heart.

In one particularly gripping story line spanning two episodes, Captain Jean-Luc Picard is taken captive and tortured by enemy combatants. Attempting to break his will and gain information, a Cardassian interrogator, Gul Madred, employs psychological and physical torture by making Captain Picard look at a display of lights and declare that there are five lights when there are actually only four. Each time the captain refuses to concede, his captor administers excruciating pain.

This regimen is repeated mercilessly for days. Finally, and unbeknownst to him, an agreement is brokered that ensures Captain Picard's freedom. Nevertheless, knowing that Picard will soon be rescued, the Cardassian leader attempts to prove his gaslighting effective even up to his last moments with the captain. The goal is no longer information; he just wants to break Picard. Once again, the lights shine blindingly on the captain as Madred employs his masterful manipulation skills anew. Madred assures the captain that his ship has been destroyed. He further torments Picard by telling him that the information the Cardassians sought is no longer needed and thus his defiance under pain of torture was ultimately for nothing. For no reason other than pure masochistic pleasure, Madred will continue torturing Captain Picard for years to come.

Or . . . the captain can live out the rest of his days in comfort, being treated with the dignity of a Cardassian crew member. He will be given food, warm clothing, women, allowed to pursue history and philosophical studies as he desires. All Madred requires of Picard is to tell Madred how many lights he sees. The captain knows that Madred wants him to say there are five lights, when in reality there are only four. Picard looks at the lights. He appears bruised and frail. He can hardly support his own weight or stand upright. Clearly, the torture has taken its toll. There is a long pause. Madred repeats himself, "How many lights?"

Behind Captain Picard, a door opens and three Cardassian soldiers enter the room to extract Picard from his tormentor and escort him to his ship. Undaunted, Madred whispers to the captain, who is still squinting at the lights in consideration that this is his last chance before the guards seize him. Madred implores Picard not to be a stubborn fool and demands to be told how many lights there are. Before Picard has the chance to answer, one of the soldiers barks at Madred that the Captain was expected to be cleaned up and prepared for transport back to his ship before the guards arrived. Turning to their hostage, the head guard explains to Captain Picard that these men have come to escort him to his ship. The jig is up. The trick didn't work. The captain looks up again at the light, considering. Weary though he is, he musters the strength to raise a hoarse voice and defiantly exclaim: "There! Are! *Four!* Lights!"

Back on his own ship, we are privy to a private conversation that the captain has while debriefing with the ship's counselor, Deanna Troy. Through a worn, raspy voice, Picard confesses how effective his torture had actually been:

COUNSELOR: I read your report.
PICARD: What I didn't put in the report is that at the end, he gave me a choice—between a life of comfort or more torture. All I had to do is say that I could see five lights when, in fact, there were only four.
COUNSELOR: You didn't say it?
PICARD: No. No. But I was going to. I was going to do anything. Anything at all. But more than that, I believe that I could see five lights.[8]

I share this story because in it we observe that under the excruciating pain of torture, the only thing that Captain Picard could control—could grasp onto—was the right view of reality. Without hope of rescue, and stripped of everything, his sanity was his last worldly possession, his last place of refuge. In an era when those who profess the name of Jesus are deliberately causing others to question their understanding of reality, simply maintaining our understanding of who God *really* is, is an act of worship.

Where white Christianity has manipulated so many, papering over deep wounds and turning entire congregations against those audacious enough to escape the abuse, our simply saying "I still believe" is a miraculous, mutinous act of worship.

Protecting our mental health in the face of calculated efforts to steal our peace is defiant worship. Clinging to any resources that help affirm the true identity of Jesus as suffering servant, not patriotic celebrity, is worship.

Maintaining fellowship, though it be selective, is worship. Where the church is actively working to distort the identity of Christ in so many ways, defending our sanity, grasping to Jesus's hem in hope, is worship, and that worship gives us hope for healing.

Conclusion

Returning to *Star Wars,* I posit that Kylo Ren doesn't get enough credit for his sage advice helpful to all of us processing our grief over church-inflicted trauma: "Let the past die. Kill it if you have to. That's the only way to become what you are meant to be."[9] Maybe it's because he was a mass murderer and acolyte of evil. Nobody's perfect. But his words still ring true for me.

As nonchalant as I may seem about anger, even as an Enneagram 8, I'm fully aware that anger is not sustainable or a healthy long-term strategy for processing grief. At least, it's not healthy by itself. I advocate that we use anger as our catalyst—a motivator to inspire us to move in whatever way is necessary to accomplish freedom. That may mean being willing to confront and challenge the status quo. It may be willingness to escape abusive relationships of all sorts. Regardless, my goal has not been to drive you into nihilism, joining suffering souls for the sake of company. My goal is to free you from a two-dimensional canvas into a three-dimensional world where you can find supportive, God-loving brothers and sisters in Christ who will show you the fullness of God's love as it was always intended for you. As the saying goes, "I sat with my Anger long enough until she told me her real name was Grief."[10] We are wounded greatly because we loved greatly. And now it's time to move forward.

Where can we find hope in the future of white Christianity? In my opinion, we cannot. Our hope is no longer in white Christianity. Notwithstanding that, I do believe there is cause for hope. We find hope in comforting brothers and sisters who were spiritually abused and traumatized by religion because we see that our own pain was not wasted and that God can use our brokenness and our quest for healing to mend the wounds of others. Our hope springs from fellowship with those convinced there's more to the gospel than Platitude Jesus and Instagram Church. We find hope when we speak for the downcast and, in the distance, we hear an amen. We find hope when others join the chorus speaking out about who God really is, when the table grows longer to make room for more people. We hope when teaching our children about a richer, truer faith than the one handed to us by white Christianity. We hope in the promise that Christ will have his bride, the church of the faithful, and that wrong will be made right in the end. Our hope is in communion with other believers who challenge us and help us see a little more clearly.

> **We are wounded greatly because we loved greatly. And now it's time to move forward.**

This is the hope that Martin Luther King Jr. encouraged us to take back with us to the cities and villages in which we live: that every valley will be exalted, every mountain made low, and the crooked places made straight. This righteousness is more than a social freedom from a caste system created by our culture; it is the freedom to lift our hands in worship, free of spiritual and emotional chains. Selah. Our hope is no longer found in the institution of faith but in the authentic living out of our faith in a way that brings emancipation for all. Our hope is in being the church, not being part of the church. Our hope is knowing that as we do this work, our heavenly Father looks down and sees a little bit of Jesus at work in us.

Epilogue

Closing Arguments

*A*t some level, all trial lawyers are narcissists. We go to law school dreaming of a day when we'll have the opportunity to stand in the well of a courtroom, delivering powerful closing arguments in important cases to a captive audience sitting in the jury box. But while closing arguments feel like the most significant part of a trial, they are, from a legal perspective, one of the least significant.

As the name suggests, closings are situated at the end of the case, after all the evidence has been presented to the jury—no new evidence is presented to the jury by the attorney during closing remarks. Closings allow attorneys to summarize the evidence admitted during trial through their perspective and urge the jury to act in accordance with that understanding. In fact, before the attorneys begin their closing remarks, the court often instructs jurors that they have been given all of the law, facts, and evidence that they need to decide the case. I mention this because I feel the need to remind you in these last pages that if you have made it this far, you have all the tools that you need to begin securing your freedom from spiritual abuse. Namely, the rejection of white Christianity as the objective standard for faithfully interpreting the gospel, a commitment toward your own healing, and the unquenchable fire that stirs inside you.

Ladies and gentlemen: *you have every right to be angry*. The anger toward white Christianity that burns inside you is not manufactured from imagined slights or dramatized hypersensitivity.

Rather, it is the natural, and God-inspired, reaction to intentional, systematic attempts to diminish your soul. Efforts to convince you that, somehow, you are not entitled to the same fullness of dignity as our brothers and sisters in the majority culture. Efforts to quiet you by telling you that your voice is unworthy of being heard in the fullness of its volume—lest you be perceived as . . . angry. Efforts to convince you that you are divisive for challenging Christianity's complicity with racism.

Let's review how far we've come since beginning this journey. Early on, we established that when God's heart burns in anger toward injustice, ours should too. Therefore, we have every right to be angry about the church's complicity with racism. Further, demanding minorities quietly assimilate into white Christianity, with its tolerance of racism, is spiritual abuse. Subsequently, we used the framework of legal analysis to correctly analyze what it means to be a Christian—what the gospel means to the marginalized and what is expected of Christ-followers. Further along, we surveyed American jurisprudence, exposing how turning a color-blind eye toward racial justice has been ineffective in our democracy and injurious to our faith. We discussed the importance of breaking our silence and removing our masks, both of which white Christianity imposed upon us and we adopted for survival in that ecosystem.

We've discussed how Christian whiteness teaches an impoverished form of the good news—a new Jim Crow theology—that is out of sync with the truth-telling mission of the gospel. We examined the utility of anger as a motivator for our spiritual liberation and an essential part of breaking the ties that bind. We came to appreciate that we must take responsibility for our own liberation from spiritual abuse and that God's grace accompanies us as we leave spiritually abusive environments. Last, we identified the hope that we take with us as we set out in uncharted territory to rebuild our fractured faith. Friends, you now have all the tools needed to embark on this journey successfully. Moreover, you do not venture out alone. Rather, in departing from white Christianity, we join along with countless others who have embraced the need to do so and reclaim their wholeness.

White Christianity has stolen enough from us. As you close this book and set about the work of reclaiming your wholeness, know that you already have everything you need to do so. Use the songs, the meditations, and the reflections herein to create new forms of worship, new community, and a new love for the God we worship. We may not be in Kansas anymore, but we have all we need to get home and reclaim our wholeness. In the words of Tracy Chapman, "Remember the Tin Man found he had what he thought he lacked. Remember the Tin Man, go find your heart and take it back."[1]

If you take nothing else away from this book, let it be the affirmation of your worth as one of God's image-bearers, the assurance that the gospel is supremely concerned with the welfare of the marginalized, and the need to fight for your sanity in the midst of those hell-bent on depriving you of it. God shares our anger and wants more for us than we've been led to believe. Let us carry this righteous anger with us like a torch in dark places that never allows us to forget what we are walking away from. Let the intensity and voluminosity of that light bear witness that we are far from alone in our journey. Let that lead us to reclaiming our wholeness.

Questions for Reflection and Discussion

1. How willing is your church to talk about issues of racism and social justice? Is it a natural part of preaching, prayer, and group discussion? Does the church react only when current events demand? Does it avoid addressing them altogether?

2. On pages 13-14, white Christianity is defined, in part, by its indifference toward the effects of racism on the church. What examples of apathy or "all lives matter" evasion have you witnessed in your faith community?

3. Have you questioned your faith or considered leaving the church due to its complicity with racism? How has the church's racism, misogyny, or LGBTQIA+ bigotry played a part in your evolving spiritual identity?

4. How would you respond to those who claim the gospel is unconcerned with issues like racism or social justice?

5. How can the church move beyond performative actions toward meaningful change? What practical steps can the church take to create a safe space for minorities to express their concerns and experiences and to foster a culture of empathy and understanding for minorities?

6. Have you ever felt you had to keep silence or wear a mask in order to survive in a certain environment? How does doing so affect a person long-term? What difference does it make if church is one of those environments?

7. Consider the public statements of Brandt Jean and Jonathan

Isaac in response to racist violence (pp. 130–33). Why should or shouldn't Christians celebrate these perspectives from Black Americans?

8. Have you ever felt that anger is sinful or not appropriate for followers of Christ? How can you reframe your understanding of anger as a powerful and potentially righteous emotion?

9. The differences between repentance, forgiveness, reconciliation, restitution, reparations, and restoration are explored on pages 195–200. Making use of these terms, how would you describe the path forward for practitioners of white Christianity and Black Christians?

10. What overall conclusions do you take away from reading and discussing this book? How will those conclusions direct your future actions?

Is It Time to Go?
Personal Inventory

Spend time reflecting on these questions privately, by journaling, or in conversation with a trusted friend. Your responses may shed valuable light on your decision to remain or leave your current congregation.

1. How do you rate your church's response to issues of racism and social justice? Does the church proactively address and discuss these issues, react only when current events demand, or avoid addressing them altogether?
2. Have you ever felt the church's response to racial injustice was inadequate or performative? What effect did this have on your faith?
3. How do the teachings and practices of your church align with your values and understanding of Scripture? Do the church's actions align with its own professed values and teachings? Do you find yourself compartmentalizing your faith from the place you worship?
4. Does the church provide opportunities for you to utilize your gifts and talents authentically?
5. How would you rate the support and understanding you receive from church leaders and fellow members regarding your experience as a minority? What improvements are needed?

6. How open are church leaders to dialogue and to addressing concerns about racism and discrimination?

7. Have you ever tried to discuss with church leaders the church's willingness to address racism from the pulpit? If so, how was it received? If not, why not? Does the thought of doing so reveal any anxieties or a lack of security in the worship environment? Do you believe their response could be productive, or do you believe that it's a lost cause?

8. What practical steps could the church take to create a safe space for minorities to express their concerns and experiences? What changes would you need to see to trust that your church was moving beyond performative actions toward meaningful change?

9. Does the idea of leaving your church bring on feelings of fear, sadness, or guilt? What would it take for you to feel confident about leaving an unsupportive community behind?

10. Where might you find a spiritual community that welcomes you in the wholeness of your identity? If such a community does not exist in your area, how can you help build one?

Notes

Introduction: Since I've Laid My Burden Down

1. *Terminator Salvation*, directed by McG (Warner Bros., 2009).
2. In 1 Cor. 2, Paul writes of the wisdom of God in contrast to the wisdom of humans. His comparison crescendos in vv. 14–16: The natural person does not accept the things of the Spirit of God, because to the natural person they appear to be folly and cannot be understood because they are spiritually discerned. "For, 'Who has known the mind of the Lord so as to instruct him?' But we have the mind of Christ." I see believers spend a lot of effort (usually defensively) to locate themselves on a political spectrum that encourages binary labeling: conservative/Republican/right vs. progressive/liberal/Democrat/left. All of these, as well as centrism, are insufficient to encapsulate the view of societal issues that I believe Jesus calls us to as believers. Therefore, in this book, when it becomes necessary to label a view with political or societal implications that is most in conformity with God's will, I'm borrowing from Paul to call that view "the mind of Christ" (NIV).
3. "Beth Moore Sounds the Alarm," *The Disrupters* (podcast), season 2, episode 3, October 8, 2020.

Chapter 1: Lift Every Voice and Sing

1. Jessica Martínez and Gregory A. Smith, "How the Faithful Voted," Pew Research Center, November 9, 2016, https://www.pewresearch.org/fact-tank/2016/11/09/how-the-faithful-voted-a-preliminary-2016-analysis/.
2. Justin Nortey, "Most White Americans Who Regularly Attend Worship Services Voted for Trump in 2020," Pew Research Center, August 30, 2021, https://www.pewresearch.org/short-reads/2021/08/30/most-white-americans-who-regularly-attend-worship-services-voted-for-trump-in-2020/.
3. Mark Murray, "Poll: 61% of Republicans Still Believe Biden Didn't Win Fair and Square in 2020," Meet the Press Blog, NBC News, Sept. 27,

2022, https://www.nbcnews.com/meet-the-press/meetthepressblog/poll-61
-republicans-still-believe-biden-didnt-win-fair-square-2020-rcna49630.

4. On December 19, 2021, former president Trump spoke during Sunday
morning's service to approximately 6,000 churchgoers at First Baptist Church
in Dallas at the invitation of pastor Dr. Robert Jeffries. A month earlier,
Cornerstone Church in San Antonio, Texas, hosted the ReAwaken America
conference where political coconspirators Michael Flynn and Michael Lindell
(the MyPillow guy) spoke. A viral video from the event showed the church's
auditorium filled to capacity with attendees chanting "Let's Go, Brandon!"
The phrase became coded language synonymous with "F*ck Joe Biden" after
a NASCAR crowd chanted the phrase on live TV and it was misinterpreted
as "Let's go, Brandon" by Kelli Stavast, who was interviewing the winner,
Brandon Brown, at the time.

5. If you don't catch this reference already, you're in for a treat. In the fall
of 2020, a video of televangelist Paula White's rhythmic (?) prayer calling upon
angels from Africa and South America to aid Donald Trump's bid for reelection
went viral online. Wyatte Grantham-Philips, "Pastor Paula White Calls on
Angels from Africa and South America to Bring Trump Victory," *USA Today*,
updated November 6, 2020, https://www.usatoday.com/story/news/nation/2020
/11/05/paula-white-trumps-spiritual-adviser-african-south-american-angels
/6173576002/.

6. J. Crum (@jcrummusic), "How you speak in tongues but can't apologize?" Twitter, April 21, 2022, 12:25 p.m., https://twitter.com/jcrummusic
/status/1517192736096542723?s=46.

7. Dani Di Placido, "'Anti-Woke' Author Who Can't Define 'Woke' Goes
Viral," *Forbes*, March 16, 2023, https://www.forbes.com/sites/danidiplacido
/2023/03/16/anti-woke-author-who-cant-define-woke-goes-viral/?sh
=3bb058e95b3e. See https://youtube.com/shorts/W7iWEEcPKoQ.

8. Louis D. Brandeis, *Other People's Money and How the Bankers Use It*
(New York: Frederick A. Stokes, 1914), 92.

9. James Bryce, *The American Commonwealth* (London: Macmillan, 1888),
2:325.

10. Hat tip to April Ajoy (@aprilajoyr), "A late response to Matt Chandler
calling deconstruction sexy," Twitter, January 17, 2022, 7:59 p.m., https://
twitter.com/aprilajoyr/status/1483257707226411011?s=46; Chandler's original
comment: https://www.youtube.com/watch?v=X_r8IMU647g

11. Dr. Thema Bryant (@drthema), "Truth telling will cost you,"
Twitter, July 23, 2022, 7:18 p.m., https://twitter.com/drthema/status
/1550998898147074048?s=21.

12. "Lift Every Voice and Sing," text by James Weldon Johnson, music by
John Rosamond Johnson.

Chapter 2: More Than Fine

1. *The Italian Job*, directed by F. Gary Gray (Paramount Pictures, 2003).
2. "Read the Full Transcript of Joe Biden's ABC News Town Hall," ABC News, October 15, 2020, https://abcnews.go.com/Politics/read-full-transcript-joe-bidens-abc-news-town/story?id=73643517.
3. In August 2019, Craig Barr filed suit against Popeyes Chicken in Hamilton County, Tennessee, because the food chain ran out of chicken sandwiches. Janelle Griffith, "Tennessee Man Sues Popeyes for Running Out of Chicken Sandwiches," NBC News, August 30, 2019, https://www.nbcnews.com/news/us-news/tennessee-man-sues-popeyes-running-out-chicken-sandwiches-n1048321.
4. In a widely circulated story that has since been debunked by Snopes, a Chinese couple reportedly divorced, and the husband sued his wife, when she gave birth to a child he thought to be ugly. The man initially thought the woman was having an affair but later learned that his wife had previously had plastic surgery but failed to tell him. Again, this story is most likely a hoax. "Chinese Man Sues Wife for Being Ugly, Wins $120,000," KDVR, Denver, CO, October 26, 2012, https://kdvr.com/news/chinese-man-sues-wins-120000/.
5. In fairness, maybe they didn't hold their noses. Maybe COVID-19 stole their sense of smell. More on polling data: Frank Newport, "Religious Group Voting and the 2020 Election," Gallup, November 13, 2020, https://news.gallup.com/opinion/polling-matters/324410/religious-group-voting-2020-election.aspx.
6. Justin Nortey, "Most White Americans Who Regularly Attend Worship Services Voted for Trump in 2020," Pew Research Center, August 30, 2021, https://www.pewresearch.org/short-reads/2021/08/30/most-white-americans-who-regularly-attend-worship-services-voted-for-trump-in-2020.
7. Julia Duin, "She Led Trump to Christ: The Rise of the Televangelist Who Advises the White House," *Washington Post*, November 14, 2017, https://www.washingtonpost.com/lifestyle/magazine/she-led-trump-to-christ-the-rise-of-the-televangelist-who-advises-the-white-house/2017/11/13/1dc3a830-bb1a-11e7-be94-fabb0f1e9ffb_story.html.
8. Jessica Taylor, "Citing 'Two Corinthians,' Trump Struggles to Make the Sale to Evangelicals," NPR, January 18, 2016, https://www.npr.org/2016/01/18/463528847/citing-two-corinthians-trump-struggles-to-make-the-sale-to-evangelicals.
9. Perhaps unsurprisingly, the one bit of Scripture he did recall during the interview was "an eye for an eye." Rebecca Shabad, "Donald Trump Names His Favorite Bible Verse," CBS News, April 14, 2016, https://www.cbsnews.com/news/donald-trump-names-his-favorite-bible-verse/.
10. Nick Niedzwiadek, "Trump Goes After Black Lives Matter, 'Toxic

Propaganda' in Schools," *Politico*, September 17, 2020, https://www.politico.com/news/2020/09/17/trump-black-lives-matter-1619-project-417162.

11. Safia Samee Ali, "'Not by Accident': False 'Thug' Narratives Have Long Been Used to Discredit Civil Rights Movements," NBC News, September 27, 2020, https://www.nbcnews.com/news/us-news/not-accident-false-thug-narratives-have-long-been-used-discredit-n1240509.

12. Sungil Han, Jordan R. Riddell, and Alex R. Piquero, "Anti-Asian American Hate Crimes Spike during the Early Stages of the COVID-19 Pandemic," *Journal of Interpersonal Violence* 38 (2023): 3513–33, https://www.ncbi.nlm.nih.gov/pmc/articles/PMC9168424/.

13. "Report: Online Hate Increasing against Minorities, Says Expert," United Nations Human Rights, Office of the High Commissioner, March 23, 2021, https://www.ohchr.org/en/stories/2021/03/report-online-hate-increasing-against-minorities-says-expert; Chrysalis L. Wright, Ashley Lopez, Beatriz Coelho, and Caitlyn Koerner, "Online Racism: Has the Internet Caused More Harm Than Good?," *Amplifier Magazine*, Fall/Winter 2023, https://div46amplifier.com/2022/12/14/online-racism-has-the-internet-caused-more-harm-than-good/.

14. Martin Pengelly, "Trump Dodges Question over Whether Any Past Partners Had Abortions," April 2, 2016, *Guardian*, https://www.theguardian.com/us-news/2016/apr/02/donald-trump-marueen-dowd-interview-abortion-past-partners.

15. Kristin Kobes Du Mez, *Jesus and John Wayne* (New York: Liveright Publishing, 2020), 257–61, 294.

16. In a June 16, 2015, campaign speech.

17. July 2015 at Family Leadership Summit, Ames, Iowa.

18. On March 3, 2013, after Brande Roderick, a *Celebrity Apprentice* contestant, stated she (figuratively) got down on her knees to beg a male team member for an opportunity, Trump said, "It must be a pretty picture, you dropping to your knees."

19. https://www.npr.org/2024/02/19/1232438349/donald-trump-golden-high-top-sneakers; https://www.cnn.com/2024/03/28/us/donald-trump-bible-christianity-cec/index.html

20. Zach W. Lambert (@ZachWLambert), "I'm committed to racial justice because of the Bible," Twitter, August 1, 2022, 8:29 a.m., https://twitter.com/zachwlambert/status/1554096987649314816?s=46.

21. Kate Boyd, *An Untidy Faith: Journeying Back to the Joy of Following Jesus* (Harrisonburg, VA: Herald Press, 2023), 75; Sylvia C. Keesmaat and Brian J. Walsh, *Romans Disarmed: Resisting Empire, Demanding Justice* (Grand Rapids: Brazos, 2019), 12.

22. "More than Fine," by Jonathan Mark Foreman, on Switchfoot, *The Beautiful Letdown*, Sony Music Entertainment, 2003.

Chapter 3: Mad as Heaven

1. Matt. 18:6–7; 23:13–39.

2. *Avengers: Infinity War*, directed by Anthony and Joe Russo (Walt Disney Studios Motion Pictures, 2018).

3. Nicodemus comes to Jesus in the night and confesses to Jesus, "Rabbi, we know that you are a teacher come from God, for no one can do these signs that you do unless God is with him" (John 3:2, ESV). Thereafter, Jesus informs Nicodemus that he must be born again. However, as the conversation is depicted, Nicodemus doesn't ask Jesus about salvation—rather, Jesus volunteers it to him.

4. E.g., Ps. 105:3: "Glory in his holy name; let the hearts of those who seek the LORD rejoice." Ps. 111:9: "He provided redemption for his people; he ordained his covenant forever—holy and awesome is his name."

5. A comment reportedly made by the then president in January 2018. Though he vaguely denied this specific language was used, he has never denied making insulting or similarly derogatory remarks regarding these countries.

6. Pastor John MacArthur reportedly stated privately in a meeting, then confirmed again in an interview in 2021, that, in his opinion, CRT is the most dangerous controversy of the last 100 years.

7. To some, "murder" may feel like an exaggerated description of George Floyd's death. However, it is precisely the charge for which his killer stood trial and was convicted. Steve Karnowski, "Chauvin Murder Conviction Upheld in George Floyd Killing," Associated Press, April 17, 2023, https://apnews.com/article/chauvin-murder-appeals-court-6941a6074dcc310c85e4f3eab2be97eb.

8. Campbell Robertson, "A Quiet Exodus: Why Black Worshipers Are Leaving White Evangelical Churches," *New York Times,* March 9, 2018, https://www.nytimes.com/2018/03/09/us/blacks-evangelical-churches.html.

9. Dara T. Mathis, "The Church's Black Exodus: Pastors' Silence on Racism and COVID-19 Is Driving Black Parishioners Away from Their Congregations," *Atlantic,* October 11, 2020, https://www.theatlantic.com/politics/archive/2020/10/why-black-parishioners-are-leaving-churches/616588/.

10. Martin Luther King Jr., *Stride toward Freedom* (New York: Harper & Row, 1958), 40.

11. Lucille Clifton, "Why some people be mad at me sometimes," in *How to Carry Water: Selected Poems*, ed. Aracelis Girmay (Rochester, NY: BOA Editions Ltd., 2020).

12. Credit to Mike Ere and Timm Stafford at *Voxology* podcast, who are constantly challenging listeners with this vital question.

13. See Kaitlyn Schiess, *The Liturgy of Politics: Spiritual Formation for the Sake of Our Neighbor* (Downers Grove, IL: IVP Academic, 2020).

Chapter 4: Pass Me Not

1. Sam Cooke, "A Change Is Gonna Come," 1954, https://www.archives
.gov/exhibits/documented-rights/exhibit/section4/detail/change-is-gonna-come
-lyrics.html.

2. "History of Hymns: 'Pass Me Not, O Gentle Savior,'" Discipleship
Ministries of the United Methodist Church, June 14, 2013, https://www
.umcdiscipleship.org/resources/history-of-hymns-pass-me-not-o-gentle-savior.

3. "Pastor Dewey Smith Sings—Pass Me Not," YouTube, January 7, 2010,
https://youtu.be/FTfXVkTMOHo; "Pass Me Not by Fantasia (Life Is Not a
Fairytale)," YouTube, July 2, 2010, https://youtu.be/Es0ofgENfjg.

4. While I no longer ascribe to this belief, I was raised believing in a literal
reading of the creation narrative in Genesis and the historicity of the fall, both
of which are still commonly taught in evangelicalism. For those interested,
there are entire books on the problem with this theology, including *Original
Blessing: Putting Sin in Its Rightful Place* by Danielle Shroyer (Minneapolis:
Fortress Press, 2016).

5. "The Shadow Proves the Sunshine," on Switchfoot, *Nothing Is Sound*,
Sparrow Records, 2005.

6. In 1967 King confessed as much during an interview with NBC News
at Ebenezer Baptist Church in Atlanta. Speaking of the speech he gave at the
Lincoln Memorial in 1963 (the "I Have a Dream" speech), and America's
involvement in the Vietnam War, King stated, "I must confess that that period
was a great period of hope for me and I'm sure for many others all across the
nation. Many of the Negroes who had about lost hope saw a solid decade of
progress in the South. . . . But I must confess that that dream that I had that
day has at many points turned into a nightmare. Now I'm not one to lose
hope. I keep on hoping. I still have faith in the future. But I've had to analyze
many things over the last few years, and I would say over the last few months.
And I've gone through a lot of soul searching and agonizing moments. And
I've come to see that we have many more difficult days ahead and some of
the old optimism was a little superficial and now it must be tempered with
a solid realism." This quote begins at 21:56 of "MLK Talks 'New Phase' of
Civil Rights Struggle, 11 Months before His Assassination," NBC News on
YouTube, https://www.youtube.com/watch?v=2xsbt3a7K-8&t=1284s.

7. Robin J. DiAngelo, *White Fragility: Why It's So Hard for White People to
Talk about Racism* (Boston: Beacon Press, 2018), 30, 31, 63.

8. Lina Mann, "The Enslaved Household of President Thomas Jefferson,"
White House Historical Association, November 20, 2019, https://www
.whitehousehistory.org/slavery-in-the-thomas-jefferson-white-house.

9. Slaughter-House Cases, 100 U.S. 303, 307–8 (1880) (emphasis added).

10. Plessy v. Ferguson, 163 U.S. 537 (1896). As the court would later
explain in overturning this case, *Plessy*'s "separate but equal" doctrine justified
segregation by erroneously reasoning that "equality of treatment is accorded
when the races are provided substantially equal facilities, even though these

facilities be separate." Brown v. Board of Education of Topeka, 347 U.S. 483, 488 (1954).

11. State v. Treadway, 126 La. 300, 300 (La. 1910). The Treadways were found not guilty at the trial court level, but the state appealed, attempting to secure a conviction after having presented its evidence at trial and lost. This is significant because due process and double jeopardy laws now prevent the state from appealing an acquittal. The appellate history here shows a level of vindictiveness in the prosecution.

12. Brown v. Board of Education, 347 U.S. 483, 494.

13. Brown v. Board of Education, 347 U.S. at 490.

14. Accordingly, the Supreme Court revisited its decision a year later in Brown v. Board of Education of Topeka II, 394 U.S. 294 (1955). In a unanimous opinion, the court made clear that the states were expected to comply with the previous year's ruling. However, the court gave little instruction on timing other than that the states were to do so "with all deliberate speed."

15. Griffin v. School Board, 377 U.S. 218 (1964).

16. The Lovings were arrested in 1958 and sentenced to a year in jail in 1959. However, the judge agreed to suspend their incarceration on the condition that they agree not to return together to Virginia for twenty-five years. The Lovings only sought legal intervention in 1964 after years of navigating the difficulty of visiting family in Virginia under this agreement grew too burdensome.

17. Loving v. Virginia, 388 U.S. 1, 10 (1967).

18. Morgan v. Virginia, 328 U.S. 373 (1946).

19. Morgan v. Virginia, 328 U.S. 373; Gayle v. Browder, 352 U.S. 903 (1956); Boynton v. Virginia, 364 U.S. 454 (1960).

20. Bailey v. Patterson, 369 U.S. 31, 33 (1962).

21. "March on Washington for Jobs and Freedom," National Park Service, updated November 20, 2023, https://www.nps.gov/articles/march-on -washington.htm.

22. Heart of Atlanta Motel, Inc. v. United States, 379 U.S. 241, 261 (1964).

23. Shelby County v. Holder, 570 U.S. 529 (2013).

24. Jasleen Singh and Sara Carter, "States Have Added Nearly 100 Restrictive Laws since SCOTUS Gutted the Voting Rights Act 10 Years Ago," Brennan Center for Justice, June 23, 2023, https://www.brennancenter .org/our-work/analysis-opinion/states-have-added-nearly-100-restrictive-laws -scotus-gutted-voting-rights.

25. Allen v. Milligan, 599 U.S. 1, 143 S. Ct. 1487 (2023).

26. Jones v. Alfred H. Mayer Co., 392 U.S. 409 (1968). Stewart was quoting an 1866 speech by Illinois Senator Lyman Trumbull, a coauthor of the Thirteenth Amendment.

27. University of California Regents v. Bakke, 438 U.S. 265 (1978); Grutter v. Bollinger, 539 U.S. 306 (2003); Students for Fair Admissions, Inc. v. President and Fellows of Harvard College, 600 U.S. 181 (2023).

28. Stephanie Condon, "After 148 Years, Mississippi Finally Ratifies 13th Amendment, Which Banned Slavery," CBS News, February 18, 2013, https://www.cbsnews.com/news/after-148-years-mississippi-finally-ratifies -13th-amendment-which-banned-slavery/.

29. "Michael Che's Civil Rights Update," *Michael Che Matters,* Netflix, 2016, YouTube video, https://www.youtube.com/watch?v=AeN_SVoJet0.

Chapter 5: A New Lens for a Color-Blind Church

1. "James Baldwin and Paul Weiss's HEATED Debate on Discrimination in America," *Dick Cavett Show,* originally aired May 16, 1969, YouTube video, 3:06–3:39 and 10:16–11:26, https://youtu.be/hzH5IDnLaBA.

2. "Read Martin Luther King Jr.'s 'I Have a Dream' Speech in Its Entirety," NPR, updated January 16, 2023, https://www.npr.org/2010/01/18/122701268 /i-have-a-dream-speech-in-its-entirety.

3. In May 2023, Ted Cruz posted that King would be ashamed of how profoundly the NAACP has lost its way. Nigel Roberts, "Martin Luther King's Daughter Bernice King Responds to Sen. Ted Cruz's Criticism of NAACP Florida Advisory," BET, May 23, 2023, https://www.bet.com/article/bbzqt3 /bernice-king-ted-cruz-naacp-florida-travel-advisory-mlk-daughter-response.

4. Rebecca J. Laurent (@Theculturedconscience), Instagram, June 22, 2021, https://www.instagram.com/p/CQa_4sKDzXy/.

Chapter 6: We Break the Silence

1. Benjamin Young (@bjyoung1990), "When speaking of civil and social issues of justice and liberation I have often heard the following from white Christian conservatives," Threads, August 5, 2023, https://www.threads.net /@bjyoung1990/post/CvktbOqgHOB/.

2. Malcolm X, "If You Stick a Knife in My Back," interview, YouTube video posted November 5, 2011, https://www.youtube.com/watch?v =XiSiHRNQlQo.

3. David Maraniss and Sally Jenkins, "Jerry Jones Helped Transform the NFL, Except When It Comes to Race," *Washington Post,* November 23, 2022, https://www.washingtonpost.com/sports/interactive/2022/jerry-jones-black -coaches-nfl/.

4. Andrew DeMillo, Anthony Izaguirre, and Nicholas Riccardi, Associated Press, "Republican 2024 Hopeful Ron DeSantis Is 'Blazing a Trail' on School Book Bans," NPR, May 26, 2023, https://www.pbs.org/newshour/amp/politics /republican-2024-hopeful-ron-desantis-is-blazing-a-trail-on-school-book -bans. In January 2024, NBC News reported that the Escambia County Public School District pulled several titles from its shelves and began to scrutinize the biographies of Oprah Winfrey and Beyoncé, the diary of Anne Frank, and *The Autobiography of Malcom X* as well. Marlene Lenthang, "Florida School District Pulls Over 1,600 Books for Review to Possibly Be Banned—Including

Dictionaries," January 11, 2024, https://www.nbcnews.com/news/amp
/rcna133436. Among 300 titles caught in the dragnet of banned books was
Little Rock Nine by Marshall Poe; "2022–2023 School District Reporting
Pursuant to Section 1006.28(2), Florida Statutes," Florida Department of
Education, https://www.fldoe.org/core/fileparse.php/5574/urlt
/2223ObjectionList.pdf.

5. As one of the preeminent poets of our generation stated, "These days,
you can't see who's in cahoots, 'Cause now the KKK wears three-piece suits."
Chuck D, Public Enemy, from "Rebirth," track 2 on *Apocalypse 91 . . . The
Enemy Strikes Back*, Def Jam Recordings, UMG Recordings, Inc., 1991.

6. Kyle "Guante" Tran Myhre, "Not a Lot of Reasons to Sing, but Enough,"
November 22, 2020, https://guante.info/2020/11/22/nottheshark/.

7. "Our Changing Population: Spokane County, Washington," USAFacts,
updated July 2022, https://usafacts.org/data/topics/people-society/population
-and-demographics/our-changing-population/state/washington/county/spokane
-county/?endDate=1998-01-01&startDate=1997-01-01.

8. "North Idaho and Spokane Have Been a Historical Hotbed for Violent
White Supremacists," *The Spokesman-Review*, March 27, 2024, https://www
.spokesman.com/stories/2024/mar/27/north-idaho-and-spokane-have-been
-a-historical-hot/

9. In the practice of law, we spend a lot of time educating juries about the
differences between, and value of, direct and circumstantial evidence. Direct
evidence supports the veracity of an allegation without need for any additional
inferences. Examples of direct evidence include DNA, fingerprints, video
evidence, and photographs. Generally speaking, once you see those things,
if you accept them as true, you don't have to ascertain the value they have as
evidence. The evidence stands directly for the proposition it's presented to
prove.

By contrast, circumstantial evidence is used to create inferences that may
support the allegations made. For example, in a case where someone is accused
of robbing a bank at gunpoint, the relevant circumstances may include the
fact that the accused was seen purchasing the same sort of weapon used in the
crime. The inference is that because the same sort of weapon was utilized, the
gun purchased is the same one used in the commission of the crime. Other
circumstances may support the same inference: sudden large purchases, a one-
way airline ticket to a country without extradition, an internet browser history
that includes "what is the best way to get away with robbery?" (You'd be
amazed at the things I've seen.) Combined, these circumstances strengthen the
ultimate proposition: the defendant committed the crime.

Because it requires additional inferences to prove the ultimate proposition,
circumstantial evidence is sometimes assumed to be less potent than direct
evidence. Thus juries are often hung up on the value of testimony in cases
where there are two conflicting sides to the story. However, as we're discussing

the testimony of minorities detailing their experiences with racism, it is important to note that—in a legal context—live testimony is *direct* evidence if you find it credible.

10. Dan Glaister, "Seinfeld Actor Lets Fly with Racist Tirade," *Guardian,* November 22, 2006, https://www.theguardian.com/world/2006/nov/22/usa .danglaister; https://www.cracked.com/article_33171_when-jerry-seinfeld -helped-michael-richards-make-the-worlds-cringiest-apology.html.

11. Dion Lim, "'I'm Not Racist': Solano County Auto Shop Owner Speaks Out about Controversial 'China Virus' Promotion," KGO-TV, San Francisco, December 28, 2020, https://abc7news.com/solano-county-free-smog-check -moorhead-auto-center-fairfield-coronavirus-impact-china-virus-term/9149904/.

12. Biba Adams, "Kelly Loeffler Runs Facebook Ad Darkening Rev. Warnock's Skin Color," Yahoo! News, January 5, 2021, https://news.yahoo .com/kelly-loeffler-runs-facebook-ad-193628867.html.

13. Minyvonne Burke, "Announcer Who Called High School Basketball Team Racial Slur Blames His Diabetes," NBC News, March 13, 2021, https://www.nbcnews.com/news/us-news/announcer-who-called-high-school -basketball-team-racial-slur-blames-n1261040.

14. Credit Mike Erre and Timothy Stafford, *Voxology* podcast. See episode 349, "Image - Part Seven: Gotta Have Faith, Faith, Faith," https://podcasts .apple.com/us/podcast/voxology/id1049250910?i=1000559363379.

15. Kelsey Payton, "A few things I'm learning from Jesus in this passage," Facebook, September 30, 2022, https://m.facebook.com/story.php?story_fbid =pfbid0f9teXMtiboCnU5cYpGNGdjsSgT6MKehwP2q5tirSdFffmALFbruRg NjM96w5Nr84l&id=504983671.

Chapter 7: We Wear the Mask (No Longer)

1. Samuel Stebbins and Evan Comen, "16 Most Segregated Cities in America," 24/7 Wall St., updated January 11, 2020, https://247wallst.com /special-report/2018/07/20/16-most-segregated-cities-in-america-3/2.

2. Tyler Burns, "Permission to Be Black with A.D. Thomason," *Pass the Mic* (podcast), February 2, 2021, https://podcasts.apple.com/us/podcast /permission-to-be-black-with-a-d-thomason/id1435500798?i=1000507455845.

3. Tyler Burns, "Leave LOUD: Tyler Burns' Story," *Pass the Mic* (podcast), March 15, 2021, https://podcasts.apple.com/us/podcast/pass-the-mic /id1435500798?i=1000513112150.

4. Emily and Amelia Nagoski, *Burnout: The Secret to Unlocking the Stress Cycle* (New York: Ballantine, 2020), 94; referencing Lepore and Revenson, "Relationships between Posttraumatic Growth and Resilience: Recovery, Resistance, and Reconfiguration," in *Handbook of Posttraumatic Growth: Research and Practice*, ed. L.G. Calhoun and R.G. Tedeschi (Mahwah, NJ: Lawrence Erlbaum Associates, 2006).

5. See "Who We Are: A Chronicle of Racism in America," The Who We Are Project, https://thewhoweareproject.org/the-film.

6. As a reminder, *Brown v. Board* was the case that, on paper, officially ended lawful segregation (known as the "separate but equal" policy) in primary school public education. Brown v. Board of Education of Topeka, 347 U.S. 483 (1954).

7. Jemar Tisby, *The Color of Compromise* (Grand Rapids: Zondervan, 2019), 38.

8. Comments posted in 2022 on Baylor University's Facebook page by white Baylor graduates after Brittney Griner was arrested in February 2022 at a Moscow airport and sentenced to nine years of hard labor in a Russian gulag for possessing minor amounts of hashish oil in a vape pen cartridge. She was freed in a prisoner exchange in December 2022.

9. "Smile," by Charles Chaplin, with lyrics by John Turner and Geoffrey Parsons, on Nat King Cole, *The World of Nat King Cole,* Capitol Records, 2005.

Chapter 8: The New Jim Crow Theology

1. Peter Jesserer Smith, "Brandt Jean to Amber Guyger: 'I Forgive You, I Love You, Give Your Life to Christ'" (blog), *National Catholic Register,* October 3, 2019, https://www.ncregister.com/blog/brandt-jean-to-amber -guyger-i-forgive-you-i-love-you-give-your-life-to-christ. Video is available at Bill Hutchinson, "Extraordinary Act of Mercy: Brother of Botham Jean Hugs and Forgives Amber Guyger after 10-Year Sentence Imposed," ABC News, October 2, 2019, https://abcnews.go.com/US/jury-deciding-sentence-police -officer-amber-guyger-wrong/story?id=66002182.

2. CBS News, "Mother of Man Slain by Cop Says Son's Hug Should Not Be 'Misconstrued' as 'Complete Forgiveness,'" October 3, 2019, https://www.cbsnews.com/news/amber-guyger-trial-botham-jeans-mother -reacts-to-sentencing-and-emotional-hug/.

3. Diana Chandler, "Man Forgives Brother's Killer, Offers Her Christ," *Baptist Press,* October 3, 2019, https://www.baptistpress.com/resource-library /news/man-forgives-brothers-killer-offers-her-christ/.

4. Kyle Sweitzer, "Brandt Jean's Ultimate Act of Forgiveness," Acton Institute, July 14, 2021, https://rlo.acton.org/archives/121922-brandt-jeans -ultimate-act-of-forgiveness.html.

5. Smith, "Brandt Jean to Amber Guyger."

6. Rhina Guidos, "In an Act of Christian Love, a Murder Victim's Brother Publicly Forgives His Killer in Court," *America: The Jesuit Review,* October 3, 2019, https://www.americamagazine.org/faith/2019/10/03/act-christian-love -murder-victims-brother-publicly-forgives-his-killer-court.

7. "Brandt Jean Receives 2019 Ethical Courage Award from ILEA," Center

for American and International Law, December 4, 2019, https://www.cailaw
.org/institute-for-law-enforcement-administration/News/2019/brandt-jean
-received-ethical-courage-award.html.

8. Mike D. Sykes II, "Jonathan Isaac Says He Didn't Kneel during the
National Anthem Because 'All Lives Are Supported through the Gospel,'"
USA Today, August 1, 2020, https://ftw.usatoday.com/2020/08
/jonathan-issac-national-anthem-kneel-black-lives-matter.

9. I recall an event early in our time at TFI when, during the closing
moments, one of the associate pastors wanted to make a point that there are
so many things in the world to find joy in. The last example was the joy they
received when an Asian woman who was interning with the church would greet
them in the mornings. Then the speaker imitated the intern's accent for comedic
effect. There was a mix of laughter and grimaces in the congregation. A group of
Asian international students were sitting in the row in front of me. Seeing how
this hit them, I leaned forward and apologized to them. Red flag in hindsight,
but I justified it by saying this wasn't the head pastor, I hadn't observed anything
like this before, and the rest of the sermon was good. I know this concern was
taken to people in leadership, but there was never a public apology.

10. Kate Boyd, *An Untidy Faith: Journeying Back to the Joy of Following
Jesus* (Harrisonburg, VA: Herald Press, 2023), 49.

11. Andrew Lawler, "Church Unearthed in Ethiopia Rewrites the History of
Christianity in Africa," *Smithsonian Magazine,* December 10, 2019,
https://www.smithsonianmag.com/history/church-unearthed-ethiopia-rewrites
-history-christianity-africa-180973740/; and Emma George Ross, "African
Christianity in Ethiopia," Metropolitan Museum of Art, October 2002,
https://www.metmuseum.org/toah/hd/acet/hd_acet.htm.

12. Some call this dynamic "implicit bias." While I recognize the existence
of implicit bias, I think it too often affords the benefit of ignorance to prejudice,
which is a conscious bias. A bias is only implicit if the culprit doesn't
consciously consider their prejudice. But how often is a racial or cultural bias
100 percent unconscious? For example, a stereotype we believe only applies
to 1 percent of a culture is still a conscious bias when we realize it doesn't
apply to the other 99 percent. Knowing this bias exists, even if we can't fully
articulate the nature of the bias, eliminates its unrevealed nature. Understanding
that, no cultural bias—conscious or unconscious—should remain within us as
believers.

13. Mike Kelsey, "TSF with Mike Kelsey: Q&A + Mike & Friends," *That
Sounds Fun* (podcast), June 22, 2020, https://podcasts.apple.com/us/podcast
/tsf-with-mike-kelsey-g-g-mike-friends/id944925529?i=1000479246800.

Chapter 9: Angry Gets S*** Done

1. I feel the need to emphasize that grief is unique to each person and each
loss. We may process through the various stages differently each time. The
stages may not come in this order. We may experience more than one stage at a

time. We may move through one stage only to find ourselves back in that stage again. We may travel through peaks and valleys. But the big takeaway is that no one, including yourself, should have expectations of how you grieve. The process is what the process is, and it takes as long as it takes.

2. Credit to my friend Johnna Harris for this analogy.

3. *American Gods,* season 1, episode 2, "The Secret of Spoons," created by Bryan Fuller and Michael Green, Starz, 2017.

4. "Advocating for Abuse Reform in the SBC" with Keith Myer, Emily Snook, and David Bronson, *Bodies Behind the Bus* (podcast), episode 48, https://podcasts.apple.com/us/podcast/bodies-behind-the-bus/id1601586078?i =1000615988114.

5. Associated Press, "The DOJ Is Investigating Southern Baptists following Sexual Abuse Crisis," NPR, August 13, 2022, https://www.npr.org/2022/08 /13/1117362904/southern-baptists-doj-investigation-sexual-abuse.

6. Kathryn Post, "Grove City College Condemns 'Alleged Drift into CRT Advocacy,'" *Christianity Today,* April 25, 2022, https://www.christianitytoday .com/news/2022/april/grove-city-college-critical-race-theory-crt-jemar-tisby -rep.html.

7. Mike Cosper, "Who Killed Mars Hill?" *The Rise and Fall of Mars Hill* (podcast), June 21, 2021, https://www.christianitytoday.com/ct/podcasts/rise -and-fall-of-mars-hill/who-killed-mars-hill-church-mark-driscoll-rise-fall.html.

8. "Advocating for Abuse Reform in the SBC."

9. Thomas L. Shaffer, *On Being a Christian and a Lawyer: Law for the Innocent* (Provo, UT: Brigham Young University Press, 1981), 50. See also Joseph Allegretti, *The Lawyer's Calling: Christian Faith and Legal Practice* (New York: Paulist Press, 1996), 75.

10. Cyndia Hammond, "Our country nees a big lesson in intent vs. impact," Facebook, July 24, 2020, https://www.facebook.com/baylordia/posts /pfbid02WCkrrm6ggva1oZgUDQfBDjgnveVRkUesuN2ETZsZ7Qe46b2ej B4XFGtUbd1AiwQol.

11. "Emily & Amelia Nagoski, Burnout—XOXO Festival (2019)," YouTube, October 17, 2019, https://youtu.be/BOaCn9nptN8.

Chapter 10: Burn It All (Take Nothing with You)

1. Gary Thomas, *When to Walk Away: Finding Freedom from Toxic People* (Grand Rapids: Zondervan, 2019), 17.

Chapter 11: The Cavalry's Not Coming

1. A close cousin of the Cavalry Refusal is the Deus Ex Machina (literally, God from the machine) trope wherein the divine hand of fate, luck, or another force intervenes at the last moment in the place of the cavalry. This device fairly characterizes situations where the unexpected or implausible is introduced to the story to aid the protagonist in accomplishing what is

necessary. The antithesis of the Deus Ex Machina is the Bolivian Army Ending. In this trope, the good guys ride out expecting death . . . and they die. In hindsight, the audience realizes that the real enemy was the protagonist's fear of an unavoidable end and the "victory" was facing that fear with dignity. Examples include *The Chinese Connection, Thelma and Louise, Butch Cassidy and the Sundance Kid*, and *The Alamo*. Spoiler alert.

2. David Hayward (@nakedpastor), "Deconstruction affects everything because your religion did," Instagram, February 2, 2023, https://www.instagram.com/p/CoKTXMQqZOB/?igshid=MzRlODBiNWFlZA==.

3. Unrecommended reading, cited for legal purposes only: John Eldredge, *Wild at Heart: Discovering the Secret of a Man's Soul* (Nashville: Thomas Nelson, 2011).

4. Kaitlin B. Curtice (@KaitlinCurtice), "A relationship to the church that consists of 'maybe if I stay things will change/I'll find community' is an abusive relationship," Twitter, November 4, 2021, 9:30 a.m., https://twitter.com/kaitlincurtice/status/1456267732068962312?s=46.

5. James H. Cone, *A Black Theology of Liberation*, 20th anniv. ed. (Maryknoll, NY: Orbis, 1990), 58.

6. Michael Gorman, *Apostle of the Crucified Lord: A Theological Introduction to Paul and His Letters,* 2nd ed. (Grand Rapids: Eerdmans Publishing, 2017), 376 (emphasis in original).

Chapter 12: Permission to Leave

1. T. J. Webb (@tjwebbmd), "My advice: leave anyway," Twitter, January 5, 2022, 1:39 p.m., https://mobile.twitter.com/tjwebbmd/status/1478813487962984450.

2. *Boyz n the Hood,* directed by John Singleton (Columbia Pictures, 1991).

3. Campbell Robertson, "A Quiet Exodus: Why Black Worshipers Are Leaving White Evangelical Churches," *New York Times,* March 9, 2018, https://www.nytimes.com/2018/03/09/us/blacks-evangelical-churches.html.

4. Dwight McKissic (@pastordmack), "Tweet thread non minority evangelical pastors ought read," Twitter, September 30, 2022, 9:56 a.m., https://twitter.com/pastordmack/status/1575862129475084294?s=20.

5. Ashley Irons, Ryan Holmes, and Elijah Misigaro, *We Talk Different* (podcast), https://podcasts.apple.com/us/podcast/wetalkdifferent/id1161601126?i=1000465927338. See also Howard Zinn, *You Can't Be Neutral on a Moving Train: A Personal History of Our Times* (Boston: Beacon Press, 1994).

6. F. F. Bruce, *The Acts of the Apostles* (London: Tyndale, 1952), 97, quoted in Blue Letter Bible, s.v. *metanoeō*, accessed March 14, 2024, https://www.blueletterbible.org/lexicon/g3340/esv/tr/0-1/.

7. Rob Reimer, *Soul Care: 7 Transformational Principles for a Healthy Soul* (Franklin, TN: Carpenter's Son Publishing, 2016). Note: Reimer references the dynamics of repentance with a different view from my own.

8. "Leave Loud: Malcolm Foley," *Pass the Mic* (podcast), May 30, 2022, https://podcasts.apple.com/us/podcast/leave-loud-malcolm-foley/id1435500798?i=1000564486307.

Chapter 13: A Newer Hope

1. Spoken by Jyn Erso in *Rogue One: A Star Wars Story* (Walt Disney Studios Motion Pictures, 2016).

2. Paul V. Burnett Jr. (@vanderNumber2), "Jesus couldn't do much with people from his own community who rejected His divinity," Twitter, November 27, 2022, 10:06 a.m., https://twitter.com/vandernumber2/status/15968982479181112771?s=12.

3. Kate Shellnutt, "Willow Creek Investigation: Allegations against Bill Hybels Are Credible," *Christianity Today,* February 28, 2019, https://www.christianitytoday.com/news/2019/february/willow-creek-bill-hybels-investigation-iag-report.html.

4. 1 Cor. 1:21–27; Rom. 8:19–21; 1 Pet. 5:10.

5. "'She Deserves Better' with Sheila Gregoire," *Bodies Behind the Bus* (podcast), episode 45, April 19, 2023, https://podcasts.apple.com/us/podcast/bodies-behind-the-bus/id1601586078?i=1000609614092.

6. Psychology Glossary (website), s.v. "Musterbation," https://www.psychology-lexicon.com/cms/glossary/46-glossary-m/13256-musterbation.html.

7. "Tyler Burns—Don't Negotiate Your Dignity," YouTube, September 1, 2023, https://youtu.be/1hPz3DtgNeI?si=5c2vPhIM5aJaGvxl.

8. *Star Trek: The Next Generation,* "Chain of Command," parts 1 and 2, 1992.

9. *Star Wars: Episode VIII—The Last Jedi*, directed by Rian Johnson (Walt Disney Studios Motion Pictures, 2017).

10. Author unknown, possibly C. S. Lewis.

Epilogue: Closing Arguments

1. Tracy Chapman, "Remember the Tin Man," on *New Beginning,* Sony/ATV Music Publishing, 1995.

Printed in the USA
CPSIA information can be obtained
at www.ICGtesting.com
CBHW071955070924
R15548000001B/R155480PG13922CBX00001B/1